NO MISSION TOO DIFFICULT!

OLD BUDDIES OF THE 1ST DIVISION TELL ALL ABOUT WORLD WAR II

BLYTHE FOOTE FINKE

Edited by Steven Weingartner with John F. Votaw

CONTEMPORARY
BOOKS
A TRIBUNE NEW MEDIA COMPANY

Library of Congress Cataloging-in-Publication Data

No mission too difficult! : old buddies of the 1st Division tell all about
   World War II / [edited by] Blythe Foote Finke.
         p.   cm.
      ISBN 0-8092-3259-6
         1. World War, 1939–1945—Personal narratives, American.
      2. United States.   Army.   Infantry Division, 1st—History.
      I. Finke, Blythe Foote.
      D811.A2N67   1995
      940.54'1273—dc20   95-35776
                                                                    CIP

Parts of "East Chicagoan Leads Capture of Sicily Town," by
H. R. Knickerbocker, are reprinted with permission of the
Chicago Sun-Times, © 1994.

Parts of "Undershirts Save Yankees from Own Bombers as They Battle
Along Rocky Rock Road to Troina," by Don Whitehead, are reprinted by
permission of the Associated Press.

The chronology was compiled by Steven Weingartner with editorial
assistance by Andrew E. Woods.

Published by Contemporary Books, Inc.
Two Prudential Plaza, Chicago, Illinois 60601-6790
Manufactured in the United States of America
International Standard Book Number: 0-8092-3259-6
10   9   8   7   6   5   4   3   2   1

Dedicated to the 1st Division

Contents

Foreword

There is something special about the 1st Division. In a sense its organization in the spring of 1917 represented the beginning of the modern American army. When the United States entered World War I, not a single division was in existence, so the War Department hastily pulled together four infantry regiments and assorted artillery and other units and filled their ranks with recruits to bring them up to strength. Soldiers of the 2nd Battalion of the 16th Infantry Regiment were the first Americans to parade in Paris on July 4, 1917, and some of them were among the first AEF casualties that fall. When the war ended sixteen months later, the 1st Division had so distinguished itself that General John J. Pershing issued a general order which stated: "The Commander-in-Chief has noted in this Division a special pride of service and a high state of morale, never broken by hardship nor battle."

Over the next twenty years, the division garrisoned old coast artillery forts on the East Coast and went about the peacetime routine in a spit-and-polish manner. The story told in this volume picks up during the mobilization period before Pearl Harbor and carries the division through the terrible battles of North Africa, Sicily, France, and Germany.

Blythe Foote Finke, the wife of John Finke, one of the stalwarts of the 16th Infantry Regiment, listened to her husband and his comrades tell their war stories and conceived the idea of a history of the division during World War II based on their reminiscences. She interviewed fourteen veterans and also got written memoirs from two of them. Most served in the 16th Infantry Regiment, most were officers or became officers in the course of the war, and several, including her husband, stayed in the army after the war.

Given the division's prominent role in several of the hardest campaigns in the war and the resulting cost in casualties, it is not surprising that some fifty thousand men (more than triple its basic strength) served in its ranks during World War II. Admittedly, fourteen is not a sizeable sample, but, as the reader will find, the experiences of these men were varied and broad enough to serve the author's purpose in getting across what it was like to be in this famed division during that war.

Memories are like snapshots which have been pasted in albums. Oral historians open up those albums and then place their findings in a different format. Some authors collect a few and simply let their subjects, more or less, tell their own stories at length. Others blend bits and pieces of their interviews together with information from records, letters, and other sources to obtain their story. This book follows the different course of grouping excerpts of varied length to get across a particular incident or mood.

From the prewar maneuvers to the battlefields, the skillfully and sensitively selected excerpts re-create vividly in tint and tone those long-ago events. The connecting explanatory passages— "The Record"—as well as the division chronology help the reader keep the quoted accounts in proper context.

What one finds in these pages is not a full-scale history of this unit but rather the human experience of war with its highs and lows. There are poignant moments and ones of horror and others of frivolity. One comes away from this book with not only a better understanding of what war was like for the men who fought and a greater appreciation of the camaraderie and the pride that these men of the 1st Division share, but also why that division has always been outstanding.

> Edward M. Coffman
> Professor Emeritus
> University of Wisconsin–Madison

Preface

The collection of oral history impressions that follows is the creation of Blythe Foote Finke, an army wife whose discerning intellect and keen ability to look for the significant story in an interview session show through brightly in this work. She stuck with the project over a period of years, worked hard to place the manuscript with a publisher, and didn't quit when commercial presses seemed indifferent to military memoirs. Mrs. Finke, her steadfast husband, John, and their many friends convinced me that publication was warranted. With the creation of the Cantigny Military History Series in 1993, the opportunity to publish *No Mission Too Difficult!* arrived. We then turned the manuscript over to our editor, Steven Weingartner, who further shaped and organized the interview transcripts into narrative form and wrote passages that provide historical context to the first-person accounts. That task completed, we approached the people at Contemporary Books to see if they might be open to the idea of publishing Mrs. Finke's manuscript in collaboration with the Cantigny First Division Foundation. They were quick to see the virtues of her work and agreed to bring it out under their imprint.

Originally Mrs. Finke had intended for her book to encompass the entire combat history of the 1st Division from World War I through the Gulf War. In due course, however, this intent was altered by the dominant nature of the World War II section. The sheer length of it, not to mention the fascinating character of the stories it comprises, demanded stand-alone treatment. Adding weight to that demand was the fifty-year anniversary of World War II, which has done so much in recent years to spark a resurgence of interest in that conflict. Time and funds permitting, the remaining sections of the manuscript dealing with World War I, Vietnam, and Desert Storm will appear as separate publications. In the meantime we are pleased to present, after much work and deliberation, *No Mission Too Difficult!*

John F. Votaw
Executive Director
Cantigny First Division Foundation
August 1995

Acknowledgments

The author and editors thank Dr. Edward M. Coffman for his informative, graceful introduction to *No Mission Too Difficult!* Dr. Coffman has been a longtime friend of the Cantigny First Division Foundation and the First Division Museum. His interest in the project and helpful criticism have strengthened the book.

Andrew Woods, the reference librarian of the museum's Colonel Robert R. McCormick Research Center, assisted the editors in the preparation of the chronology. The contributors, or their family members, provided the personal photographs, and the research center located the excellent supplementary combat action photos. The Society of the First Division and its executive director, Arthur L. Chaitt, kindly permitted us to use the maps from *Danger Forward: The Story of the First Division in World War II* and to rely on the book as a source of information.

Finally, we thank the *Chicago Sun-Times* and the Associated Press for granting permission to reprint articles by H. R. Knickerbocker and Don Whitehead, respectively. If we have overlooked anyone, our error was unintentional.

The stories and anecdotes provided by the contributors are the strength of the book. The editors have tried to ensure that the facts are correct, but the interpretations and conclusions are the contributors' alone. If any errors in "The Record" sections remain, the editors accept responsibility for those oversights.

Introduction

My husband, John, is a gallant infantry officer who served with the 1st Infantry Division during World War II and afterward, and was decorated for extraordinary heroism in battle. In the course of more than thirty years, while attending the division's reunions, I have met many of his fellow officers and enlisted men from the Big Red One, and have always come away from these events impressed by their camaraderie. It is obvious from the way they relate to one another that the intangible bonds between them are very strong, linking the veterans of every conflict in which the 1st Division has participated, from the First World War through Operation Desert Storm.

I have heard these men tell their stories at the reunions and at smaller gatherings in our home. They constitute a diverse group, hailing from big cities, farms, small towns, and everywhere in between. They represent a wide range of professions—among them are corporate executives, educators, farmers, factory workers, and businessmen of every stripe. Not a few were career soldiers. Once they get together, however, their post–1st Division identities, whether civilian or military, fade away. It is as though they have once again become members of the Big Red One; as though they have come home, but with one crucial difference: they no longer recognize differences of rank. Instead, all are equal because all were once members of the division.

Listening to them talk, one soon becomes aware that they share a lot more than mere membership in the same division. Though their recollections may be either serious or humorous, all are informed by feelings of intense pride. And just as pride is a common thread that runs through all their stories, so too is it a characteristic of all veterans of the 1st, no matter when and where or in what war they served. All have known the rigors of training and the hazards of combat; they have endured much and accomplished more, and they are proud of it. All are proud of their decorations and derive immense satisfaction from the recognition accorded them as result of service in the two world wars, the war in Vietnam, and the Persian Gulf War. And all take pride in the commanders under whom they served.

While attending a 1st Division reunion in Normandy on June 6, 1989—the forty-fifth anniversary of D-Day—a veteran explained their pride as the product of a "shared experience of hardship in battle and military service." He drew an analogy between the very best silver and the Big Red One. Both, he observed, possess a certain hallmark quality that makes them superior to others of their kind: with the former, it is sterling; with the latter, it is the spirit of camaraderie among its men. In other words, he said, camaraderie is to the 1st Division what sterling is to silver.

General George C. Marshall, Chief of Staff of the United States Army in the Second World War, was known for his remote personality; but even he could not resist the pull of this essential bond, instilled in him while serving as G-3 when the 1st Division went to France in World War I. In his *Memoirs of My Services in the World War, 1917–1918* (Boston: Houghton Mifflin Company,

1976, pages 117–18), he summed up feelings about "this great combat organization" upon leaving it for another assignment. "Bigger problems were to come," he wrote, "but never again that feeling of comradeship which grows out of the intimate relationship among those in immediate contact with fighting troops. Whatever else was to happen to me—in that war or in the future—could be but a minor incident in my career."

During World War II a member of the 1st Division echoed Marshall's sentiments when he wrote:

> I am . . . with my men and my heart is happy. One never realizes the utter loneliness or separation until he has had the privilege of living [with] and being part of the finest group of men on the face of the earth. These are men who see and live the intimate relationships of mutual sufferers in the greatest of ordeals. I've had an honor never to be equaled in being part of a group that will ever stand as a symbol of greatness to all who witnessed or knew how they measured up to the supreme test without faltering or wavering.

It is by virtue of their mutually felt pride and comradeship that veterans of the 1st are able to establish an almost immediate rapport with each other whenever they first meet and at every meeting thereafter. One veteran I know recently likened that rapport to being tuned in with his fellows in the sense that they were all integral components of a smoothly running machine.

Upon hearing veterans of the 1st reminisce about their service with the division, I have come to realize how rarely one encounters among men and women the sort of lifelong friendship and loyalty that binds these men. I also feel privileged to share, if only after the fact, their once-in-a-lifetime experiences. In World War II those experiences were gained over the course of 443 days of combat—89 in North Africa, 36 in Sicily, and 318 in Western Europe. Through it all, no mission was too difficult for the 1st Division to tackle. And its tasks were often formidable indeed. One of its sternest tests came at Omaha Beach on D-Day. There, as is well known, German defenders exacted a bloody price in dead and wounded from positions on the heights overlooking the beach. Yet the men of the 1st endured and ultimately overcame the enemy.

Writing about the extraordinary courage and tenacity they displayed that day, war correspondent Ernie Pyle, who witnessed the landings, used the term "pure miracle" to describe what he saw. The men of the division are proud of that reaction from Pyle; he enjoyed a deserved reputation among GIs as a writer who could be trusted to "tell it like it is" in his dispatches.

Also witness to the 1st Division's deeds at Omaha Beach was a beloved Catholic chaplain—alas, now gone—who not so long ago recalled, "I never saw anything so big and impressive in my life. . . . If I had gone no further than that beach I would have thanked God for the opportunity to help those brave men." General Omar Bradley was similarly grateful when he declared, "I always thank God for the 1st Division. . . . Any inexperienced division might not have made it that day" (Omar Bradley, *A Soldier's Story*, New York: Henry Holt and Company, 1951, page 272).

A colleague of Ernie Pyle, *New York Times* correspondent Drew Middleton, once remarked that the 1st Division "fights with cool, seemingly effortless efficiency." Of course the division's fighting qualities, not to mention the success it achieved, did not go unnoticed by the enemy, or unremarked either. "Where the 1st Division was, there we would have trouble," a German General Staff officer observed after the war.

At a reunion in my garden, one veteran summed up his feelings about his buddies when he said, "We became very good friends at an early age, the formative years of our lives when we were in our twenties. We felt [as if we were] an elite group and became almost arrogant in our sense of pride in the division. Pride kept us going." Whereupon another of those present commented, "Yes, there was tremendous pride in getting the mission accomplished, a tremendous warmth among us. Although promotions might be slow, we were happy. There was no competitive jealousy as is often felt in other branches of the service. Get the job done, that was the only objective."

Yet another World War II correspondent once told a historian, "The 1st Division is not just a military unit. The thing few people realize is, it is one of the world's minor religions." Between 1990 and 1991, I was fortunate to interview more than a dozen practitioners of this "religion." I am deeply grateful to one and all for sharing their experiences with me. I also want to thank the 1st Division Headquarters at Fort Riley, Kansas, and the U.S. Army Military History Institute, Carlisle Barracks, Pennsylvania. A special word of thanks goes out to John Votaw at the First Division Museum at Cantigny in Wheaton, Illinois, for his excellent advice and support, without which this project would never have gotten off the ground; and to Steven Weingartner, whose excellent work as both editor and writer did so much to make it a reality.

Blythe Foote Finke
Fort Belvoir, Virginia
July 1995

Prologue

The outbreak of World War II in Europe on September 1, 1939, found the United States in an isolationist mood that precluded, for the time being at least, any direct involvement in that conflict. And a good thing too, for the truth is, the nation was wholly unprepared to fight a large-scale war. Raw numbers tell the story best. Germany, for example, invaded Poland with more than 1.5 million men organized into five armies comprising six armored divisions, eight motorized divisions, and twenty-seven infantry divisions. Poland, weak by comparison, fielded thirty infantry divisions, eleven cavalry brigades, and two motorized brigades. In contrast the United States Army had just under two hundred thousand men parceled out, for the most part, into five under-strength and ill-equipped infantry divisions and one cavalry division. Only four of the divisions were based in the continental United States; the other two were based in the Hawaiian and Philippine Islands.

Among the former was the 1st Division. Known as the "Big Red One" because of its shoulder patch—a red numeral on an olive-drab shield—the division was constituted on May 24, 1917, as the First Expeditionary Division, and it was officially organized on June 8. The first American division sent to France (lead elements arrived at Saint Nazaire on June 26, 1917), the Big Red One also won the first American victory of the war at the battle of Cantigny, May 28–31, 1918, and was a key participant in virtually every other American action, notably the battle of Saint-Mihiel and the Meuse-Argonne offensive (September–November 1918). Not coincidentally, the Big Red One suffered the most casualties of any American division, with more than twenty-two thousand killed, wounded, and missing in action by war's end.

Following the Armistice on November 11, 1918, the division occupied a sector near Coblenz, Germany, until August 1919, when most of the soldiers returned to the United States. For the next twenty years the division was headquartered in Fort Hamilton, New York, with its component units dispersed to various posts on the East Coast. In World War I the division had a "square" structure, with twenty-eight thousand men organized into four infantry regiments (the 16th, 18th, 26th, and 28th) numbering forty-two hundred men each, three artillery regiments with fifteen hundred men each, and many smaller support units. In the autumn of 1939, however, the army converted to a "triangular" structure; accordingly, the division was reorganized to consist of three infantry regiments (the 16th, 18th, and 26th), while the 28th Regiment was assigned to the 8th Infantry Division.

The 16th Infantry was constituted shortly after the outbreak of the American Civil War on May 3, 1861, as an offshoot of the 11th Infantry Regiment; the 18th Infantry was formed on the same date. Both regiments served with distinction throughout the Civil War, participating in many of that conflict's biggest battles; they also served in the Spanish-American War, the Philippine Insurrection, and World War I. The 26th Infantry was the younger partner of the group; constituted on February 2, 1901, two years after the cessation of hostilities with Spain, it served in the Philippines and World War I.

With the triangular structure, each regiment numbered thirty-three hundred infantrymen. Regimental combat teams were formed for specific missions by adding quartermaster, medical, ordnance, engineer, reconnaissance, signal, and artillery troops.

In addition to organic cannon companies within the infantry regiments, the division had four artillery battalions: the 5th, 7th, 32nd, and 33rd Field Artillery. Each had a complement of about 520 men. Collectively known as 1st Division Artillery or more commonly, 1st Divarty, these battalions contained venerable units by U.S. Army standards: Battery D of the 5th (Alexander Hamilton's Battery) had a history that extended back to 1776 and the Revolutionary War. The 7th was constituted on July 1, 1916, and assigned to the 1st Expeditionary Division on June 8, 1917. The 32nd and 33rd were constituted on July 5, 1918, and assigned to the 1st Division on October 1, 1940.

The division also included the 1st Engineer Battalion, formed in 1846, and additional service troops. The overall strength of the division in World War II was nominally fifteen thousand men, although this figure varied with the circumstances.

In the two years preceding the events of December 7, 1941, Congress, responding to increasingly ominous developments in Europe and Asia, enacted legislation aimed at readying the nation's military (and indeed the nation itself) for possible entry into the war. The institution of the nation's first peacetime draft (June 1940) along with the passage of generous appropriations bills provided the army and the navy with three much-needed commodities: men, money, and the matériel that only money could buy. A prime beneficiary of this congressionally mandated largess, the 1st Division put it to good use in a training regimen that included participation in several large-scale maneuvers.

In November 1939 the division moved to Fort Benning, Georgia, to spend the winter. In May 1940 the division proceeded to the vicinity of Sabine, Louisiana, to participate in the Louisiana maneuvers, where it functioned as a triangular unit for the first time. The division returned to Fort Hamilton in June. That same year the 3rd Battalion of the 18th Infantry and the 3rd Battalion of the 16th Infantry went to Culebra, Puerto Rico, to practice amphibious landings. On February 4, 1941, the division moved its headquarters to Fort Devens, Massachusetts, with the rest of the division soon following. In 1941 as well, the division practiced landings at Buzzard's Bay, Massachusetts, and underwent additional amphibious training in August with the 1st Marine Division at New River, North Carolina.

In the autumn of 1941 the division was involved in the First Army's maneuvers in North Carolina. It returned to Fort Devens in the first week of December shortly before the Japanese attack on Pearl Harbor. More amphibious training at Virginia Beach, Virginia, in January 1942 was followed in the spring by infantry training at Camp Blanding in Florida, and air-ground tests and demonstrations at Fort Benning, Georgia. Upon the conclusion of the Benning exercises, the division moved to Indiantown Gap, Pennsylvania, on June 21, 1942, to assemble and organize for overseas movement in August.

During this period the division actually began preparing for expeditions to Martinique, the Azores, and the west coast of Africa, only to have each operation canceled at the last minute. The division was then part of the First Army's VI Corps; but between May 1941 and February 1942 the division was also a component of the I Amphibious Corps, and therefore under navy control.

On May 15, 1942, the 1st Division had been officially redesignated an infantry division. By then the Allies were fighting what was in effect two separate wars: one in Asia and the Pacific; the other in Europe (including the Soviet Union), North Africa, and the Middle East. The Allies' Europe First policy, formulated by American and British military planners in the opening months of 1941, gave priority to defeating Germany. Not incidentally it determined where and against whom the 1st Division would direct its efforts. So it was that one of the U.S. Army's best divisions would be sent to do battle with the enemy deemed most vital to defeat at the earliest date: Nazi Germany.

Part i

Preparing for War

Chapter 1

Subway Soldiers

The Record

On the eve of America's entry into the war the men of the 1st Division were a typically diverse group. Very few, mostly officers and NCOs, were career soldiers. The rest were essentially civilians in uniform. Some had been drafted into the army, others had enlisted; in either case they tended to have no prior military experience. In the minority were those who were acquainted with military life through National Guard service or participation in college and high school ROTC programs.

Charles Hangsterfer

Back in the Depression days I was fortunate enough to go to Gettysburg College, where they had an ROTC program. I found that in your junior and senior years they paid you sixteen cents an hour for every drill you attended and also provided a uniform. I always thought I looked pretty good in a uniform, and I got to thinking, well, the fact is, there are no jobs. I didn't know what I wanted to do, so I thought maybe I'd go into the army. I entered

the army after I graduated as a second lieutenant under the
Thomason Act. This annually took a thousand graduates from
colleges and universities that had ROTC programs. Out of the
thousand, a hundred were selected for regular army commissions.
This was back in 1940. I was assigned to the 16th Infantry of the
1st Division, which was based at Fort Jay on Governor's Island
in New York. But my first tour of duty was at Fort Benning,
Georgia, where I was sent on detached service from the regiment.

The Record

*At Fort Benning the newly minted Second Lieutenant Hangsterfer
took a refresher course for officers, then attended a three-month officers communications school, the first to be offered at the post. Upon
graduation he rejoined the 16th Infantry at Fort Jay.*

Charles Hangsterfer

The reason I never became chief of staff of the United States
Army was that, back in those days, there was no set date for
Thanksgiving. In 1940 President Roosevelt had changed the federal government's date for the holiday from the fourth Thursday
in November to the third Thursday. But the states were allowed
to set their own dates, and in Pennsylvania, where I had gone to
college, it remained the fourth Thursday. So I reported to Fort
Jay in New York on the third Thursday thinking that Thanksgiving would not be celebrated until the following week. I was
wrong. The army celebrated Thanksgiving on the third Thursday because that was the day the federal government had mandated.

I compounded the error by interrupting Major Edward
O'Neill, the 16th Regiment's adjutant, at Thanksgiving dinner.
He never said hello, just cut me down to size by saying, "Don't
you know enough not to report for duty on a holiday?" In effect

he was telling me that I had violated a venerable army tradition. And that's why I never became chief of staff of the army. Instead I became the officer who had made the big mistake of reporting for duty on a holiday. As a result, I also became the officer Major O'Neill remembered whenever someone was needed for "special" duties.

The next day I reported to Captain B. M. Kelley, the Headquarters Company commander. Lieutenants Joe Denbeau, Phil Nertig, and George Sawyer were Headquarters Company's officers. They practically jumped for joy when I showed up. They said, "Here is a new man to go on maneuvers in our place."

The reason for their glee soon became apparent. In those days regimental headquarters companies had three communications platoons, one for each battalion, consisting of a message center, a wire section, and a radio section. The platoons were, of course, commanded by officers, namely Lieutenants Denbeau, Nertig, and Sawyer. They knew that HQ Company was sending one platoon on the battalion-sized amphibious landing maneuvers that were scheduled for December. They also knew that I would be commanding that platoon. This was confirmed when Captain Kelley advised me not to get too comfortable at Fort Jay because I would be going on maneuvers with the 3rd Battalion as the communications officer.

Early in December, 3rd Battalion departed from Fort Jay and went to Edgewood Arsenal, Maryland. It was then I found out why the headquarters officers had done their little dance: the battalion was quartered out in the open in tents in the middle of winter. It was very cold in those tents, and I never did figure out how to bank the Sibley stoves they gave us so there would be heat in the morning.

Our training consisted of practicing amphibious landings on the Gunpowder River. Amphibious equipment was in short supply—we had no landing craft—so we used large rowboats instead.

The boats reminded me of Viking ships (less the dragon figure-head on the prow!) or the whaleboat Captain Ahab used to chase Moby Dick. The first part of our training involved learning how to row and steer. Boat teams were organized according to boat capacity and the number of rubber hip boots available. We had to use the boots because the Gunpowder River did not have a sloping beach and was too shallow to get the boats close to the banks. This meant that the troops had to disembark in two or three feet of water. But because there weren't enough hip boots for everyone, they were issued to the troops of the first wave only. After these men had gotten ashore, the exercise came to a halt while they took off the boots and gave them to the troops of the second wave who were waiting on the beach. The second-wave troops put on the boots, climbed aboard the boats, rowed back to the middle of the river, turned around, and returned to assault the beach. Then they removed the boots and gave them to the next group. The same procedure was followed until every-body had a chance to experience the scheme of maneuver. After use by the first wave, however, the boots were wet and usually frozen stiff, which further slowed the operation.

Often during the landing exercise someone from the post would come to warn us that chemicals were being tested nearby and a toxic cloud was headed our way. When that happened we beat a retreat to a safe area until the danger passed. (We had been issued gas masks that were for training purposes only but not the real thing.)

After we got our boots off and we were sure there weren't any gas experiments, we proceeded with the exercise. The wire section would lay a wire line for everyone to follow to the objec-tive so they wouldn't get lost. Little did they realize that I was the greatest one in the world to get lost. We did what the bat-talion CO wanted us to do, but I explained to him that in com-bat some other means would have to be used because the wire men would be too busy laying wire to double as point men. I suggested that the rifle companies lay engineer's tapes, which would be more visible than the black wire. This idea worked out very good in later night landings. At least I never got lost.

Sometime after that we conducted landing exercises in Puerto Rico. When we arrived in Puerto Rico we did not use rowboats. We had to climb down into whaleboats from rope ladders hung alongside the transport. These boats were normally used for transporting seamen when they went ashore on liberty, and were not too well suited for beach landings. They got stuck on the beach, and we had to push them off so the next wave could get ashore. Many times we couldn't free them, which meant waiting until high tide before they would float. With all the makeshift equipment we had to use, we learned a lot about the problems of assault landings.

After Puerto Rico, instead of going back to Fort Jay to resume being "Subway Soldiers" [the unofficial nickname for 16th Infantry troops], we sailed to Boston, then proceeded to Fort Devens, Massachusetts. Here we were given the mission of preparing the camp for the entire 1st Division. It would be the first time since World War I that all the division's regiments and other units were together in one place.

After a short training period at Fort Devens, the division went on maneuvers in North Carolina. We lived in tents in the woods. I was a city boy and never liked woods with all their bugs and snakes. I must have been overheard complaining because I received orders to report to the navy in Norfolk, Virginia, to practice landing maneuvers with them.

When I arrived in Norfolk, I was still in the boots and britches that I had been wearing for two days because I couldn't get the boots off without help. The ship I was ordered to report to was in dry dock, so I was relocated onto the ship conducting landing exercises off Virginia Beach.

All the navy landing craft were the latest type; however, they still had the same problem getting stuck on the beach. Since I had a lot of experience pushing boats off the beach, I made a pest of myself telling the navy what to do. Then I was assigned to the ship's communications room to stand watch, partly because I was with the navy to learn about ship-to-shore communications, but more just to keep me out of their hair. I liked this duty because all I did was ride ashore, get my feet wet, then ride back to the ship, all the time complaining about how wrong things were.

While on watch I encoded and decoded messages. During this time Pearl Harbor was bombed. One night after the Pearl Harbor attack, a message came in saying that an unidentified dirigible was headed our way. I gave the message to the watch officer. The next thing I knew, an admiral came down to the radio room. When he saw me, he asked the watch officer what I was doing in the code room. The watch officer knew I was very skilled with the machine because of my knowledge of Morse code and quickly made this fact known to the admiral. After an exchange of several messages, it was finally discovered that the dirigible was one of ours, on submarine patrol off the coast.

The Record

As an army officer (he was now a first lieutenant), Hangsterfer was woefully ignorant of navy procedures in general and, in particular, the customs specific to his ship. His ignorance got him into trouble on two occasions, the first occurring when the ship's executive officer caught him lounging in the wardroom with his feet up, sitting in a covered chair the captain used for watching movies. Called upon to explain himself, Hangsterfer said that "some wise guy told me the covered seats were for guests." This was the truth, but the XO did not believe him; and in any case, the XO pointedly informed him, Hangsterfer "was not a guest, but a member of the crew."

Hangsterfer subsequently decided to ask the XO to transfer him back to his unit. He approached the XO while the latter sat at the senior officers' mess table in the wardroom. Without thinking, Hangsterfer seated himself at the table to make his request—his second serious breach of navy etiquette. He committed still another when he took the opportunity to protest his place at the wardroom's table. "I was upset with the wardroom eating order," recalls Hangsterfer. "I was a first lieutenant, but I was sitting at the end of the mess table with the ship's warrant officers, whereas I should have been sitting ahead of the ensigns."

In making his displeasure known to the XO, Hangsterfer was motivated by reasons of appetite rather than concerns about securing his proper standing in the mealtime hierarchy. It was navy custom for trays of food to be passed from the head of the table, where the senior officers sat, to the other end, where the lowly warrant officers were ensconced. By the time the trays got down to warrant officer territory, both the quantity and quality of the food were severely diminished, with all the best and biggest portions having disappeared en route. This was a matter of crucial importance for a self-confessed big eater like Hangsterfer. ("I was a growing boy," he explains.)

The XO was persuaded and Hangsterfer was allowed to move ahead of the ensigns. Not for long, however. "The problem was, I ate too much." This was the last straw for the XO, who "told me that he didn't have any orders to release me but that he would do everything he could to get rid of me."

The XO was as good as his word. Shortly thereafter Hangsterfer received orders to report to Fort Devens.

Charles Hangsterfer

But I wasn't there very long either. I don't think they liked me too much in the regiment, because I was assigned to the advance detail to get the camp ready in Camp Blanding, Florida. I had done such a good job getting Fort Devens ready, and I guess they figured I would be able to help down at Camp Blanding.

The 36th Infantry Division, Texas National Guard, was stationed there, and their people were still fighting the Civil War. I will never forget a gin mill where we went. When the 36th Division men played "Deep in the Heart of Texas" on the juke box, they demanded that everybody stand at attention. Well, the people in the 16th were Subway Soldiers from New York, and they weren't about to stand up for "Deep in the Heart of Texas," or "Deep in the Heart of Anyplace." So we had big fights all over the place. When the rest of the 1st Division came down, it was the same thing.

What the 1st Division would do to deal with the 36th was to send the smallest guy in the outfit into any juke joint. He would play "Deep in the Heart of Texas," then put his hat on and his feet up on the table. The Texans would say, "Hey, stand at attention!" And he'd reply, "Up yours!" They would try to make him stand up and we'd have a big riot and the MPs would have to be called. Finally, the situation got to be critical. So a joint parade of the two divisions was held, and it was explained to us that the 1st and 36th were not enemies, but on the same side, and that we shouldn't fight each other, but save all that fighting for what was to come.

CHAPTER 2

"Are You, Sir, a Member of the Army?"

The Record

Upon graduation from the U.S. Military Academy at West Point in 1936, E. V. Sutherland was assigned to the 16th Infantry Regiment at Fort Jay, where he served as executive officer of F Company. In January 1937 he and his wife embarked from Brooklyn army base on the army troop transport St. Mihiel *en route to his first permanent assignment on Luzon Island, in the Philippines. They remained there for the next two years, with Sutherland serving as executive officer of a howitzer platoon, regimental stables officer, and company commander in the 57th Infantry Regiment (Philippine Scouts). They returned to the United States in 1939. After taking foreign service leave, Sutherland reported to Fort Benning in September to attend a course at the Infantry School. While waiting for the term to begin, he served as a platoon leader in the 24th Colored Infantry Regiment (School Troops).*

In January 1940 the Infantry School course was terminated, and

*all officers were assigned to field duty. Sutherland joined the 1st
Division, which was assembling at Sand Hill on the Benning reservation. He served as executive officer of Service Company, 16th
Regiment, through the end of the year. After participating in the
Louisiana maneuvers, he was detached from the 16th to attend a
course in infantry communications at the Infantry School. In the
autumn of 1940 he was assigned to the 99th Antitank Battalion then
forming at Fort Lewis, Washington.*

E. V. Sutherland

The army was in the process of creating three such battalions,
each with an armament of thirty-six 37mm guns, towed. My first
assignment was as S-3; I subsequently served as the CO of Headquarters Company. In the first role I enjoyed the business of writing, training, and employment stuff. Our doctrine was based
largely on German doctrine. We were starting in grammar school
in this business.

Our battalion equipment was derisory. Instead of thirty-six
guns we had thirty-six pine poles supported on bipods fabricated
from two-by-fours. We could practice selection of gun positions,
but only if our imaginations were active. I can't recall when we
got our first gun. I do remember one day when I was out as S-3
looking at training. I called on B Company. I came across the
CO standing in a tight mob of his soldiers, who were all craning
their necks to look at a 37mm breechblock. That, for a time, was
all the hardware we had.

In HQ Company things were a wee bit better. We had some
pretty good radios—big, bulky jobs, but at least a step up from
the hand-cranked SCR 131s we had in the Philippine Scouts. I
found it interesting that most of the Communications Platoon
seemed to be Japanese-Americans.

Our battalion was attached to the 15th Infantry Regiment. As
a consequence my wife and I got invited to the 15th's regimen-

tal officers' parties. Good fun. There were two majors in the 15th whose names I recall: Eisenhower and Mark Clark. My best friend was Major McElroy. He had taken over Headquarters Company in the 57th Philippine Scouts when my CO was ordered back to the U.S. McElroy was not a West Pointer, but a veteran of World War I. A hands-off boss, great fun, and a good hand with liar's dice at the officers' club at Fort McKinley [on Luzon]. I sought his help when I was struggling to write training manuals for the 99th. A good practical head, and he never condescended to me.

In late autumn of 1941 I received orders to go to the staff college at Fort Leavenworth, Kansas. My wife and I packed the car, and with our son Alec we headed east in the first week of December. Our trip was abbreviated, however. We stopped for gas near Roosevelt Dam and heard a blasting radio broadcast: "Japs bomb Pearl Harbor!" I paid damn little attention to it, thinking that this was a copycat program based on Orson Welles's Martian invasion drama. That this was not so was made clear that evening in Flagstaff, Arizona, when, dressed in civvies, I was registering at a hotel. A cop approached me and asked, "Are you, sir, a member of the army?" I said, "You bet." His response was, "Then please return to your assigned post at once."

So Elly and I drove to Denver, and I put her and Alec on the sleeper for New York City. I saw a remarkable thing in Denver, and I should have saved it: a big headline in the local paper that said, "New York City Bombed." Incipient panic countrywide, I guess.

My solo drive back to Fort Lewis had its seriocomic moments. I drove through the Rockies and the Cascades (lots of snow!), and in Utah I was run off the road by a skidding trailer truck. My car came up against a handy telephone pole. The doors busted open, and I was tossed out and flipped over a barbed wire fence. I was knocked silly, but came to without a personal dent after melting some snow. The car was still ticking over nicely. I had to tie the doors shut with a bit of rope. Awkward!

Next day in the Cascades somewhere, I saw a great long train snaking below me, flatcars loaded with a clutch of antiaircraft cannon. All went well until after dark, close on to midnight, I guess. I came into Olympia, Washington, in a sort of blizzard. I heard shouts, and was quickly circled by a vociferous mob of shouting townsfolk. They started to rock the car, apparently to turn it over. My lights were on. Talk about incipient panic! This rather sobered me up.

When I got to Fort Lewis it was completely blacked out. The battalion area was deserted, the barracks doors swinging in the wind. It was about three in the morning, and with the exception of one or two frozen sentries, I saw no one until I found the only inhabited building—the substantial brick headquarters of the army's IX Corps. I worked my way past the guards and found myself in a lighted office with a major on duty. I learned that the 15th Infantry had all gone to the woods somewhere and so had the 99th AT Battalion. (Subsequently I learned they had been sent to Gray's Harbor down near Astoria on the Columbia River. Their mission was to deploy what 37mm guns they had against an expected Jap landing.)

When morning came I was interviewed by the IX Corps adjutant general. He said my service with the 99th was over and that I was forthwith assigned to G-2, the intelligence section. Colonel Lehman, a cavalryman, was my boss. In my new job I slept, walked about deserted Fort Lewis during the day, and reported for duty at six P.M. A series of quiet nights, I remember.

Three things stand out in my mind about this period. First was the night we received the teletype from Sixth Army informing us that the two great British battle cruisers, *Repulse* and *Prince of Wales*, had been sunk off the Malay Peninsula by Jap planes.

(This is getting serious! I thought.) Next was a surveillance job by a 15th Infantry platoon near Olympia. They staked out a farm house and watched through the nights as a naked bulb was lighted periodically. One cerebral doughboy started to copy down the dots and dashes, pages of this stuff through the weeks. It ended up in the hands of the signal lads at IX Corps and was handed on to Sixth Army experts. There the damn thing was decoded. It defied elucidation, and no wonder: the mysterious blinking bulb was being lit and dowsed frequently by an aged crone with bladder trouble, and the light celebrated her all-too-frequent trips to the biffy! (The authorities found this out after a warrant was obtained and the old lady's house was invaded.) The third thing I remember: the teletype again. A Jap sub had invaded Puget Sound and was prowling around the bottom just off the Seattle docks—or so the report went. Embarrassingly, no corvettes under U.S. flag were available, so the Canadians decently sent one down from Victoria. The Jap sub slouched off in its own good time. I thought, Was this for real?

Some weeks into 1942 my orders to report to the newly established Tank Destroyer Command in Temple, Texas, came through. This looked good to me and Elly, who had rejoined me by this time. So—another long car trip.

The headquarters of Tank Destroyer Command was, I discovered, in rented rooms over a village jewelry store on Temple's main street. As assistant G-3, I worked directly for Colonel Herbert L. Earnest, a horse cavalryman and a fine gent. (Later he was commanding general of the 90th Division in France and became my longtime correspondent and friend.) Here we were, about ten junior officers working under Brigadier General Tindall (cavalry), and our task was to write training manuals and dream up doctrine for tank destroyers (of which there were none)! The operations in North Africa's Western Desert and Libya were big news, and I think our braintrusters in the War Department actually figured that the war—or at least some of its critical encounters—might be settled there.

At this time the British had had some great successes in the desert, and so had the Germans. The back-and-forth struggles from the frontier of Egypt to the Gulf of Sirte had captured the imagination of our thinkers. Our little fraternity over the jewelry shop had grand plans: eventually, we thought, we would field about seventy tank destroyer battalions with high-velocity rifled cannon on armored platforms—and to hell with towed guns! And big plans were afoot to activate the now-renowned and immense Fort Hood, Texas. Gentlemen, we told ourselves, we are on the eve of great things!

I really liked this work. And I liked the feeling that, at least as far as developing doctine and tactics was concerned, we were starting with a clean slate.

CHAPTER 3

"The Ladies Will Be Down in a Minute"

The Record

Paul Bystrak was born in 1920 in the small town of Sobotiste in what was then Czechoslovakia (Sobotiste is now in Slovakia near the border with the Czech Republic). At the time of his birth his parents had already applied for and received permission to emigrate to the United States, but because of a mix-up in paper work he was not allowed to accompany them. His mother came to the United States in December 1920, leaving him in the care of her parents. His father, then serving in the Czech army, joined her in August 1921 upon receiving his discharge. Bystrak remained in Czechoslovakia with his maternal grandparents for the next six years. In due course his father became a naturalized American citizen, which automatically conferred citizenship status on his son. Thus legitimized in the reckoning of American immigration authorities, young Bystrak was allowed to emigrate in August 1927 under Red Cross sponsorship. His family settled in Binghamton,

New York—a town that, like so many others, was hard-hit by the Depression.

Paul Bystrak

Things were rough in 1938–39. My father worked in a shoe factory, and he got down to working just two days a week. I was the oldest of three sons, so I had to baby-sit, cook, and clean house in addition to going to school. Upon graduating from high school in 1937, I started to work on a local farm at $2.50 a week, plus room and board. This did not appear to promise much of a career, so I enrolled in a local business school.

One day a former student, now in the army, visited the school. He was wearing his uniform, and after seeing him all dressed up and learning that the army paid $21 a month, I decided this was the way to leave Binghamton, the housework, and probably a future in the shoe factory.

When I went to enlist in November 1938, the recruiting sergeant told me there were very few men with a high school and business school education applying for the army. He really wanted to enlist me but had no vacancies, except in the infantry or artillery—and only overseas. I didn't know anything about the army, so I asked to join anything. He said, "No, no—with your education I'll keep you out for a good assignment." I was finally enlisted on May 3, 1939, for the post quartermaster detachment at Fort Wadsworth, New York. This was the home of two battalions of the 18th Infantry Regiment, 1st Division.

This first assignment was a mistake, because only people with prior service in the infantry or artillery should have been assigned to the quartermaster. The small detachment had no facilities for training, so I had no recruit training of any kind. (This would prove embarrassing later on.) I became a clerk because I could type with all my fingers. Within three months I had put on forty pounds. My uniform was sloppy. I looked terrible.

Around August 1939 we received a telegram in the office asking for volunteers to join the 1st Division quartermaster. They wanted four volunteers from each detachment in the corps area. I put my name on first, then placed the notice on the bulletin board. I wanted to get into the 1st Division quartermaster because the 18th Infantry soldiers looked so different. They looked like real soldiers.

My detachment commander was a West Point lieutenant. He didn't want to let me go because typists were hard to come by. But he couldn't get anybody else, and he had to meet the quota. So finally he approved my transfer.

In September 1939 I transferred to the 1st Division Quartermaster Battalion at Fort Hamilton, New York. Fort Hamilton was just across the bay, so it really wasn't much of a move. The 1st Division was being reorganized into a triangular division, and the quartermaster (which had been a regiment in the old setup) would now be a full battalion.

Our portion of the unit was the headquarters of the battalion; the truck company was at Fort Jay; the maintenance unit was at Madison Barracks, New York. In about a month we received orders to go to Fort Benning. We went down there as the Quartermaster Battalion, and I thought this was one of the better units. But we wound up digging all the latrine holes for the infantry units that were coming after us. So there I was, digging holes three feet wide, six feet deep, and nine feet long. After digging holes for awhile and getting a lot of blisters, I found out that A Company of our battalion needed a clerk. I asked for a transfer. When my first sergeant found out I could type, he said, "You aren't going anywhere. You're going to stay here." I became the assistant company clerk, which was not an official position. I stayed and eventually was made company clerk.

In the spring of 1940 the 1st Division went on the Louisiana maneuvers along with some National Guard units. We went down with the whole division. In addition to being a clerk, I had become a motorcycle driver. We had motorcycles with sidecars. I never was a very good driver of a car or a motorcycle. It soon became common knowledge among the officers that they should never ride with me if they wanted to get anywhere.

An interesting thing happened to me—interesting because I was an unsophisticated country boy who didn't know anything about life. It happened when we were bivouacked at Charles Lake, outside New Orleans. Some of the fellows started talking about the "houses" of New Orleans and how nice they were. Four of us got a taxicab driver to take us to a nice "house," and he drove to a southern mansion with pillars from ground to roof. We knocked on the door, and a black man in a tuxedo opened the door and said, "Come on in, gentlemen." He introduced us to the madam. She said, "Would you care for a drink, gentlemen?" She called us "gentlemen" even though we were all privates. So we had a free drink. We couldn't afford to pay for one.

Then she said, "The ladies will be down in a minute." Somebody was playing the piano, and pretty soon the ladies started coming down a long, winding staircase in evening gowns, really beautiful. As they started to move around the room the madam said, "Would you like to join and talk to some of the girls?" So we started to mingle with them, but then one of the fellows said, "How much money do we have?" So I looked in my pockets, and I guess I had about forty cents. We all dug through our pockets, and I think we came up with about $4 between the four of us. One of the boys was real sharp. He said, "I got to go tell the cab driver to leave and not wait for us." Of course, we had no cab waiting for us. He just got out of there and disappeared. The three of us who remained hung around feeling more and more embarrassed, trying to figure out how we could get out of there too. After a while the other two said, "Well, we better go find out what happened to him." So they left me there by myself, and finally I had to tell the madam that I didn't have any money. So I left.

We returned from the Louisiana maneuvers in 1940 to Fort Hamilton. Other 1st Division units went back to their original bases. Later in the summer of 1940 we gathered in northern New York for more maneuvers. One of the lieutenants wanted to go visit a house and insisted on a driver taking him there. I didn't want to go. It was night, and I had to take him on my motorcycle in the sidecar. We didn't quite make it to the house—before we got there, he asked to go back to the base camp. I guess he didn't think I would get him to the house in one piece. He did not appreciate my driving at all.

I made corporal in 1940. This was considered quite an achievement, since at the time, the 1st Division was all regular army. I wasn't quite ready to be a corporal, however. Once, shortly after I got my stripe, I was given a detail to dig a hole. I did not know how to give orders, so I went down and started digging the hole myself. It was easier than trying to get the fellows to do it. The first sergeant saw what I was doing, and called me over and chewed me out; he told me I was supposed to be telling other people to dig holes, not showing them how to do it. So I learned fast.

We went back to our bases in the summer of 1940. Upon returning to Fort Hamilton, I was selected to go to a quartermaster noncommissioned officers school in Philadelphia. On the first day of school we all assembled on a small parade ground. By this time I had absorbed some of the 1st Division mystique. I had lost weight and got my uniform tailored, with the big red one patch on my shoulder. One of the instructors said, "You look like a soldier. Take this squad and give them foot drill." There were sergeants and staff sergeants in the squad with many more years of service than I. I asked them if they knew how to give foot drill and would one of them take the squad. A sergeant suggested that

I move the group behind a building and he would take over. My first military command was "Turn around and walk behind the building." That night (and a few more) in the barracks, with the help of some beer and my friend the helpful sergeant, I practiced giving commands by the field manual. And that was how I learned to give the proper commands for foot drill.

In November 1940, upon completion of the course, I returned in the late afternoon to Fort Hamilton. By then the company had received many new men. Some of my friends had been promoted, and I was told to take over a platoon of our company for reveille and other formations. Someone suggested going to Brooklyn to celebrate. Around midnight, in a beer joint across the street from the Brooklyn Port of Embarkation, a fight started. I received a bad cut above my left eye and bled heavily. The civilian and military police broke up the fight and told my friends and me to get out of there. The next morning, with my eye closed and blood all over my uniform, I called out the platoon for morning reveille. My appearance created quite a myth about what a tough, mean corporal I was.

In the winter of 1940–41 the 1st Division was ordered to Fort Devens. Civilian contractors were building wooden barracks, and as fast as they could be completed, units moved in. During our stay there I was promoted to sergeant and later staff sergeant. I organized the new personnel center for the Quartermaster Battalion. During this time each unit was indoctrinated to understand why the 1st Division would have to start accepting draftees.

At Fort Devens we had opportunities to enjoy the night life in Boston, Lowell, Lawrence, and Fitchburg. On one occasion after a *long* night, we arrived at Fort Devens shortly before reveille. I wanted to properly perform my duty as a platoon sergeant, so I decided to take a quick cold shower. Maybe too quick—when one of the men in the platoon came into the shower room, he gave me a look and asked why I hadn't taken off my uniform. I had gone into the shower without undressing. As I said, it had been a long night!

During our stay I decided to try my hand at something new. I got myself assigned to the Quartermaster Division Supply Section. In this new area, one of the most complicated tasks we faced was to receive and distribute the new jeep. No one knew exactly what this vehicle was capable of doing, so allotments were made to the various units for testing new uses and concepts.

In the fall of 1941 the 1st Division joined many other units in conducting maneuvers in North and South Carolina. The quartermaster went back to Fort Devens on December 6. As I unloaded our men and equipment, I recall thinking that it would be a good idea to celebrate our return. I had managed to pick up a bottle of Four Roses, and I asked some of the other sergeants to my room. This was Sunday, December 7, 1941. While having a drink, the radio music was interrupted with the news of Pearl Harbor.

Everyone thought that we would be shipped overseas immediately, but this was not to be. In 1942 the division moved to Fort Benning to test new air and ground tactics. Later we moved to Camp Blanding and had some exciting evenings trying to prove we were tougher than the Texans of the 36th Infantry Division.

CHAPTER 4

"Now We Will Get You Down in the Grease Pits"

The Record

As if to belie Europe's alarming descent toward war in the spring of 1939, the New York World's Fair opened on April 30 of that year with "Building the World of Tomorrow" as its official motto. The fair shut down for the winter on October 31, 1939, and reopened for a second and final season on May 11, 1940. In the interim the theme of the fair had been changed to "Freedom and Peace," which, given recent developments on the other side of the Atlantic, must be regarded more as wishful thinking than an accurate reflection of reality. By then, of course, the German conquest of Western Europe was in full cry (the invasion of France and the Low Countries had commenced the previous day), and the prospects for freedom and peace in the world at large were grim indeed. A 1st Division honor guard detachment was stationed at the fair in both 1939 and 1940; William Campbell joined the unit at the start of the second season and stayed until the fair closed for good on October 27, 1940.

William Campbell

I went into the service because as a lad I had always wanted to.
During the Depression I wanted to go to West Point, but unfor-
tunately I was not able to get in. So I thought I would go to Virginia Military Institute instead. On my way to VMI, I was riding
on a train just outside Washington, D.C. As I walked through
the cars somebody hollered, "Hey, Yank!"

It was an old friend, Coy Baldwin. He and I had gone to a
military prep school together in Danville, Virginia. He said,
"Where are you going?" I replied, "Well, I am going down to
VMI." He was with a friend, and they invited me to sit down.
They had a fruit jar full of corn whiskey, and they invited me to
have a drink with them, so I did. Everything went well. I got off
the train and I matriculated in the school. But two days later I
found out I had entered Virginia Polytechnic Institute, not VMI.
I stayed there anyway and graduated in May 1939. Then I went
home to Newport, Rhode Island.

While I was at home I received a letter telling me I could go
into the army on the Thomason Act. Under the terms of the
act, the army selected a certain number of men and usually gave
them a commission in return for a year's service. I went in on a
seven-month program, so I did not receive a regular army commission. However, I was allowed to go on extended active duty.
I entered the army on December 1, 1939, with orders to report
for active duty in the 18th Infantry Regiment, down in Fort Benning, Georgia.

When the bombshell went off in Europe in September 1939,
the 1st Infantry Division was sent on maneuvers up in Plattsburgh, New York. From there the regiments returned to their
regular homes in Plattsburgh, Fort Wadsworth, Fort Hamilton,
and Governor's Island. Then they left their families at these bases
to go into the field down in Fort Benning, Georgia, for more
training. Myself, I was a bachelor, so I had no problems with the

move. We lived in the field and it was quite cold sleeping in can-vas tents on canvas cots. We weren't properly equipped for the weather; we didn't even have sleeping bags. As a result we lost a few men to the cold, and to one thing and another. But we still went on and trained through the winter as best we could.

In 1940 we went on the Louisiana maneuvers. Then we returned to our home stations in New York and took thirty days' leave. When I came back from leave most of the officers got orders for more in-the-field training, but not me. After a few days I went down to headquarters and asked why. Captain Bar-ber said, "We are holding you here. You are under consideration for the World's Fair."

I thought he was being facetious, kidding me. But it turned out to be true—the division was sending a provisional battalion of specially selected troops to Camp George Washington at the World's Fair, and I was to be one of them. So I went with Andrew Lipskin and Archie Cameron on the World's Fair detail. It was a beautiful summer. Believe it or not, however, I was not as happy on that detail as I was with the regiment in the field. Still, it was a wonderful time. Among other duties, I was assigned as the unit's mess officer. I stayed at Camp George Washington until late October 1940, when the fair closed out. As mess officer I was responsible for turning in all the fancy silverware and china that we used in the mess.

I reported back to Fort Wadsworth, where an officer asked me, "Young man, are you mechanically inclined?" I responded, "Yes, sir." He said, "You are going to the Automotive School at Fort Benning, Georgia." I had been at the World's Fair wearing white gloves all summer, going to dances and hobnobbing with beautiful ladies, and he reminded me what real soldiering was all about: "Now we will get you down in the grease pits before we put you in the field."

CHAPTER 5

Thrilling Days for a Young Soldier

The Record

On February 4, 1941, the 1st Division's units moved from Forts Hamilton, Jay, and Slocum, and Plattsburgh Barracks (all in New York) to Fort Devens, in Massachusetts. Well in advance of that move, however, Fort Devens was in use as a basic training facility. A local boy from just down the road, Sidney Haszard—better known by the inevitable nickname "Hap"—was one of thousands of recruits and draftees who were introduced to military life at this installation.

Sidney "Hap" Haszard

My military service began at Fort Devens on August 13, 1940. I had enlisted earlier in the day in Boston and was shipped by train to Ayer, Massachusetts, a mile or two from Fort Devens. The post was not really prepared for a large influx of recruits. However, because it was normally engaged in Civilian Military Training Corps and Reserve Officer Training Corps activities during the

summer, there was a small tent city as well as limited range facilities for basic training. There were no apparent shortages of
World War I Springfield rifles, so we did not have to learn the
manual of arms with wooden guns or broomsticks. Other shortages, specifically of uniforms, did cause some embarrassment and
a good deal of humor. During this period of influx the army was
somewhat short of the current uniform and had to outfit many
of us from reserve stocks: the old World War I stand-up-collar
blouses, baggy britches with wrap-around leggings, and heavy,
high-top brogans.

I can remember no time during this early experience that I
had a burning desire to send a picture of myself back home. I
never really mastered the art of wrapping those leggings, and one
or both of them were often at the trail. I still don't know whether
you start wrapping from the ankles up or the knees down. Under
the circumstances, anyone who had mastered the art of his leggings welcomed the opportunity to march behind one who had
not. Stomping on leggings was a great sport.

Sometime during early basic training I learned several dis-
turbing facts. First, the people who were in charge of uniform
issue were called quartermaster folks; second, I was enlisted in
the Quartermaster Corps; and third, my quartermaster post was
on some small island off the coast of Rhode Island and accessi-
ble only by ferry.

Fortunately I was afforded an opportunity to transfer to a new
cavalry unit just forming at Fort Devens. I obtained the transfer
and became one of thirteen recruits from the training center to
join a small cadre of officers and NCOs from the 3rd U.S. Horse
Cavalry. The new unit was designated the 1st Cavalry Reconnaissance Troop of the 1st Infantry Division and was to be stationed on the main post at Fort Devens.

The main post in 1940 consisted of four large brick barracks
buildings forming a quadrangle, a small PX, a post theater, and

a parade field. In addition to purely military facilities, there were some officers' and NCOs' housing, and limited activities—but nothing on the order of a modern-day military post.

Our training progressed at the pace of equipment availability, which really posed no problem. In fact the early shortage of vehicular equipment permitted uninterrupted concentration on the fundamentals of dismounted scouting and patrolling before we had to divide our time between maintenance, driving, and mounted training.

The impact of mobilization began to become apparent in early spring of 1941. With the melting of the winter snow there was a flood of construction workers and earth-moving equipment going in and out of the post on a round-the-clock schedule. As the new division cantonment area began to take shape, elements of the 1st Infantry Division began preparations for movement to Fort Devens from Forts Hamilton, Jay, and Slocum, Plattsburgh Barracks, and other scattered posts.

These were thrilling days for a young soldier. The buildup of a division in the process of instilling esprit de corps in its units is an exciting time. That was especially true of a division with the reputation and history of the 1st Division, with its challenging motto "No Mission Too Difficult, No Sacrifice Too Great, Duty First." The presence of Word War I heroes of the division, alive and moving around in the same unit, was an inspiring force. These included Brigadier General Teddy Roosevelt, who had commanded a company of the 26th Regiment in the war, his first sergeant, John Murphy, and other veterans.

Not everyone in the service at this time shared the same feelings. As the fall of 1941 approached, some of those who had been drafted for one year began to sense that their release from the service at the appointed time might not be a sure thing. Thus a new acronym was coined: OHIO. It had nothing to do with the state of Ohio, but stood for a threatened action. If not released on time, some of these folks vowed that they would go "*Over the Hill In October.*" But as far as I know, the threats were never carried out.

By October, the 1st Division was involved in the 1941 North Carolina maneuvers. At the completion of maneuvers, while en route back to Fort Devens, our convoy stopped about 210 miles from Baltimore to drop me off. My troop commander, Captain James B. Quill, handed me orders to report to Fort Holabird in Baltimore, where I was to spend three months at the Motor Transport School taking motorcycle mechanics courses. Captain Quill wanted to make sure I knew where I was going; he also wanted to know how I planned to get there (I was going to hitchhike), and whether I had enough money to get by until I was back in a military post. He shook my hand, slapped me on the back, wished me good luck, and the convoy moved on. The next time I saw James B. Quill was after the war. He was then a major general.

The 1st Division returned to Fort Devens for only a short time before moving south to Camp Blanding, Florida, in January 1942. When I rejoined the reconnaissance troop, Captain Quill was gone and Captain Francis Adams was commanding. In addition to a change of troop commander, we were to get a new division commander, a cavalryman of some note, Major General Terry de la Mesa Allen. (He replaced Major General Donald Cubbison in June 1942.) The reputation that preceded General Allen had nothing to do with being an Eagle Scout. In fact, the stories we chose to accept seemed to favor a deviation from the norm.

Our troop cadre was made up of horse-cavalry officers and NCOs. I have come to realize over the years that these old horse-cavalry NCOs often embellished their stories with trimmings which were not always pure fact. To hear them tell it, Terry Allen was coming to us almost directly from arrest in quarters some place in Texas, or one of those other western territories. There was also a rumor floating around that he drank whiskey! Nevertheless, we were delighted with the stories.

After a few months at Camp Blanding, we moved north to Fort Benning for additional training. It was from there that most of us got our last leave prior to departure for overseas. It was also there that a friend, Second Lieutenant Paul L. Skogsberg, demonstrated that he knew opportunity when he saw it. Skogsberg's fun-loving attitude had not endeared him to his new troop commander. As a result he was chosen to stay behind and hold the fort, so to speak, while the other officers went home on leave. This turned out to be a fortuitous detail. As acting troop commander, Skogsberg received a message from the division authorizing the troop commander to recommend one second lieutenant for promotion to first lieutenant. Skogsberg recommended Second Lieutenant Paul L. Skogsberg.

Several weeks later Captain Adams received notification of the orders promoting Second Lieutenant Skogsberg to first lieutenant. Later, Skogsberg admitted he didn't feel the troop commander's heart was really in it when he offered congratulations. In fact, upon tracking down the source of the orders a few days later, the commander discovered the complete story behind that unusual promotion. When he chastised Skogsberg for not requesting a recommendation from him, Skogsberg told him that the message was not personally directed to Captain Adams, but to the troop commander. As such he, Skogsberg, thought he could handle this minor administrative matter. Skogsberg's decisiveness won him a slot on the advance party overseas.

CHAPTER 6

"We Are Not Going to Get Involved in This War"

Tom Lancer

In World War I my father, Major Thomas F. Lancer, M.D., served as regimental surgeon in the 324th Field Artillery Regiment, which was a National Guard regiment. The regiment served in France from the early summer of 1918 until the Armistice. One night in the Argonne as my father was caring for some badly wounded men, his aid station received a large concentration of gas. It was raining. An orderly was holding a blue flashlight, and it was very difficult for my father to see what he was doing. He thought that the gas concentration was not sufficiently high to be dangerous, and he took off his mask so he could see enough to stop his patients from bleeding to death. In doing so he got a dosage of gas which ultimately caused his death in 1927 at the age of forty-five. After World War I my father said, "The Germans aren't beaten yet. We are going to have to fight them again." And when I was in high school he told me to be sure that if I didn't go to one of the military academies, I should get a reserve commission, which I proceeded to do when I got to college.

The Record

Lancer attended Manhattan College, New York, and graduated in 1930 with a liberal arts degree. ("Not very valuable in job hunting.") His was the first college class to graduate after the Depression began, in 1929, and jobs were scarce. Lancer was fortunate enough to enlist in the New York State Police (which was then mostly horse-mounted), serving with that organization through most of the decade. He also attended law school at Saint John's University in New York, graduating in 1938. In 1939 he joined the FBI, and he was working as a special agent when the Germans invaded Poland on September 1 of that year.

Tom Lancer

Everyone was saying, "We are not going to get involved in this war." I knew we were. My estimate was that we would be in it by the spring of 1942. I was off by about four months. In any event I trotted around to what was then the War Department in Washington and instituted action to go on active duty. I was ordered to report to the headquarters of the 7th Field Artillery at Fort Benning in early 1940. I proceeded there and started my military career.

The 7th Field Artillery was part of the 1st Division artillery and was commanded by Colonel Carlos Brewer, who later became a major general. My commander was Captain Chaplin, a World War I veteran and a very nice gentleman.

After I arrived in the spring of 1940 we received new command cars. These were the high ungainly cars which we had copied from the Germans, and they were quite useless. Not long after we got them, a soldier driving one turned it over and was killed. My battery commander directed me to conduct a line-of-duty investigation, which I did. When I turned in my report he was quite pleased with me. A short time thereafter I was directed to report to the division provost marshal, Major Brookner Brady.

Major Brady had a copy of my report, and he asked if I had written it without help. I assured him that I had and that it was not a very difficult thing, considering my past experience and training. Major Brady said he would like to have me transfer from the artillery to the military police in the 1st Division.

I was then interviewed by the chief of staff of the 1st Division, Colonel Thomas Leslie Crystal. He asked if I gambled. I told him I did not. He said, "Remember, a military police officer must be like Caesar's wife—above reproach." I said, "Yes, sir." He said, "I will approve your transfer." I then moved from artillery to the military police, and remained there for the rest of my career.

CHAPTER 7

In for the Duration

Steve Ralph

I was there at Fort Devens with the 16th Infantry when the 1st Division was assembled for the first time since World War I. We were a patriotic bunch, happy to serve our country, but also fully aware of the neat proviso that our tours of duty were limited by our call-up orders to a term of one year.

That little proviso sprouted wings and flew out the window on December 7, 1941. No one knew where they were going or—for that matter—when. There were a lot of mixed rumors—mostly latrine types. But we all knew that we were in for the duration.

At one time we were part of the amphibious forces of the Atlantic Fleet, composed of the 1st Infantry Division, the 1st Marine Division, and certain naval combat and combat support elements. Eventually, we would probably have been put aboard ships and sent to occupy and neutralize outlying Vichy French–controlled thorns in our side such as Dakar and the rest of Senegal, Martinique, and other French possessions on the eastern and western shores of the Atlantic. We actually prepared for the invasion of Martinique. This was after the fall of France and, later, the occupation of Vichy France by the Germans. While they lasted, the Vichy French were not at all delighted by our presence in any part of the Atlantic Ocean.

CHAPTER 8

"What Happens When You Have Four Balls?"

Everett Booth

I was drafted on April 11, 1941—Good Friday—with seventy-five men from East Chicago, Indiana. We all got on the train and arrived at Fort Benjamin Harrison, in Indianapolis. We were issued uniforms but were there for only a few days. They didn't have shoes to fit me, but I still had my black oxfords. My parents were so concerned about me that they came down on Easter Sunday to check me out. I thought it was kind of funny when my mother told me how they pulled up there to the post and saw these two soldiers in blue fatigue uniforms, with those duffy hats that President Roosevelt's wife had designed. My mother said, "Lem, look at them. Isn't it terrible? Oh my gosh, it's Everett!" So, that's the first shakeup she had about the army.

They moved us down to Camp Shelby, Mississippi, where I was assigned to the 151st Infantry Band. At the first reveille formation under battalion headquarters that I attended, the commandant says, "Who's that guy over there in the black shoes?"

He called the first sergeant over and said, "Be sure he gets some army shoes." And that is what happened. They were about three sizes too large, but I got proper army shoes.

I was assigned to the medics and also attached to the band, so I sent home for my clarinet. The day I got it, the band people were in one row of tents and the medical people were in the row next to us. I got my exercise book out and took my clarinet and started blowing on the thing. Pretty soon some big, tall, lanky guy opened the door, bounced into the tent, and said, "Oh. I thought you were playing that by memory" and walked out. This fellow's name was Melvin Webster. His father was head of the clarinet department at Selmer Clarinet in Elkhart, Indiana. Later on I found out that all the guys in the band were in these tents and heard me blowing my horn. They were impressed— particularly Mel Webster.

There were some good reasons for being in music. I was able to get into the dance band. The air force, down around the coastline, didn't have bands, so we went to Gulf Port, Biloxi, and Mobile to play for the air force dances. You know, that was kind of a good deal, and a lot of people would have liked it, but I got tired of it. Every morning we went out and practiced marching thirty-inch steps. Every afternoon we sat down in the auditorium and played classical music. It didn't seem the way to serve in the army, particularly after the Japanese attacked Pearl Harbor. So I asked for assignment to Officers Candidate School in finance, since that was my background. The adjutant said, "I'm sorry, there are no openings, but there are openings at the Infantry School." I said, "Fine."

I went to the Infantry School at Fort Benning and became a brand-new second lieutenant, graduating in a class of thirty-five in June of 1942. There was a large group of us assigned directly to the 1st Infantry Division. We were stationed at Indiantown

Gap, Pennsylvania, awaiting transfer overseas; one battalion, an advance party, was already over.

Well, here I was, a brand new Second "Louie" with an old army outfit, assigned to the 3rd Platoon, K Company, 16th Infantry. My first day there I went in to check my barracks. I looked for my platoon sergeant, Sergeant Palowitz. I think he was dozing in the corner some place—he had a private to check on things. When I showed up, the private buzzed Sergeant Palowitz, who quickly reported to me as a very good infantry sergeant should. Now, he's six feet four, I'm looking up at him, and the guy has eighteen years of military service behind him—and for several years he was the heavyweight boxing champion of the army. So you can imagine how I felt, a brand new Second "John," in the army only about a year, and I've got this guy to contend with. So I said, "We'll carry on just the way you've been doing things." His reply was, "Sir, we'll do it just the way you want to." Then I found out that I had corporals in the outfit with twelve years of service. Apparently some had been booked down to private many times and gone back up in rank.

The Record

In June, the 1st Division moved from Fort Benning to the Indiantown Gap Military Reservation in Pennsylvania preparatory to the voyage to Great Britain, where it would assemble and conduct combat training. The division's new (albeit temporary) home in Britain would be Tidworth Barracks, a former cavalry post near Salisbury, Wiltshire, just fifty miles southwest of London.

The first units to make the Atlantic crossing were an advance headquarters detachment and the 2nd Battalion of the 16th Infantry Regiment; they departed by ship from Brooklyn, New York, on July 1. Charles Hangsterfer made the trip as a communications officer in the 2nd Battalion.

Charles Hangsterfer

On the move from Indiantown Gap to the Brooklyn Port of
Embarkation, the road guides somehow managed to direct the
convoy to the road to Baltimore instead of New York. When the
error was discovered, the convoy did a 180-degree turn. From
then on it was every truck for itself. It was a miracle all the trucks
made it to the port in time for departure.

But they did make it, and the battalion, together with the
advance headquarters detachment, went to England. There our
job was to get Tidworth Barracks ready for the rest of the division. On the ship over I was issued a book on the customs of the
British people. According to the book, one of their customs was
to invite a soldier home for tea. On my first trip to London after
getting Tidworth ready, I noticed a subway stop named Piccadilly
Circus. I thought to myself, these are brave people to have a circus still running in spite of the bombing blitz I had heard so
much about. As I was strolling around the square at the Piccadilly
subway stop, a lady passing by me paused to say, "Do you want
to go home with me, Yank?" Whereupon I said, "Do you mean
for a cup of tea?" She said, "I'll give you a cup of tea if you want
one, but it will still cost you two pounds." I knew that two pounds
was about equivalent to eight bucks, so I respectfully declined her
kind invitation, as I thought it outrageous to pay that much for
a cup of tea!

Back at Tidworth, while I was making a reconnaissance of
the training areas, I spotted a wire line. Being a commo officer,
I had a professional interest in what the British had in the way of
wire communication. So I followed the wire line, and as I did two
English soldiers jumped out of the brush and ordered me to put
my hands up. I protested that I was an American and on their
side, but they prodded me with their bayonets and directed me
toward their headquarters.

I was taken to be interrogated by their intelligence officer.

He asked for my identity card, which I had left back in my room on the post. All I had in the way of identification were my dog-tags. It was not enough for the Brit intelligence officer, who thought he had bagged a real live Kraut. But just to be sure he asked, "Who is Babe Ruth, and what happens when you get four balls?" Of course I knew the answer to that one, and that's how I was able to convince him that I was an American. The Brit officer then took me to his battalion CO, who told me not to interrupt their exercise and to leave the area at once.

Forty years later, when I returned to Tidworth Barracks to present a plaque for the division headquarters building, I recounted this incident to a mostly British audience. I told my listeners that I was the first Yank captured by the British since the War of 1812. The story received a small chuckle, especially when somebody asked me: "What *does* happen when you have four balls?"

The Record

The rest of the 1st Division departed Indiantown Gap on July 30, arriving in New York City on August 1. That same day it boarded HMS Queen Mary *at Pier 90. A former passenger liner converted to a troopship, the* Queen Mary *weighed anchor at 10:45 A.M. for the transatlantic crossing, which it completed without incident when it docked at Gourock, Scotland, on August 8.*

Upon arriving at Gourock the men of the 1st Division boarded trains that took them to Tidworth Barracks.

The division spent a little over two months at Tidworth, training feverishly for the inevitable day when it would be committed to combat. After completing an amphibious exercise in Scotland on October 18, the division embarked on transport ships in the Firth of Clyde, where the greatest assault convoy ever assembled was staging for Operation Torch—the invasion of North Africa.

PART II

Campaign in
North Africa

CHAPTER 9

Egyptian Adventure

The Record

Prior to Operation Torch, the war in North Africa was fought primarily in Egypt and Cyrenaica (northeast Libya), in an area extending west from El Alamein in Egypt across five hundred miles to El Agheila on the border of Tripolitania. The arena of combat encompassed the Western Desert and the adjacent coastal strip as well as the fertile region of the Jebel Akhdar (Green Mountains) in the Cyrenaican bulge. For more than two years Axis and British armies had conducted a series of campaigns that swung, pendulum-like, across the length and breadth of the disputed region, alternately gaining and losing vast expanses of territory without producing decisive results. By the first week of January 1942, however, the advantage seemed to lie with the British, who had captured all of Cyrenaica and advanced past Mersa Brega to the outskirts of El Agheila. But their advantage was only apparent, and on January 21, 1942, an Axis army commanded by General Erwin Rommel went on the attack, driving the British Eighth Army out of Mersa Brega and advancing to the Gazala-Bir Hacheim vicinity by February 4. Here

Rommel's forces halted and the front remained stable for more than three months while the adversaries rested and recouped their strength for the next round.

On May 26 Rommel resumed the offensive with an assault on the so-called Gazala Line. In the ensuing battles of the Cauldron (May 31–June 2) and Knightsbridge (June 11–13), Rommel's forces destroyed the bulk of British armor and sent the battered Eighth Army reeling back in disarray through Helfaya Pass, just inside the Egyptian border.

It was at this low point in British fortunes that E. V. Sutherland, recently of Tank Destroyer Command in Temple, Texas, arrived on the scene.

E. V. Sutherland

In May of 1942 General Earnest asked me if I would fancy going out to the Western Desert to have a look-see at how the British and Germans were doing—he thought we might get some good hints from them. I leapt at the chance, and luckily my wife was in accord with my decision.

The whole affair started off with a satisfying aura of craftiness. My orders were highly classified: I was to report to the commanding general, British Eighth Army, as a "combat observer." Getting there smacked of a Le Carré story. I wore civilian clothes en route from Texas to Miami, where I was told to sit in the bar of a certain hotel on my first evening in the city and wait to be contacted.

This I did. I didn't have to wait long. A young man approached me and asked if I was Sutherland. Satisfied that I was, he handed me an envelope and told me to report to such-and-such a building at the Miami airport at 7 A.M. the following day. "Wear a uniform," he told me.

At the airport I was met by a uniformed PAA [Pan American Airways] pilot busily checking out his DC-3. We loaded expeditiously. My flying companions were a platoon of tankers from Fort Knox under the command of a young fellow named Snyder. We stopped at Trinidad, landing in a raging rainstorm, then flew on to Dutch Guiana, where we stayed overnight. From Dutch Guiana, we flew to Forteleza, Brazil, then to Natal, on the northern bulge of Brazil.

Natal was a big place with lots of air traffic but no accommodations. I put my blankets on the floor of an empty hangar. Soon I discovered that I had insufficient priority to get a lift. The place was mobbed with State Department types and other folks with high-priority travel orders.

I hung around Natal about four days. Having no success in getting anyone to take me seriously, I got into the habit each night of having my chow packed by a Portuguese woman in a nearby hut, then stationing myself on the airstrip complete with baggage. About the fourth such evening I stood watching as three DC-3s were loaded. A gangling air force lieutenant came up and asked if I wanted a ride to Africa in his plane. He was the navigator. I piled on and found that the fuselage had been stripped bare except for two rows of great galvanized gasoline drums, cradled in two-by-four frames, with tubes running to the wing tanks. That was the only way the DC-3 could extend its legs for a flight across the ocean.

I was the only passenger on that plane. The Fort Knox tankers were still grounded while the State Department feather merchants got all the preference.

We took off, three DC-3s, at about sundown, bound for Fish Lake, Liberia. It was nice and cool aloft, and I soon made a bed on the gas drums and snoozed. Somewhere near dawn the navigator woke me and took me up to the cockpit to peer ahead. Neither of the other DC-3s was in view, but ahead was a long high bank of white cloud. "Africa," he mouthed to me, above the rush of wind through the open windows. (Incidentally, the skipper of the flight was a Second Lieutenant Hubbard, who had graduated shortly before from Midland Flying School in Texas and was making his first over-water flight. Quite an introduction to the business of flying!)

I overnighted in Fish Lake. The next morning I got a ride on another DC-3, this time loaded with a platoon or more of British soldiers in full kit. In spite of a heavy load, we made the flight to Accra, Ghana, and thence to Lagos, Nigeria, in good shape.

Here the trip was temporarily interrupted. A couple of days later, when we attempted to take off with that heavy load of troops, the landing gear collapsed. I found myself stranded for two days in Lagos. This proved to be no hardship, as Lagos was just an old-fashioned West African port city, not the deadly enclave of high-rises and pollution it is today. A wild-mustached Pole, working for British Overseas Airways, tipped me off to an old-fashioned hotel, one with three stories of wide verandahs, reminiscent of Saratoga's best in the old days. My stay there was mighty pleasant: I had tea in bed both days, and aside from trips to the airfield to seek out the possibilities of a ride, I led the life of a nineteenth-century sahib.

I finally did catch a ride on my third trip to the airfield. Boldly, I went up to an air force captain as he was inspecting the tires of his plane and asked him for a ride. He said, "Sure enough." The plane was a Lockheed Lodestar fitted out as a command post for some senior Russian general. It had several tables, comfortable chairs, extensive radio communications equipment, and so on. The captain and I were the sole passengers on this dream, which took me across the continent en route to Cairo.

I had a comfortable ride north to the great walled city of Kan and straight on to Maiduguri, where we landed for the night. The airfield was still under construction there, with hundreds of almost naked blacks pulling great rollers, packing the gravel. Accommodations were primitive: a circular wattle hut, a kerosene lamp, a canvas bunk.

While undressing, a strange thing happened. A bearded figure wearing a bush jacket, slacks, and pith helmet appeared at the door. I knew his voice at once. It was Leroy Miller, West Point class of 1934, K Company, and no great friend of mine when we were cadets—hazed me pretty sharply. But this time I was pleased to see him, and we talked at length.

He was assigned as an observer with the French army in Africa. He had come down to the Maiduguri airstrip that night from his slot up by Lake Chad, about one hundred miles to the north, to buy some whiskey. At Lake Chad he was assigned to the then almost-unknown General Jacques LeClerc, later to become the renowned commander of the French 2nd Armored Division—the first unit to enter Paris in 1944.

We set down next afternoon at the busy airstrip at Omdurman near Khartoum. In contrast to the gentlemanly solitude of my nights in Lagos, I passed this night in a vast hangar with two or three hundred others, all British servicemen as far as I could see. I went with someone to a nightclub in Khartoum—actually a rock garden four stories in the air with strings of electric bulbs and a dance band of sorts. All the hostesses were Hungarian ladies who couldn't speak a word of English. Fascinating!

The next stage of the trip, which took me north along the Nile, was an easy one. I was impressed with how terribly narrow the Nile and its green shores looked in the great waste of the desert.

In Cairo I put up at Shepheard's posh and venerable hotel. There I found Ralph Eldridge, another major from the Tank Destroyer Command who was sent to Egypt at about the same time I was on similar orders. Our instructions directed us both to report to the CG [Commanding General], British Eighth Army, in the Western Desert.

We hopped rides on various convoys, and in a few days' time arrived at Eighth Army. The troops were quartered in tents and

trailers near the coast, somewhere between Mersa Matruh and
Sidi Barani. Things were in a shambles there. The big battles of
Knightsbridge and the Cauldron and so on, while not complete
disasters for the British, had severely wounded them, and Rommel was on the move. General Ritchie, the Eighth Army commander, was up to the hilt in troubles: the whole army was in one
massive flap, with columns, massive crowds of trucks, and other
vehicles streaming back east. Ritchie, trying to sort this out, was
of course unavailable to receive us. Ralph and I slept in the open
and never got near his headquarters. By hopping rides we got
around a bit, up as far as Helfaya Pass, the British front. It looked
like a mess of worms, the British future did. After some days of
this Ralph and I got orders handed to us from Major Henry Cabot
Lodge, whose rank and prominence had admitted him to Ritchie's
circle. "Return to Cairo at once," the orders said.

We started to hitchhike our way back, getting somewhere
south of Alexandria, and were dumped at an ammo supply depot.
We were dog tired, and I lay up against a pile of boxes and fell
asleep. Ralph, meantime, had chummed up with a British officer
and had pointed to my recumbent form: "A very sick officer." An
impertinent but useful lie! To make a long story short, we were
invited onto a light British plane—a Lysander, I think—and lifted
off to Cairo as guests of General Oliver Leese, who was bound
on some weighty errand to GHQ, Middle East.

We found Cairo in a state of agitation. We reported to Middle East Command, the American outfit overseeing the transshipment of American aircraft up the Persian Gulf to the
Russians. Luckily for me the chief of staff to General Maxwell
(the commander of Middle East Command) had been one of my
physics professors at the U.S. Military Academy.

Ralph and I put up at Shepheard's. The atmosphere was like
Brussels on the eve of Waterloo: the evenings saw urbane British
officers on leave from the desert dancing to a graceful band in

the gardens, with their ladies dressed as for Ascot. Groppi's was crowded, the nightclubs were full. But the overall sense was one of guarded anxiety. Was Rommel coming, as the Gyppos [Egyptians] hoped and the British dismissed as silliness? Ralph and I, having seen the American headquarters already loaded on trucks, its destination across the Red Sea, felt uncertain. We agreed we would go south up the Nile if the crunch came, and we filled our canteens and added lots of pills to the contents. We would grab a felucca and go it alone! Ah, youth!

The Record

Rommel's forces captured Tobruk on June 21, 1942, Mersa Matruh on June 27, and Fuqua on June 28. By June 30 they had driven to the outskirts of El Alamein, where the British were preparing to make a final stand. El Alamein was a mere 150 miles from Cairo, a comparatively short haul when measured against the distances Rommel had covered in the preceding weeks. Nevertheless, it was as close as he would get to that city.

E. V. Sutherland

Rommel was overstretched and somehow the British dug in. Within a few days Ralph had orders to report to Port Tewfik, somewhere near the southern end of the Suez, to do a logistics job for Middle East Command. I was ordered back to Eighth Army, this time by windowless troop train.

I put down at a big replacement camp south of Alexandria, then went by truck to a desert spot southeast of Alamein Station and north of the Quatarra Depression. There I found myself assigned to an antitank battalion of the 22nd Armored Brigade, 7th Armored Division, Major Ronald Crouch commanding. I remained with this unit until September. No heavy engagements, but lots of movement to various parts of the line then being es-

tablished by General Claude Auchinleck, now in command of
Eighth Army.

The primitive nature of the battalion's armament interested
me. It had sixteen six-pounder guns divided into four groups, or
troops. Crouch, being of cavalry instincts, preferred to engage
with his guns mounted, firing over the trucks' tailgates, instead
of dismounting and digging them in as we Americans probably
would have prescribed. Anyway, a lovely experience there, and I
developed a tremendous respect for the Tommy trooper. Hard as
nails—and resilient!

Before long Churchill sent Montgomery out to take over the
Eighth Army from Auchinleck. Both Churchill and Montgomery
came out to the field for the evening, and I saw the prime min-
ister as he talked to a select circle of officers with Montgomery
at his side. Crouch, already somewhat famous thanks to his two
escapes from Italian and German hands, and his Military Cross
and DSO, was presented to Churchill. I saw all this from close by!

From then on there was the great buildup along the Alamein
Line. Morale was rising, and massive reinforcements were coming from the U.K. Hundreds of tanks from the U.S. were being
brought up under cover of night. In late August or early September I was again ordered back to Cairo and assigned forthwith
to Middle East Command as assistant G-3. It was a bloody
sinecure—this was a logistics headquarters, and there wasn't much
for me to do. This time I lived in a good flat on Cairo's main
drag with my friends the C/S and the G-4. Good fun, and my
responsibilities were almost nil.

For two weeks or so I commanded Heliopolis District in
northern Cairo. I was the only person assigned there. I inhabited a huge deserted mansion where my only companion was the
Greek girl who was my secretary. My in-box was always empty.
A derisory job, comic-opera stuff, and I thought it best for me
to get back to a real job in the States. General Maxwell, curse

him, was nasty enough; he said I was his, and by God, I'd stay. Then, by a stroke of luck, Henry Cabot Lodge happened by headquarters. He was on his way home, and he sympathized with my lot and agreed to smuggle two letters back with him: one to my wife and one to General Bruce, now commanding the burgeoning Tank Destroyer Command at Fort Hood. This did the trick. In a week I had a message in my hands signed by General Marshall: "Return to Fort Hood by quickest available transport."

Back in Texas my job was S-3 at the Basic Training Center, Tank Destroyer Command. Our job was as the name implies: take the recruit and make him a soldier. This was really unnecessary, since we weren't dealing with recruits—the student body consisted of already-formed tank destroyer battalions from many places throughout the country. In any case, our aim was to create a cohesive, disciplined unit, somewhat schooled in tank destroyer doctrine, but thus far lacking advanced maneuver skills. When we finished with a battalion it was shipped to the Advanced Training Center, also at Fort Hood, for the necessary conditioning that would enable it to pass the overseas deployment test. It was all pretty thorough in concept, but we were still unable to provide the final necessary ingredient: actual battlefield experience.

For some period Tank Destroyer Command enjoyed heady times. The program for the battalion's creation was massive. After Montgomery burst out of Alamein, however, the truth was all too clear, even to tank destroyer enthusiasts: our program was too big to support. The final battles would be in the Med and on the continent, not in the desert, and the necessity for vast manpower drafts into infantry, logistics, and so on made our vision out of date.

One day General Bruce called me into his office. Behind closed doors he frankly advised me of the big cuts that were coming in the tank destroyer program. And, with a wink and a nod, he informed me that he himself was going "back to the infantry." The implications were clear: Why don't you consider it?

I did. I immediately applied for relief from the command and for orders overseas as a "casual" officer. This meant going to Europe as an unassigned officer, to take my chances as to what fate should offer. Though I didn't dream of it at the time, Dame Fortune had me in line for my third and final period of service with the 1st Infantry Division. But not before other seriocomic interludes.

CHAPTER 10

Invasion

The Record

In the first two weeks of October 1942 hundreds of warships and transports concentrated in Scotland's Firth of Clyde to form the Algeria component of the Operation Torch invasion force. (At the same time another force, tasked with the invasion of French Morocco, was assembling on the East Coast of the United States.) The armada departed the Clyde in two convoys on October 22 and 26, passed through the Strait of Gibraltar on November 6, and arrived off the coast of Algeria on November 7. The invasion commenced at 12:55 A.M. on November 8, with the 1st Division going ashore on beaches near Les Andalouses and Arzew, respectively located just west and east of Oran.

Here the enemy was not the Germans but French forces nominally loyal to the collaborationist government in Vichy, France. The defenders had reasons for enmity toward both the Allies and the Germans, and their ambivalence was reflected in their inconsistent reaction to the invasion. The Americans soon discovered that French resistance could run the gamut from none at all to fierce fighting:

where some French units were only too eager to surrender to the Allies, others bitterly contested every inch of ground.

Everett Booth

Our division troops departed Indiantown Gap between July 30 and August 1, 1942. We boarded HMS *Queen Mary* on August 2 in New York City. It took only five days to cross the Atlantic Ocean, and we didn't have an escort because the naval vessels couldn't keep up with our ship.

We landed in Glasgow, Scotland, and they moved us down to the southern coast of England for a short period. From there we went to the Firth of Clyde in Scotland, where we lived on British ships and practiced landing maneuvers every day. We were there for a couple of months, all in preparation for the invasion of North Africa.

I remember one bright moonlit night, when I saw that the ships were moving out. This was unusual, since they normally would be docked in the bay. We sailed into the Atlantic and down toward Africa.

The navy landed us at Arzew and we encountered no resistance at the beach, which was fine since we were all screwed up. It took about an hour for all the troops on the beach to figure out where they were and where they were going. Finally everyone figured it out and took off. Our regiment, the 16th Infantry, went over a pretty good-size hill, and my platoon, which belonged to K Company, was given the mission of flank protection for the entire regiment. So, as the regiment went over this hill, my platoon took a little path to the left side. At one point we strayed almost a mile from our regimental troops. We came back by way of another road, and somewhere along the way I said to my platoon sergeant, "You know, we're going to see a railroad track here in a couple of minutes." Sure enough, the railroad track showed up. I remember thinking then that apparently our training and preparation in studying maps had been pretty good. We got back to the bottom of the hill, and as we approached it we saw the regiment coming down. We met exactly as planned, but one hour later.

Not long after that, I remember, I was lying in a grape orchard on my stomach, receiving machine-gun fire. The entire outfit was in the same predicament. I don't exactly recall how we got out of that situation, but I was always thankful for those high grapevines. A couple of weeks later I went back to that vineyard, and I tell you, those grapes weren't very high. They weren't much over a foot off the ground, so we must have had our bellies really deep in the sand.

Paul Bystrak

Paul Bystrak was a warrant officer in the 1st Quartermaster Battalion when the 1st Division shipped out to Britain. The Atlantic crossing was a memorable event in his life: "There I was on the Queen Mary," *he recalls, "a poor country boy served by English waiters with all the silver and choices!" His unit was posted first to southern England and then to Scotland.*

I was sent up to Scotland with the Quartermaster Battalion just prior to loading the ships for the journey to North Africa. The ships were mostly British with British crews and British rations, which consisted mostly of mutton. Jimmy Wright, a quartermaster and a very famous individual in our division, found out that all the troop ships coming from America needed extra rations in case something happened at sea. When they arrived in Scotland all the extra rations were deposited in a warehouse. Jimmy told me to find some trucks and go down and get as much meat as I could. So I went down with twenty-four trucks and we loaded them with fresh American beef and pork. We even found a few boxes of hot dogs, which were really something to be desired.

By this time all the troopships bound for North Africa had been loaded. The British were not used to our kind of logistics. I couldn't get them to accept the free meat. They wouldn't lower their loading devices, so I asked a company of rangers to work with me. The rangers went with me, unloaded the trucks onto a barge, then went from ship to ship and asked them to drop their nets. They called for the senior American supply man, told him that we had free meat, and asked if he would help us load it on the ship. The rangers hung themselves on the nets and passed up the cases of meat. The men on the ships used the meat to supplement the British rations.

On the way to North Africa we were on a British ship that originally had been used as a ferry between Ireland and England. Every time we ran into a storm we looked like a submarine. We were under water half the time.

The ship had one company from the Quartermaster Battalion and one company from the 1st Ranger Battalion. This was a strange arrangement, because the rangers were supposed to land first, and the Quartermaster was supposed to come last to support the invasion.

The ship had a bar, and we drank considerably. One of the ship's officers was a Scot. The night before the landing he and I drank quite a bit. We decided that we wanted to volunteer to become rangers. Of course, we had no training to qualify us for landing with them. The next morning, when I tried to join the rangers, someone stopped me. But the Scot went on and landed with them. I found out later that he was awarded a medal for what he did on the beach.

We landed on Arzew beach at the docks of some sort of French military installation. There were a lot of old abandoned vehicles just sitting there, the kind that ran on steam made from charcoal. One of the mechanics in our company was really good, so I asked him if he could try to start some of them. He went in there and was able to get about six of them running. They were the first vehicles that we could use to start moving ammunition up to the troops. I later received a promotion to chief warrant officer based on that incident.

Charles Hangsterfer

At Arzew they put me off the ship where my company was and I didn't know what I was supposed to do. I figured maybe they were going to send me home, reclassify me. But I got there and joined up with the 16th Regiment. I was made executive officer of Headquarters Company because I had told them, "Either promote me or send me home." I didn't want to be a communications officer anymore.

I didn't hear a hostile shot at Arzew. My first sight of a dead American soldier was when a power line fell down and electrocuted some men. But I didn't see anyone who had been killed by gunfire.

Sidney Haszard

Haszard remembers boarding the Queen Mary *in New York: "All twenty thousand of us, and each one was allotted one-third of a bunk; that is, we each owned the bunk for eight hours every day. On arrival in England we went to Tidworth Barracks and trained out on the open highways, with reconnaissance units traveling all over the local roads just as we had in the United States."*

After training in Scotland, Haszard's unit sailed to North Africa aboard a British ship, the Warwick Castle.

We spent almost three weeks at sea sailing around as we waited for all the convoys to assemble. In the *Warwick Castle*, the British fed us good tripe. They also fed us lots of kidney stew, and we were not accustomed to that. Some of us felt that the kidneys could have been better drained and flushed prior to being canned.

We finally went through the Strait of Gibraltar and landed at Arzew. We were "greeted" by the French, who shot at us rather halfheartedly. In the beginning we fought Frenchmen, Arabs, and colonial troops but no Germans. After three days of fighting, the division camped in the general area, and got involved in retraining the French after just getting over fighting them.

Ted Antonelli

Ted Antonelli joined the 1st Division at Fort Devens in July 1941 and landed at Arzew as a member of the 3rd Battalion, 16th Infantry. Advancing toward Oran on November 9, elements of the 3/16th became involved in the battle for the town of Saint Cloud, which was defended by French troops.

I went to North Africa on the *Warwick Castle*. We went into the Mediterranean past Gibraltar, and I recall seeing the Rock of Gibraltar. Off the starboard there were some lights in the distance. That was Tangier.

On the night of November 7, 1942, at one o'clock in the morning we boarded the landing craft. These were manned by Brits. Because the Vichy French were in North Africa, and because there was bad blood between the French and the British, it was important for us to identify ourselves as Americans. We were expected to announce, as we approached the shore, "*Nous sommes américains*" (We are Americans), "*Nous sommes vos amis*" (We are your friends), and "*n'ecoute pas*" (Don't shoot). But the fact of the matter was, we usually said, "*Nous sommes américains*," and started shooting. We were very inexperienced, to say the least.

Despite the confusion, we made it ashore. This was at Arzew just east of Oran. I don't recall any armed resistance—I think there was friendly fire. However, those who went in from Oran met severe resistance from the French.

We were supposed to make our destination by dawn, which we did, although we were not sure we were at exactly the right spot. Then at about eight o'clock in the morning we saw Everett Booth (who we called Albie) and his reconnaissance platoon come in to rejoin the company. That was reassuring.

I recall M Company—Heavy Weapons Company—coming in. Lieutenant Bob Waters, the company commander, was riding in a jeep, leading the heavy machine-gun platoon, with his leg dangling over the side in a sort of cowboy fashion. That was the last we saw of him. He was hit by a sniper shortly thereafter. He was one of our first casualties. His death sent a shock through us.

The landing itself and getting to our destination were fairly easy, although there was a lot of confusion. But there was fighting in a place called Saint Cloud. The French put up some resistance, and we were determined to form a task force to relieve our men there. Charlie Stone became the task force commander. K Company participated in that action. As we proceeded down the road toward Saint Cloud, we experienced enemy fire for the first time. Stone, who was taller than the rest of us, thought that if he walked in a crouch he would be less of a target. He bent over and split his trousers. It was humorous.

The initial reaction of most of our people when we took fire was to hit the dirt. Everybody just disappeared. We didn't move forward very much. A lot of our training was on a rifle range, where you see a target and you shoot it, but when fire is coming in your direction, what happens is, people hit the dirt. You can't see one another. You're just lying there, and it is not a good situation. That was one of the lessons we learned on the road to Saint Cloud.

Fortunately for us, the French ceased their resistance. I don't think we contributed very much toward that. But we learned quite a few lessons about command and control and what happens when you hit the dirt and nobody is there to get you moving again. One of the shocks I had was that when the enemy is shooting at you, things don't work out quite as they did in training.

After Oran was secured the 3rd Battalion went to Fleurus, and we camped in that area. Fred Gibb was our battalion commander. One night when we were moving through Fleurus we ran out of the water we had carried to the shore. This was the first time we had to use halazone tablets with water from a well. The water was brackish and tasted terrible.

In those early days of the campaign most of our movements were at night. We were afraid of enemy aircraft during the day, although there really were no enemy planes around Oran.

I saw my first casualties, the first dead Americans, on the move toward Oran. (Bob Waters had been killed earlier, but I didn't see him go down.) I recall one with a helmet. A shell fragment had hit the helmet, and his brains were . . .

William Campbell

Campbell was the regimental maintenance officer for the 18th Infantry. As such he worked closely with Cannon Company, a unit equipped with the M-10 Wolverine, a tank destroyer with a three-inch antiaircraft gun mounted in an open-topped turret on the chassis of an M-4 Sherman medium tank.

We loaded all our vehicles and equipment in Liverpool, England—the 32nd Field Artillery, the 18th Infantry, the engineers, the whole bit. My unit went aboard the *Alcenas*, a Dutch ship with a Chinese crew. We encountered heavy seas. We didn't have much of a convoy; for escorts there were a few corvettes, a little ship smaller than a destroyer. Once in a while you would see one of them on the crest of a wave. How the crews slept on those things, ate on them, I don't know. We were rolling around, banging around—it was rough. And the food was awful.

We passed Gibraltar on a bright sunny day. Axis Sally came on the radio. Not only did she announce our entry into the Mediterranean, she said it was the 1st Division on the ship and told us where we were going. They thought we were going to Egypt. We sailed past Oran and landed at Arzew. It was a dark, dark night. The British wanted to land when there was no moon, and you could see these little landing boats going in; the phosphorus in the water would light them up. We loaded the M-10s into the LCMs. No one knew if the French would shoot or not. But the landing at Arzew was unopposed.

The rangers were to go in and take out the French security detachment in a fort up on a hill overlooking Arzew. They did that. We heard it all on the radio. Our ships went in, but we had no sooner loaded the M-10s into the LCMs, when we found an M-10 that wouldn't start. We got aboard with the M-10 crew and fixed it. I was tempted to stay with them, but I went back to complete my mission, which was to get the rest of the ship unloaded.

As it turned lighter we continued to load the LCMs. At daybreak the *Alcenas* entered the harbor. I went ashore when the ship tied up at the dock. There was sniping and some shooting—a mixed affair. Because it was the first action for the 18th Infantry, the casualties ran high. The officers knew we were going into vineyard country—we had read about it—and some of the Arabs there had gotten ahold of guns and they were doing a little sniping too.

I reported to regimental headquarters just before dark. That night "Hi-ho" was the password, and "Silver" was the countersign. Everywhere you went you could hear people saying the password and giving the countersign, but it didn't keep them from shooting at each other. There was shooting all over the place, even in Arzew. Sometime during the night a sergeant from an artillery unit came into headquarters. He reported that his unit was pinned down by its own men. A section of his platoon was on one side of the road, and another section was on the opposite side. They were having a firefight with each other.

I returned to my unit to find that the M-10s had never been seen by most of our troops. At first the infantry didn't know what the M-10s were. They would see one and ask each other, "Is that ours, or is it the enemy's?" They often assumed they were the enemy's and fired on them with armor-piercing bullets. As a result many of the M-10s were pretty well pockmarked by the end of the day.

On the second day one of the M-10s had the recoil mechanism of its main gun shot out. Another M-10's engine had failed at Saint Cloud across the street from a cemetery. Our regimental commander ordered me to get the gun off that vehicle and put it on the M-10 with the damaged recoil mechanism.

We didn't have a wrecker. (We had the wrecker truck, but the boom had been removed.) There was an armored division around there, and I borrowed a wrecker from them. We drove to Saint Cloud in a jeep with the wrecker following us. The boom on the wrecker looked like a mounted gun. We got up to our front lines and asked some soldiers where the fire was coming from. They told us they thought it was coming from vineyards and houses at the end of Saint Cloud. We told them what we were going to do and asked them to give us covering fire.

There was a knocked-out French ambulance on the right side of the road. Our plan was to drive up behind it, jump into the ditch, and build up as much firepower as we could to keep down the fire coming from the houses. In the meantime the wrecker would drive down the dirt road leading into the cemetery, back around in front of the M-10, hook it up, and tow it back behind our lines.

We drove up behind the ambulance and I hopped out of the jeep. My driver was slow getting out, and I told him, "Get the hell out of the jeep—get into the ditch!" Then I got my first aimed enemy rifle shot, a French bullet fired by Arab soldiers commanded by French NCOs and officers. It whistled as it went by. Another bullet whistled by, and a guy came up to me and said, "How are you?" I said, "Why do you ask?" And he replied, "Boy, you went down so quick, I thought you were hit."

So the shooting started. We got down and started building up a base of operations. The wrecker arrived, turned around, stopped, and the driver jumped out. As he started unloading chains from the back, I said to him, "You'll be killed surer than hell." And I thought, We've got to get going; so I got up to help. I worked with him and got the M-10 hooked up to the wrecker, and we moved out of there.

That night there was sniping, a crossfire, and the British were in it. What happened was, the British were getting shot at by our troops.

CHAPTER 11

"Colonel, There Is No Rank in a Whorehouse"

The Record

On November 10 Oran was secured, and in Algiers Admiral François Darlan, high commissioner for the Vichy government, ordered his troops to lay down their arms. The next day the French in Algeria and Morocco signed an armistice with the Allies, thus ending the opening phase of the North African campaign. Next on the Allied agenda was the conquest of neighboring Tunisia, where Axis forces had seized control from the French beginning November 9 as a counter to the Operation Torch landings. Advancing eastward along the Mediterranean coast, Allied forces crossed into Tunisia at Tabarka on November 15. This movement was undertaken without the 1st Division, which had remained in the Oran area to regroup and reorganize. In the immemorial fashion of soldiers everywhere, the men of the 1st Division lost little time in sampling the pleasures of the newly conquered city.

Paul Bystrak

After the invasion we went to a house in Oran, where we became quite well known. One evening there was a long line of officers and soldiers waiting on the staircase. We went right on past everybody. A colonel stopped me and said, "You have to go to the end of the line." I replied, "Colonel, there is no rank in a whorehouse." The madam came running and shouted, "*Cheri!*" and took us right in. That was rather interesting.

Everett Booth

When the fighting was over we ended up in Oran. We did MP duty—I think they called us "security troops." One of the things I wasn't quite used to was checking all the houses of prostitution. We closed them up for the enlisted men, went around and checked the rooms. If we found any soldiers, we told them to move out. We did this for about a month. It was kind of interesting. I got to know some of the madams pretty well. One invited me and my group over for a dinner she and her girls prepared every night after they were through working. We went and it was quite a meal. And that was *all* it was—we ate dinner and left. But I don't know what time it was when we left—late in the evening, I think.

John Finke

John Finke was a first lieutenant serving as assistant provost marshal at Tidworth Barracks just prior to Operation Torch.

En route to Oran I commanded twelve MPs guarding twenty-four U.S. Army field safes containing $2 million in gold specie for Admiral Darlan. On arrival I delivered the safes to the finance officer at II Corps headquarters. I was then assigned as assistant II Corps provost marshal in charge of "supervising orderly behavior" of the troops in Oran; I was also put in charge of an information office for visiting dignitaries and VIPs.

Among my duties during the initial post-landing phase—before I joined the 1st Division—I was responsible for inspecting and closing all *maisons-de-tolerance* catering to the baser needs of the nonenlisted personnel. After closing the Villa des Roses, where I had, on occasion, encountered several young men from the 16th and 26th Regiments (who became friends and friendly acquaintances later on), I made it my regular habit to visit Number 3 Rue Boyer as my last stop. There was good reason for this—the madam was the wife of the owner and operator of the Chantilly Club, known for its excellent kitchen. As a perk I ate with the staff, with whom I became amicably acquainted, and I sometimes sampled the wares. On one occasion I encountered a senior member of one of the other regiments. He told me a sad story to explain his presence with one or two of his younger staff officers.

He had made a date with a very attractive army nurse. Having promised himself a wonderful meeting (the lady had previously indicated her intent to cooperate in this endeavor), he decided to ask his surgeon (in strictest confidence, of course) if there were any way to enhance his "potentiality," so as to ensure mutual satisfaction and a delightful "climax" to the relationship. The faithful doctor so informed him and gave him medication of a most highly classified nature. The officer was assured that it was absolutely foolproof and guaranteed to give power and lasting perfection.

So far, so good. He took the medication. He met the maiden. They had a lovely dinner and an early evening. Then the roof fell in. She had unexpectedly and unavoidably received a monthly visitor. There would be no uplifting and delightful heavenly climax. What to do now? The medicine was working! His young staff officer presented him with an alternate course of action: Number 3 Rue Boyer.

On arrival at that address the madam told him that she regretted exceedingly that she had to close up, as the II Corps provost representative (me) was expected for supper. I arrived, ate, and, hearing some faint noises of jollity—and noting the absence of the madam—I inquired as to her whereabouts. I received some equivocal answers and insisted on checking. I was met at the door of the salon by the young staff officer, who at first wouldn't let me enter. Finally his patron called me in, explained his predicament, and requested my cooperation. When I granted it—the solution to the problem seemingly already having taken place—I was invited to join the principals. I offered my thanks, but had no intention of any follow-up; my application to the 16th Regiment, 1st Division, had been approved, and I was awaiting my orders. I was also a little apprehensive about serving in a unit whose principal was so beholden to me and whose young staff officer was in on the story. I was wiser than I knew. The staff officer was shortly thereafter promoted to a higher rank and transferred to the Pacific Theater of Operations.

Sidney Haszard

We stayed in the Oran area until December or January. We were out in some lonely place, flat as a pancake, and it could be the blackest place in the world at night. You couldn't see a thing until the stars came out; then the sky was bright and beautiful.

The worst thing about those early days in North Africa was the dysentery. A lot of us had it. I never understood how anybody with dysentery could even think about surrendering. You just had to lie there until you got better. If you were captured I don't think anyone could have made you walk anywhere when you were suffering like that.

Our rations were less than appetizing. They were mostly British Compo-Rations. These came in packets containing crackers, cans of sardines, plum pudding, cans of steak-and-kidney pie, stew, sour candy balls, orange marmalade, and tea. The mess stewards would separate the rations by category, open the packets, and dump the contents into pans. Then they heated it up and laid it out in standard mess-line style, just as if they were serving us real good food.

Another major problem was the yellow jackets and flies going from one latrine to another, and finally into our rations. It was a lucky man who could get through a whole meal without crunching a yellow jacket between his teeth.

The Arabs sold us tangerines and grapes at exorbitant prices. They also offered bottles of wine for $100 or so. We always had to bargain with them, but it didn't make much difference. Eventually some stupid GI would pay the asking price, like five dollars for something that wasn't worth more than fifty centimes. The Arabs didn't lose any time. They would dicker for almost anything: knives, tangerines, oranges, wine, whatever. The GIs played the game because, as a matter of fact, it was fun to dicker with the Arabs.

Everett Booth

Once I bumped into this little Arab kid at a French military installation. Apparently he was a runner, doing odd jobs around the place. When the French introduced me to him, they mentioned that I was from Chicago. His remark was, "Oh, gangster—boom, boom, boom!" We formed a relationship. I had a picture taken with my arm around him, and it appeared in a Chicago newspaper. It also appeared in the *Hammond Times* and the caption read, "Yank and His Brother in Arms."

Charles Hangsterfer

We stayed around outside Oran at Saint Leu. There were some Arabs and some French people there. They were real friendly. The Algerian kids dug latrines for us, but they couldn't understand why we wanted latrines. They thought, why not just do the thing right there on the ground? They didn't even have toilet paper, so we used to keep far away from them because of that. But they were cute little kids.

Frank Kolb

Algiers, capital of Algeria, was captured by the Allies on November 8 as part of Operation Torch. Frank Kolb was an unassigned member of the force that took the city. He disembarked in Algiers harbor shortly after the city fell, and was promptly sent to the 1st Division near Oran.

I left Algiers on a train headed to Oran. The only military personnel on it were privates and second lieutenants like myself, all bound for the 1st Division. We also had the German consul's wife and children and their French maid. One of our officers could speak German, and he was assigned to take her to Spanish Morocco. Her husband had been killed in the invasion. When we arrived in Oran nobody was there to meet us. Later, trucks came to take us to the 1st Division. I was assigned to the 16th Infantry Regiment and reported to regimental headquarters.

When I first joined the regiment we were in Fleurus. In mid-December my battalion moved into Oran for duty. We were housed in old French barracks overlooking the harbor. We had a three-day duty rotation—guarding the city hall with the MPs and local police on the first day, taking the next day off (except to stand evening retreat in the city square), and training on the third day. The French Foreign Legion came in from Sidi bel Abbes to stand retreat on Christmas Eve. Admiral Darlan, former commander of Vichy French forces in North Africa, was assassinated the same day. [Editor's note: Darlan was shot to death by a follower of his rival, General Charles de Gaulle.] My company was supposed to be off on Christmas Eve, but we were sent to the square anyway, to keep people moving and to prevent a riot.

John Finke

On December 13, 1942, I was transferred to the 16th Infantry with assignment as a platoon leader in 2nd Platoon, D Company. We were quartered at Tafaraoui Airfield outside Oran, a bunch of lieutenants living together in trenches about five feet wide, eight feet long, and two feet deep covered with pup-tent halves joined together. There was no way to keep up a decent appearance in such conditions. But just before Christmas we were switched to the 3rd Battalion. We moved into an Algerian winery, which was apparently not functioning. It was heaven! Our quarters were empty open-air vats measuring twelve feet deep and twelve feet wide. Each vat housed two officers. The roof over us was nearly nine feet above the top rim of the vat, and there were eaves wide and deep enough to keep rain from falling inside on either the wine or any alien tenants then in residence. We each had a folding cot and a sort of small table for personal belongings. To enter these palatial quarters we went to the second story and walked along two-foot-wide aisles from vat to vat; then we descended rickety homemade ladders to the floor.

Here we spent Christmas interrupted by several twenty-four-hour alerts, some of them practice drills and others real; for example, I remember on Christmas Eve and Day we were on top-degree security because of the assassination of Admiral Darlan. When I heard that he had been murdered, I wondered what happened to the $2 million we had brought to him from England. I never found out.

Chapter 12

Into Tunisia

The Record

In the final week of November the 1st Division began to be committed on a unit basis to the Tunisian front. Among the first units to go was the 3rd Battalion of the 26th Infantry, which was flown east to Youk les Bains in southern Tunisia and then deployed in outposts guarding the south and east approaches to the Atlas Mountains. On November 23, the 5th Field Artillery Battalion joined the British V Corps and elements of a U.S. 1st Armored Division task force in northern Tunisia. The 5th remained under British control until February 7, 1943. In early December, the 18th Infantry Regimental Combat Team, to which William Campbell belonged, was also attached to British V Corps. The 18th fought alongside British units (notably the Coldstream Guards) in battles at Longstop Hill and Medjez el Bab during the abortive Allied drive on Tunis in late December.

William Campbell

We stayed at Arzew on an Arab farm, out in a field. We had no bathing facilities, so we kept clean by taking baths in the Mediterranean. The civilian population was very sparse, and we didn't have much contact with them. We did have some social meetings with the French; there was a small detachment of French soldiers there, and they gave me my first taste of couscous.

Before we moved up to Medjez el Bab we went to a soldiers' dance. A family was there, Hasidic Jews from Spain, I think. They invited us to dinner on Sunday. The dinner started at noon and ended at 4:00 P.M. It was fabulous.

My CO was the provisional battalion commander, and he decided to have a parade on December 7, 1942, to commemorate the first anniversary of the attack on Pearl Harbor. It seemed ridiculous, but we had the parade. As we were coming back from the parade a jeep came down the road and stopped. An officer in the jeep told us, "Prepare to move out. We are moving out tonight at nine o'clock." So we went back and packed up. But it was dawn before we left, and then it was only to the outskirts of town. Then we were moving toward Tunis, although I didn't know it at the time.

Everett Booth

After a month or so, we moved out into Tunisia. One night there was a transportation unit moving our battalion, and one of the drivers lost contact with the truck in front of him. That scared the shit out of him, I guess, and he decided to turn around and go back. He turned the whole doggone column with him so that half the regiment was going in the wrong direction. Somebody finally stopped this guy and got us headed back the right way.

Charles Hangsterfer

We didn't go into Tunisia as a whole division, but piecemeal. By the time my regiment—the 16th—got there I was regimental headquarters company commander and regimental communications officer as well.

Two of our battalions were attached to the British. We had one battalion spread all over the place. There was nothing in the textbooks that showed any semblance to this military operation except that we were occupying some ground. The enemy up there, the few that we saw, were Italians. I remember once seeing an Italian soldier coming down the road. When he spotted us he said, "Hey, don't shoot me. I'm from Brooklyn. I just happened to be over in Italy and they put me in the army. I'm glad to see you folks!"

That was my first experience with the enemy real close—this poor guy from Brooklyn, drafted by Mussolini into the army.

Frank Kolb

Soon after Christmas, in early January, we left Oran by train for Tunisia. We had several engagements there. We did not operate as a division but were scattered out and mixed in with French and British units. For a time the company sector was so large that patrols had to go out each day to contact the unit on our flank. When we were not patrolling or in the company area, the platoon manned an outpost for twenty-four hours.

Steve Ralph

My outfit, the 16th Infantry, was with a British brigade in North Africa. We had lots of tea but godawful food such as oxtail stew and ersatz sausage because there was no meat—only fat and grain. Oh, how appetizing!

We ate meals out of communal pots while sitting on the ground. Our cooks put all the food in one pot and cooked it up. The tea was good, but our soldiers wouldn't drink it. They wanted coffee. The big thing we got was a ration of rum, enough for every soldier, and it was about 140 proof. We were supposed to water it down. We ladled it out to the soldiers. The officers got scotch and gin, but you had to buy it. A British brigade provided it, and it cost ninety cents for an imperial quart of Johnny Walker!

We had been with the British so long that it became funny. If one of our soldiers got wounded and was sent back to us after he recovered, he was wearing a British uniform because we didn't have any American uniforms to give him. In order to get the poor guy out of the hospital, they had to clothe him somehow and bring him back up to us. He'd appear in the British pisspot helmet and battle dress. It was really funny to see those guys come back looking like Brits.

Chuck Horner went completely British. He even grew a mustache. He got ahold of a Bren gun carrier—a tracked vehicle, lightly armored, with a very low ground clearance, that carried a Bren gun, a Czech-made machine gun which was like a Browning Automatic Rifle. By that time Chuck was a battalion executive officer. He got a French gimmick and hooked it on his helmet, and he carried a swagger stick. I can see him now, peering straight ahead with his hand on the Bren gun carrier, looking like Lawrence of Arabia.

Our regiment's commander, Colonel D'Alary Fechet, was a World War I veteran. He was still World War I as far as I was concerned. He came up once on inspection while we were still with the British. He asked Chuck, who was wearing British battle dress and leggings, "Young man, are you in the American army?"

Sidney Haszard

At first the African campaign was a case of loafing a lot. I remember going to places like the one just northeast of Tébessa. This was an outpost in the high desert, and I have never been so cold in my life. We made walls with empty British gas cans and put pup tents on top of them. There was a chimney at one end of the tent and a candle for light and heat. We didn't have many blankets and no winter clothing.

Initially there wasn't much action in this area. But we were a reconnaissance unit, and we traveled all over the place looking for information; and, once in a while, we got zapped. Generally we lost only one or two men at a time, but once, in an ambush, we lost a good part of the platoon. Another time, I went out on patrol in a jeep accompanied by a quarter-ton truck, searching for some of our missing men. We found two Arabs and a donkey coming across the desert, and over the back of the donkey was one of our platoon leaders, First Lieutenant P. L. Skogsberg. He had been shot in the butt. The Arabs had picked him up, saved him. When we got him on the hood of the jeep, he asked us to give the Arabs all the money in his wallet.

Paul Bystrak

In the aftermath of Operation Torch the 1st Division's Quartermaster Battalion was broken up. The maintenance platoon of Headquarters Company became the 701st Ordnance Company, and the rest of the organization became the 1st Quartermaster Company. Since there was no vacancy in either unit for a warrant officer, Bystrak was given a choice: he could either accept a commission as a second lieutenant in the Quartermaster Company or go to division headquarters in G-4 as a warrant officer. "I had no college education, and I did not really want to be an officer," says Bystrak, "so I went up to division headquarters." He was with headquarters when the division began its move into Tunisia.

As we headed into Tunisia, one of the things we found out about logistics was that there was no way an American fighting man could carry all the equipment he was issued. Someone got the bright idea that we ought to take all the barracks bags—they were called barracks bags A and B—and store them while their owners were in combat. If the troops were pulled out of combat, it was my job to get the bags to them in a rest area as fast as possible so they could change clothes and get their personal effects.

One time in a village somewhere in Tunisia, storage of any kind was hard to find. I evacuated as many Arabs as I had to out of their little shacks and put in the baggage of the whole division of fifteen thousand men. Someone thought I should have some security for the buildings. They gave me infantry men who had been wounded and were recovering; these men, as an interim assignment, were to provide security while they finished their recuperation.

I thought I had security on all the buildings. Then, during one of the movements in lower Tunisia, one of the regiments was taken out of the line for a rest. I was called and told to get their luggage up to them. They sent a British truck company to transport the bags. A major was in command. He saluted me and I said, "Major, you don't have to salute a warrant officer." He replied, "Whatever you want, sir; I'll do whatever you want." He was very cooperative. We loaded all his trucks, and they took the bags to the regiment.

Shortly afterward the inspector general of the division came down for an investigation. I asked, "What's going on?" He said, "What happened to the officers' clothing that was stored in the bags?" I said, "Nothing should have happened." Then the IG told me that all the clothes had been stolen from the officers' bags. It turned out that, despite the presence of the guards, the darn Arabs had climbed onto the rooftop of one of the buildings, removed the shingles, and gone inside. It was where the officers' bags were stored, and the Arabs were smart enough to figure out which were the VAL packs and which were the barracks bags. [Editor's note: A VAL pack was a folding suitcase, usually made of canvas, normally used by officers for personal uniforms and effects.] So they took the officers' clothing from the VAL packs, then crawled back out, covered up the roof, and left.

Between this and some other incidents, it became apparent that storing the bags was not a solution. All the men were asked to completely strip themselves and keep only what they needed for fighting. Anything they wanted was shipped home by the quartermaster free of charge, and the rest of it was turned in.

Around this time we repaired a captured shower unit. When units were pulled out of action, all the men were allowed to take showers and get complete changes of clothing, outer and inner. This became standard procedure for Europe later on, where official shower companies were assigned.

Another incident in Tunisia: we were running short of supplies, and I was asked to go up to the British army near Tunis to see if I could get clothing and rations. While I was up there, they told me the only underwear they had was female underwear that had gotten shipped there by mistake. I decided to take it, because after all, it was clean, and it would fit some of the men. I don't know who wore it though.

In order to receive a ration of rum like the British got, we had to sign certificates that we were operating in lots of inclement weather. I certified that we had inclement weather, and the division got lots of rum.

Charles Hangsterfer

The job of a regimental headquarters company commander can be compared to that of an innkeeper. Not only do you have to take care of the health and welfare of the troops, you also have to be chambermaid and maitre d' to the regimental CO and his staff.

In 1942 the table of organization and equipment did not take into account special requests such as portable latrines, which the regimental executive officer had ordered me to provide. To begin with, there were no GI specifications available from which to construct such an item. Second, there was no material readily available to assemble portable latrines. However, that made no never-mind to the regimental exec, so the company scrounger was pressed into service to find the material for the portable privy. Had we not been in combat and constantly on the move, this item would not have been as much of a problem as it turned out to be. Since there was no TO&E for a portable privy mover, nobody wanted to handle the temporary toilet; consequently, when we went to a new location, the WC became a will-o'-the-wisp, and the only one concerned about it was the regimental exec. As the innkeeper and HQ commander, I was responsible for everything my company did or did not do; therefore, I was caustically chewed out because the comforts of home were not on the dropping line.

Since I did not enjoy being berated for the missing obnoxious odoriferous object, I assigned one soldier to guard, transport, care for, clean, and control the use of the portable privy. I admonished him that he would wear it as a collar if it were left behind when we moved. Responsibility of command is a heavy burden, and when the portable toilet collapsed with the heavy burden of the regimental exec on it, my army career turned on what the soldier in charge of the PP [portable privy] did. I often wonder what he told his children when they asked him, "What did you do in the army, Daddy?"

William Campbell

I was still with Cannon Company when the 18th Regiment went into Tunisia. We had to move up behind the regiment because we had trouble with the vehicles. Denny Fowler was then CO of Cannon Company, and I worked with him—the regimental commander said he didn't want to see me unless the M-10s were with us. We didn't have much food along the way—just some canned food as well as good French bread from the bakeries in these little French towns. We also traded with the Arabs for eggs. We made it to Algiers, where we met the rest of the regiment. Then we moved up to Medjez el Bab.

We arrived there at night. It was pitch-black and the weather was horrible: rainy and foggy, with lots of mud. We went to a bivouac area near a place called Longstop Hill. The Coldstream Guards had allegedly taken Longstop Hill, but they didn't really have it, and our 1st Battalion was committed to combat on December 23rd. It was a hard-fought battle, and the battalion lost a company.

Then we got orders to pack up because we were pulling back. On Christmas morning, in the mud and rain, we moved into an olive grove. The 1st Battalion was still up on Longstop Hill, but the rest of the regiment had moved back.

We regrouped. Then the entire regiment—except the battalion that had gotten shot up on Longstop Hill—moved up to Medjez el Bab again. We stayed there for forty-five days. I was still regimental maintenance officer, but I continued to spend a great deal of time with Cannon Company.

Our supply lines were seventy-five miles long, and if possible, the only time we did any moving was at night. It was kind of a static situation. Two German Messerschmitts controlled the area. We saw them all the time—we called them Mutt and Jeff.

They would fly over our positions every day and do a little strafing. They would come down and strafe a single vehicle on the
road, let alone a convoy. One moonlit night they killed some
artillery people in a jeep.

At Medjez el Bab, there was a British observation post. One
time when the British soldiers were changing the duty shift, a
German patrol caught the ones coming off and shot them all up
and killed them. Also at night the Germans laid mines in places
like Tally-Ho Corners, which was named by the British and
located behind our positions.

Between the 18th Infantry and the neighboring British regiment was a five-mile gap, and German patrols went through
there at night. So the British sent up one hundred Scottish commandos to stop the patrols. We had a British liaison officer, Captain Guy Mansell, and he told us the commandos were coming
in. He wanted us to come over that night to meet them. So we
went over and had a few drinks with the commandos. They were
dining in that night, having a stag party. Some of the Scotties
wore kilts, and they were drinking and wrestling and carrying
on. Their colonel was wrestling too, and as he grappled with his
partner, he fell down, his kilt flew up, and that's how I got the
answer to the age-old question of what the Scots wear under their
kilts. The answer is, nothing. Captain Mansell, who was standing next to me watching the colonel, said, "Look at it, Bill—look
at those wrinkly old balls."

After a while the liaison officer asked, "Is there anything
doing around here?" We told him what we knew: there was a
house nearby where we thought there were some enemy soldiers.
About midnight, after the frolic of their stag party, the commandos had a shot of whisky, then took off their kilts, blackened
their faces, and went out on patrol in full battle dress.

They found a guard sleeping on the porch of the house. They
took care of him. Then, rather than go into the house to find

out what was there, they just set the house on fire. The Germans who came out were greeted by the commandos. Next morning, after the Scotties had returned, they had another little nip of whiskey, retired for a wee nap, then arose ready once more to do battle.

The Record

In early January the rest of the 26th Infantry Regiment and the 33rd Field Artillery Battalion joined the U.S. II Corps in southern Tunisia. The remainder of the division moved into the area between January 18 and January 24, concentrating in the vicinity of Guelma sixty miles east of Constantine. By January 25 the entire division was in Tunisia. However, due to a series of emergencies confronting Allied forces at this stage of the campaign, division elements had been committed to action separately over a two-hundred-mile front extending from Medjez el Bab in the north through the Ousseltia River Valley in the center to Gafsa in the south.

Ted Antonelli

Some elements of the division were not under the command of Terry Allen; they had been parceled out to other commanders. My regiment, the 16th Infantry, went to the Ousseltia Valley and reported to the French XIX Corps, which was commanded by General Louis-Marie Koeltz.

Our first real combat after Oran was in this valley. We were facing the Italians and the Germans, and the Germans had air superiority, so we moved at night. After one such night movement we felt a little uneasy about where we ended up, but didn't think much about it. The next day we began to receive artillery rounds in our positions. The initial reaction was that this was friendly fire and would soon cease. I was with K Company, and I was the company exec. Captain Les White was the company commander. He detailed me to take a group and go off on the left flank. While I was there the shelling continued, and it became obvious that it was enemy artillery. We were much farther forward than we were supposed to be. Evidently the battalion commander had misread the maps and we had moved up too far.

Unbeknownst to me while our patrol was on the left flank, the battalion got orders to withdraw. We didn't get the order and remained where we were, but when we looked back we could see our troops withdrawing. The withdrawal became a disorderly rout as people rushed to get away. I decided to go back to where my company headquarters had been and find out what was going on. It was there that I saw my second casualty. I thought he was a sleeping soldier, but he wasn't sleeping—he was dead.

At that point it became obvious to me that everyone had withdrawn, so we decided to withdraw too. There were about five of us and we had a jeep. We hooked up the ammunition carts to the jeep, and as we drove back, the Germans or Italians, or whoever they were, began shooting at us. We became worried about our own people not knowing who we were, since we were coming down from enemy lines. Then our ammunition carts turned over. We had to unhook them and leave them behind, but we made it back to our lines.

So the first real action we participated in was almost a disaster. We weren't where we were supposed to be. We had withdrawn in a disorderly fashion; there was considerable confusion. We were fortunate the enemy didn't press the attack against us; perhaps they couldn't. We survived our initial taste of combat, which was not exactly heroic.

Then we went into some other positions. We knew that the troops in front of us were Italians. During this period we had nightly air raids and didn't engage in any offensive maneuvers. Once, some of us spotted three Italians. By the time word got back to headquarters, they had turned into three *battalions*! That caused a good bit of confusion.

CHAPTER 13

Kasserine Pass

The Record

The main body of the 1st Division was still in the Ousseltia Valley on February 14, the date General Jürgen von Arnim's Fifth Panzer Army launched a powerful offensive against U.S. II Corps positions in the Faid Pass area, some eighty miles south of the division's sector. Spearheaded by two Panzer divisions (10th and 21st), the Fifth Panzer Army advanced through and around Faid Pass to Sidi Bou Zid, where it mauled American 1st Armored Division tank forces in two days of fighting. Meanwhile, to the south, Erwin Rommel's Panzer Army Africa, with elements of 15th Panzer Division leading the way, captured Gafsa and pushed north to effect a juncture with von Arnim at Kasserine Pass.

On February 16 the rest of the 1st Division was withdrawn from the Ousseltia Valley and dispatched to the Kasserine Pass vicinity to meet the enemy onslaught. The Germans pressed on. The two attacking armies, now united under Rommel's overall command, reached Kasserine Pass on February 19.

Charles Hangsterfer

The fighting started to get progressively worse. There was this place called Kasserine Pass—the Germans had broken through there. This was the Afrika Korps, the real soldiers who had been retreating with Rommel from El Alamein. They still had a lot of fight in them, and they knocked the daylights out of the outfits on top of Kasserine Pass. The 16th was sent down for a counterattack to keep them from breaking through any farther.

I went down with the regimental CO and his staff to Tébessa, where II Corps headquarters was located, to find out where we were going. We walked into headquarters, and you could smell the aroma of steak and french fries. Until then we had been under British control, and all we had was steak and kidney pudding and corned beef. The first time you ate their food it was great, but after you had it for lunch and dinner for two or three weeks, the steak and kidney pudding tasted like—well, I can't say what it tasted like. But it was comparable to the Spam we had later.

So we smelled steak and french fries and would have liked to eat some, but the II Corps headquarters personnel weren't gentlemanly enough to invite us old combat soldiers for dinner. They told us we were going to Kasserine Pass to fight the Germans, and that is what we did. We knocked the daylights out of the Germans. We were up on the ridge and they were down in the valley, and we just shot the daylights out of them.

William Campbell

After forty-five days at Medjez el Bab we thought we would be relieved. We were all pooped out and hoped to get a rest when Rommel made a breakthrough at Sidi Bou Zid and Kasserine Pass. He was making this push because the Eighth Army was putting pressure on him. The situation was almost like the German offensive in the Ardennes in the winter of 1944. So we moved at night to get around him, and suddenly we were caught on this road, the whole regiment bumper to bumper, and if any German planes had come over. . . .

The Record

Following probing attacks into Kasserine Pass on February 19, the Germans launched a massive assault on February 20 that broke through the Allied defense line. The Allies fell back and the Germans advanced through the pass, sending a diversionary attack west toward Tébessa and thrusting north to Thala with the 10th Panzer Division and elements of the 15th Panzer Division. At the same time the 21st Panzer Division drove north from Sbeitla to Sbiba. But the Allies, strengthened by reinforcements that included British troops and tanks and the U.S. 9th Infantry Division artillery, were able to stabilize the situation and mount counterattacks that drove the enemy back.

Everett Booth

Everett Booth describes a climactic episode in the Battle of Kasserine Pass, when Allied artillery smashed a German armored attack on the road to Tébessa on February 22.

We were advised that General Rommel was going to bring his tanks through Kasserine Pass to break through our defensive lines. The 1st Infantry Division was assigned to cover that pass. I took my platoon up one night, and we were assigned an area just at the end of the pass. We went up in darkness and found a unit from the 601st Tank Destroyer Battalion. We were relieving them, and their commander was getting his orders for their next move. He was a guy I had worked with before the war, in the purchasing department at General American. How about that for a small world! I bid adieu to the guy. I felt sorry for him because I knew where he was headed, and I knew what kind of armor and artillery he had compared to Rommel's tanks. I thought I'd never see him again.

We took over his position. The next morning we were dive-bombed by Stukas. [The Axis had air superiority at the time.] Later that morning a large group of German tanks came down through the valley. Lieutenant John McCarthy went looking for a place to put an OP [Observation Post]. When he saw where I was, he said, "Hey, how about if I join you?" I said, "Be my guest." While he watched the German tanks heading in our direction, he asked, "Why isn't the artillery firing at them?" The absence of artillery fire finally got to him and he said, "Boy, they're within my maximum range, I'm gonna fire." He gave a command to his mortars—these were 81mm mortars—to fire one round of smoke. We heard the round go out of the tube—you could hear the noise they made. Then we listened and listened and waited and waited for that damn shell to land. Well, he was firing at maximum range, and that shell went up in the air, miles I guess. Finally we saw a great big cloud of smoke on top of one of the tanks. Mac had hit the damn tank right on the head.

Shortly afterward the artillery opened up and the tanks broke their formation. The artillery gunners had had to change their range settings and that's what had held them up. We stopped those tanks primarily with artillery fire.

The next thing that happened in Kasserine Pass: Down the main drag in the middle of the pass came a bunch of two-and-a-half-ton trucks. When they got to a certain point, the troops jumped out and started firing in our direction. We found out later that these were all Italian troops. It didn't take us long to annihilate them with artillery and machine-gun fire. We cleaned that problem up. After that we headed back toward Oran.

Steve Ralph

D'Alary Fechet, the commander of the 16th Infantry, would drive you crazy. Chuck Horner and I used to laugh about this. Once, down in Kasserine Pass, I was at 2nd Battalion headquarters, and it must have been about four o'clock in the morning. Everybody was asleep but me. There was nothing going on, but they let me handle the phone calls all night because I was the oldest guy in the regiment. I got this phone call. We had these code words because Terry Allen said you had to use them. For example, a tank was called a grunt. So when you were talking over the phone you weren't supposed to say "tank"—you said "grunt." D'Alary called up. His code name was Dance. He said, "This is Dance. Let me talk with Joe Crawford," except he gave Crawford's code name. (Crawford was 2nd Battalion commander.) I said, "I am sorry, he's not here."

D'Alary said, "Have you jumped off yet?" I knew the man was mixed up—he had called the wrong battalion—but I didn't want to violate security by telling him that. So all I said was, "Sir." He got madder than hell at me, and repeated, "Have you jumped off yet?" I kept saying, "Sir." He said, "Let me speak to . . ." And he gave the code name for Horner. I got hold of Horner and explained, "The Old Man has lost his goddamned marbles. He's mixed up." So Chuck got on the phone with him and straightened him out.

What pleased me was that D'Alary said to Horner at the end of the conversation, "Apologize to that young man." He was all mixed up. The attack he was talking about was supposed to be on the other side of Kasserine Pass, not where we were. He was all screwed up.

The Record

The Battle of Kasserine Pass effectively ended on February 23, 1943, when the Germans abandoned their offensive and withdrew eastward through the pass.

Ted Antonelli

We got word that down at Kasserine Pass it had been a disaster. So we were withdrawn from our positions in the Ousseltia Valley and sent by convoy down toward the pass. This was the first time that Terry Allen was able to assume complete command and control of the whole division. The 16th Infantry participated in a counterattack. We were successful and thought we had repulsed Rommel. It turned out that he was in the process of withdrawing—at the end of his logistic capabilities. But still, the Germans withdrew in the face of our fire.

The attack on Kasserine Pass was launched, and we went into the town of Kasserine, but no Germans were there. They had withdrawn even farther. From there we went to Gafsa and then to El Guettar.

CHAPTER 14

Gafsa to El Guettar

The Record

After Kasserine Pass the 1st Division was sent to Marsott, northwest of Tébessa, to regroup. Following a ten-day rest, the division, now assembled as a unit for the first time in the North African campaign, moved out of Marsott and deployed to attack the oasis town of Gafsa and its Italian garrison.

Charles Hangsterfer

At Gafsa, the 16th Infantry was going down one road, the 18th down another, and we were all going to converge on the town. It was the first time the division had attacked together as a unit since Oran. I was riding along the road to see how the troops were doing, and I spotted this jeep with a big sign that said, WAR CORRESPONDENT.

There was nobody around. "Anybody here?" I shouted. Nobody answered. So I told my driver that I was going to take the jeep back to the regimental CP and paint out that white sign. When I entered the CP, the regimental commander saw me riding in this war correspondent's jeep and says, "Where did you get that jeep?" I said, "Down the road." He said, "Did you steal it?" "No, I didn't steal it, but I was afraid some dishonest person would, so I figured I would bring it here for safekeeping." He said, "Take it back where you found it—now." He wouldn't let me keep the jeep.

We were issued stocking caps to be worn under the helmet. It was always the responsibility of the company commander to see that his people didn't wear the stocking caps except under the helmet. One day I was outside the CP and I see this fellow who I don't know, and he's wearing a stocking cap without his helmet. I exploded. "What the hell's the matter with you anyhow, wearing a stocking cap?" I told him, "Put your helmet on and cover up that stocking cap!" I didn't know it was Ernie Pyle, the war correspondent. He wrote a lot of stories about our unit. In one of them he observed that, to date, we had spent more time on the line than the 1st Division had in World War I.

Tom Lancer

Our first attack was against the town of Gafsa in southern Tunisia. The Germans had blown out a long section of road, and we couldn't get the wheel traffic across, only infantry. The 1st Engineers were busily repairing the road. It was very important to restore the wheel traffic for supplies, ambulance evacuation, and the like. It was raining heavily and my men were strung along the road directing traffic. The date was March 17, 1943—Saint Patrick's Day—and along came Brigadier General Theodore Roosevelt in his jeep.

His jeep was called Rough Rider, and that name was painted on the front. He stopped and I immediately reported to him. He looked me up and down. It was pouring rain but he would not put up the top on his jeep. Knowing my background, he said,

"Tom, it is a great day for the Irish." Then he said, "I notice your men are all clean-shaven."

Being clean-shaven was something I insisted on when water was available, not just for appearances, but because it was good for morale. For the same reason the British Guards always polished their boots before they attacked.

The Record

Gafsa's Italian garrison withdrew and the 1st Division took the town without a fight on March 17.

Charles Hangsterfer

By this time General Patton was II Corps commander, having replaced General Fredendall on March 6. Patton was a real strict military man, but he allowed us to open the collars of our shirts and pull our neckties down to the first two shirt buttons. Everybody else had suntans, and here we were in our woolen uniforms, so he said we could undo the first button. Well, that was mighty gracious, but if you got caught without a necktie or didn't have your helmet on, you might be fined $50 or $100.

The Record

From Gafsa, motorized patrols probed in a southeasterly direction along the Gabés road, making contact with Italian forces just east of El Guettar. The division attacked the Italians on March 20, and a full-scale battle developed when the Germans rushed in strong reinforcements that included elements of the veteran 10th Panzer Division, and subsequently the 21st Panzer Division as well. The climax of the battle occurred on March 23, when the Americans repulsed several furious assaults by German armor and infantry supported by Stuka dive bombers.

William Campbell

Down at El Guettar I was lying there in the ditch with some of my soldiers, and the 88mm shells were coming in pretty heavily. A command car came and drove down the side of the road. General Terry Allen and General Patton were in the car. I thought at the time, Boy, if they want to get killed, they at least ought to let their driver get out. They were just off the side of the road and there was a little gap in the hills. The 88s were flying in there and popping around. We were just staying down, but Allen and Patton stayed there and watched for a while. Then they left.

Subsequently that day, as predicted by a British intelligence outfit, we were subjected to a tank attack. I think that is where Patton's aide was killed. It was about four-thirty in the afternoon. First the report came in that the attack would occur about four-fifty; then the British came back with a correction. It was very good intelligence. They had good contacts.

The enemy was down below our battalions, which were positioned in the hills on the enemy's flanks. Their tanks came into view and the German soldiers looked like they had just sprung up from the ground. They had been in a wadi and they were walking along with the tanks, right into our artillery fire.

Our artillery broke their attack. Out on the flank, Colonel Greer thought it was a good time to police up some of the damaged vehicles in front of us. So we went out with a wrecker into the regimental front lines to pick up the vehicles. That started the German artillery coming in. It was 75mm or 88mm artillery and, though the bursting range was pretty small, they had us pretty well bracketed, so we decided to get out of there and move back.

One day at El Guettar we were attacked by Stukas, the old dive bombers. When they dove, they flew below our line of sight; it was as if we were looking down on them from the roof of a three-story building, and they'd get down to the second floor before they pulled out and dropped their bombs. Those Stukas could really come in.

Steve Ralph

On one occasion we launched an attack with E Company. The plan of attack was that each platoon would step out smartly, every man advancing toward the enemy positions. D'Alary Fechet was down there with his entire staff except me. He left me in charge of the command post. Thank God. He took everybody else, and I mean *everybody*, and started off this attack with a platoon. It was ridiculous—I was left back in the CP with nobody. I was the only one there when General Allen called up from division. I answered, "Dagwood CP."

"Let me talk with D'Alary," Allen said.

"I'm sorry, he isn't here," I replied. "He's out on inspection."

"Let me talk to the executive officer."

"I'm sorry, he's not here. He's out with the colonel."

"How about the three [third in command]?"

"I'm sorry, he's not here."

"How about the intelligence officer?"

"I'm sorry, he's not here."

"Who the hell *is* there?" Terry finally demanded.

"Me."

I think there was probably a squad of Italians out front who opened up on D'Alary and his men with a machine gun. Pinned them down all day, and put a bullet through D'Alary's elbow. He laid out there all day long. That was the end of D'Alary.

Charles Hangsterfer

El Guettar was a real miserable place. The terrain was big hills and bridges. I remember that an armored outfit reported to our headquarters to inform us they would "whip like a snake up the valley" and beat the hell out of the Germans.

In those days every gun that shot at us seemed to be an 88, and they were really good artillery pieces—they could knock the eye out of a fly wherever the gunners could see him. So the armor didn't do too well whipping like a snake up this valley. It was the infantry that had to go up these hills, mostly with night attacks, to defeat the enemy. Colonel Fechet, the regimental commander, got wounded there, following up an attack. I was almost with him when he got hit, but I was somewhere else, splicing a wire line. But the poor old regimental commander and his S-2 were both wounded.

Sidney Haszard

Our unit, the 1st Recon Troop, often acted as a diversionary force. During the battle of El Guettar we had a hairy job of probing the German flank to make them think a real threat existed there. What we often did was move into an area at night, make a lot of noise, then quietly move out before dawn. We did that up and down the front between the regiments and units, to deceive the Germans as to where the gaps in our lines might be.

Once we got into our daytime positions, we couldn't move because we would get strafed. We didn't have any air support in those days, so we couldn't give away our positions—if we had we'd have been sitting ducks for the German planes.

Fred Dolfi

We had some tough battles at El Guettar. We lost a lot of men there. I was cited for hauling ammunition under direct fire. The Germans zeroed in with mortars and one of the mortar shells hit my jeep. I wasn't wounded, but others were. After that they called my jeep "Shrapnel Joe." It was pretty well banged up.

Ted Antonelli

Some people feel that El Guettar is where the 1st Division really came together as a fighting element. First we took positions that had belonged to the Italians, and many Italians surrendered. Subsequently we engaged a German unit that was going to attack El Guettar. We had been given considerable information about their plans. Their attack unfolded essentially in the way that we had been told, except that there was a delay of about thirty minutes. The attack was initiated by Stuka dive bombers followed by artillery and armor, and finally infantry.

We held at El Guettar although the 18th Infantry did give way, and some of our people were taken prisoner. A 601st Tank Destroyer unit, which had been forward of our position, was badly handled—they were no match for the German tanks and 88s.

We proceeded to move forward. Rommel was coming up along the coast with the British Eighth Army in pursuit. Our plan was for the 1st Armored Division to punch through. We would follow and drive on to the coast to cut off some of Rommel's elements.

I will always remember that morning when the tanks of the 1st Armored Division, with pennants flying, started to move. But that evening and the next day they were still in the same place. So began an infantry slugfest, with the 9th Division on our right and the 3rd Division on the left in the hills, moving forward inch by inch to get to the area we were supposed to reach in a few hours.

One of our problems was determining exactly where the 9th Division was located. We sent patrols to find them and they came back without success. Then it was decided that a patrol led by an officer would go out. This was unusual—up to that time I had thought that patrols were supposed to be led by NCOs. As I was company exec, I was detailed to take the patrol.

I had a good-size group, about twelve men. We left the foothills and went across the valley floor to get to the mountains, the place where we thought the 9th Division might be. While we were going across the valley we had a number of actions. German aircraft strafed us, which made us think, Why are they wasting ammunition on such a small group? We didn't know that the Germans were preparing to withdraw farther. We were also fired on by 88s. The first shot came in short and the next one came in way past us. They fired a number of rounds without being able to hit us. To fire 88s on a patrol seemed a waste. I think they were just expending their ammunition.

In the late afternoon we contacted the 9th Division and exchanged information. We showed them where the 1st Division was and proceeded back through some German mine fields, using bayonets to find where the mines were. We completed the mission, and that was how I got my first Silver Star.

CHAPTER 15

Moment of Glory

The Record

After much hard fighting, the Germans broke off contact and withdrew from the El Guettar area on April 7. Afterward the 1st Division spent a few days in the Marsott area for rest and refitting, then moved by truck convoy 150 miles north to positions northeast of Beja. On the night of April 22–23 the division launched an offensive aimed at clearing the Tine River Valley and its flanking hills for the final drive on Tunis.

Ted Antonelli

The preparations for the attack were impressive. We had air parity and possibly even air superiority. Our aircraft determined where the enemy positions were and our artillery bombarded them. We were supposed to reach our line of departure at dawn, but didn't. So it was in the full morning sun that we crossed our line of departure on the forward slope of a wheat field. We headed down into a little valley to assault the German positions in the hills in front of us. We took a lot of fire—machine-gun fire, artillery, and so on. We were in a very difficult position, on the slope of the hill in full sight of the Germans. Then we got into the wheat field. We were pinned down there and we couldn't see the Germans because the wheat was fairly high. The Germans couldn't see us either, but they were hitting us with just about everything they had.

At one point we thought we were getting friendly artillery fire. I recall being on the end of a phone line to Charlie Stone asking, "Where is the artillery hitting?" A shell fragment came within a few inches of my head. All our artillery was shut down then until it was determined whether it was our guns or German artillery firing at us. The Germans were very clever, timing their attacks to coincide with ours to cause confusion. It was possible that it was their artillery coming in, but there was also reason to believe that it was our own. So we shut down and remained in this position until night.

My company commander, Dick Cole, was missing, so I became company commander. At night we withdrew on order to a battalion assembly area. The orders were that the attack would be resumed toward morning. Since K Company had been in the assault the day before—and because there were no officers left in our company—it was decided that the assault would be led by I and L Companies with K in reserve.

We moved forward to prepare for the assault. The fellow commanding I Company had been quite a braggart about what he was going to do to the Germans. But he broke down. He cried. It was obvious he couldn't lead, so Charlie Stone decided that I Company would be held in reserve and K Company would conduct the assault.

We moved forward into a draw at dark, toward a hill. I told my men to fix bayonets. On my signal we were going to yell and scream. This had been done before by some other outfit and we thought it wasn't a bad idea to make a lot of noise.

We proceeded into the draw and got about halfway up the hill. We received fire and the men began to hit the ground. I thought back to the lesson we had learned earlier: you take heavier casualties when people hit the ground and don't go forward. As the only officer in the company, I decided that we would move forward, and we did.

We got to the top of the hill. There was some light—it was dawn. Suddenly there was an explosion in front of me, and I fell, coughing. I knew something had happened, but I wasn't spitting up blood, so I figured I wasn't hurt too bad. It turned out that a hand grenade had been thrown at me because I was the guy the Germans could see coming up the hill. We were very close to the Germans, and there were four or five of them. We took them prisoner.

We took the hill and got behind the Germans—the mission was accomplished. That was my moment of glory. I have since been told that the Germans began to withdraw and there was no further offensive action. I was evacuated to a field hospital for surgery, then taken by ambulance to a British hospital ship, the *Yorkshire*, which took me to a hospital in Oran. I had some complications and went to another hospital in Rabat. I eventually recovered and got an assignment with VI Corps. I ended up in Italy.

It is an unusual experience to serve in combat, especially close combat. I have been in combat with other units, but it is not the same thing. In Vietnam I was a general and I saw a lot of shooting, a lot of activity, but it was never the same as when I was a platoon leader or company commander. It was very different.

CHAPTER 16

"They Said They Weren't Mad at Us"

The Record

The Tine Valley campaign was characterized by fierce fighting in rugged terrain that greatly aided the defenders. By exploiting the isolating effect that rough country tends to have on combat operations, the Germans were, on one occasion, able to surround and capture elements of the 1st Battalion of the 16th Regiment. This occurred on April 30 when two platoons of the 1/16th, after seizing the crest of Hill 523, were cut off by a German counterattack and forced to surrender. Frank Kolb was one of those taken prisoner.

Frank Kolb

At El Guettar, Lieutenant Kim Richmond was hit by artillery fire. I was assigned his platoon. Richmond was back in forty-eight hours. He said if he could stand the rough ambulance ride, he figured he wasn't going to die, and thought that he would be better off with his unit.

We moved out of El Guettar and up north into the mountains. Soon after that—sometime in April—I was transferred out of 3rd Battalion (16th Regiment) and assigned to the 1st Battalion because it had lost quite a few of its officers. Colonel Taylor had told the regiment's battalion commanders that they would have to send their youngest officers as replacements instead of letting the commanders pick who to send. I was just turning twenty and was the youngest officer in the 3rd Battalion. I went to a rifle platoon in C Company, 1st Battalion. Then we went into the Beja-Mateur area, and I was one of ten officers captured.

We were on Hill 523. We took the hill during the night and the radios got knocked out. We had also laid two telephone lines and they got knocked out too. C Company was on the left flank, and the Germans proceeded to work that flank. They knocked out our first platoon. I was near the CP and we got word twice that the platoon was trying to counterattack and repel the Germans. I think finally one man came back to report they had lost the position.

By that time the Germans had gotten onto the hill, and they started picking us off one or two at a time. My platoon sergeant, "Gunner" Green, and I got picked off. They threw a potato masher at us and we jumped out. They stood there with machine guns, yelling in German, which neither of us understood. But we knew they wanted our hands up, so we put them up and went down the hill. I just knew they were going to take us down there and shoot us.

At the bottom of the hill they took everything from us, including our personal possessions. Finally a lieutenant showed up and he chewed his men out. They kept all the GI issue, but gave back our billfolds and everything else. They took us back to the company command post of a paratrooper outfit. Colonel Denholm, the battalion commander, was there and he was exhausted. The German commander saluted him and told him that the colonel's rank called for a certain respect. Then he had his orderly spread out his [the German commander's] greatcoat and Colonel Denholm lay down on it to rest.

They shipped us all back to a staging area—I'm not really sure where. There was a Red Cross guy there. Every day he complained to the Germans that he wasn't supposed to be there, that he had gotten lost and that they should turn him loose. But they never did.

This was the regular German army we were dealing with. One day they told us that an SS officer was going to take our money and give us receipts for it. They said to hide most of our money but give the SS man some to satisfy him.

The guards let the Arabs in at night to sell us food. We got the same rations as the Germans, but it wasn't very much because they didn't have much.

Then we were deloused and given a permit to enter the Greater Reich. They moved us to somewhere near Tunis. At that time we had other prisoners with us, all Americans, including a colonel of ordnance who had been on the battlefield checking out German tanks when he got captured.

The men argued with the German guards, talked about Hitler and Roosevelt. The Americans would say, "Hitler stinks!" The Germans would reply, "Roosevelt is no good!" We talked to some of the German officers, and they said they weren't mad at us; they were just doing their job—they were paid to fight.

We were never mistreated. In fact the Germans kind of looked after us when the SS men came. They told us that when we got to Germany, if we were lucky, we would get into a camp run by air force people; but if we were unlucky, we would get into the camps run by the SS. The day before we left they gave us a loaf of bread, and the French Red Cross also sent us some food. Then we went down at night to get on a ship.

When we reached the ship a bunch of British Eighth Army soldiers were there—Indian troops. It was an Italian ship with an Italian crew and German naval personnel and antiaircraft gun-

ners. Early one morning an Italian destroyer came into the harbor to escort us, and we started out of Tunis Harbor. Planes of
the U.S. Air Force, especially B-25s, were bombing the harbor
area heavily, but we still got out pretty far before one of the
planes flipped a bomb down back of the escorting destroyer and
blew it up. So our ship's captain got leery, and he started to return
to Tunis. His heart really wasn't in this.

Then the planes started bombing our ship. We got a couple
of near hits, which sprang the plates, and we started taking on
water. The captain ran us onto a sandbar right off Carthage. We
didn't have much list, and from the air we must have looked like
we were still seaworthy, so the planes bombed us before we could
get off the sandbar—bombed us a total of about seven times.
There was a British soldier killed, a German, and—I think—one
American.

The Italians said they wanted to get off the ship, and the Germans said they would have to take everybody with them on the
lifeboat. They removed the sick and wounded first and got to the
harbor all right. Then the air force came back, strafing anything
out on the water that was moving. It was impossible to evacuate
anyone else.

By then the German gun crew and the Italian crew had all
gone. A British major and Colonel Denholm decided that Denholm was the ranking officer and should take charge. We opened
up the stores and got food. We found blankets—red and white
ones—and made a Red Cross sign. We also found an American
flag and a British flag. We took down the Italian flag and ran
those up.

But the planes kept bombing us, so we sent two signal men
from the British artillery up to the bridge to flash signal lights
at them. The colonel sent me up with them, and when the
bombers flew in, the artillery men signaled SOS and PW (for
"prisoner of war") with their blinking lights. In the meantime a

British intelligence officer and one of our officers swam ashore to notify the Americans to quit bombing us. Finally, three planes came in. They flew over us and stacked up. It looked like they were coming in on us when all of a sudden the lead plane veered off course and threw his bomb wide. The other two planes never did drop their bombs.

That was the end of the bombing. Then the French got boats and came out to pick us up. We ended up in a school building. We were under Colonel Denholm's command, and he was telling everyone what to do. He had everything organized. I was sent with Buck Fagan into Tunis to try to get some food. We had a German car. We had to put a pair of pliers in the gearshift to make it work, but we managed to get to Tunis.

The Germans were still trying to get out of Tunis, and the British Eighth Army hadn't gotten there yet. Some French people told us to go to the Louis Pasteur Institute. At the institute the French gave us food, which we brought back to the rest of the former prisoners. Soon after that the British army came to town. We greeted them as they arrived. They were surprised to see us.

We got back to our unit. We had been gone a total of two weeks. Colonel Taylor had been sitting on the missing-in-action reports, so none of our families had been notified of our capture. My family would not have been notified anyway, because I had been transferred to C Company by verbal order. Personnel didn't know about it. When they had gotten the remnant of the battalion back and checked the roster, it was assumed that everybody who wasn't there was missing in action. Well, I was never on their roster, and so far as the army was concerned I was never missing in action. How I found out about this was, we were paid, I think, $20 a month for rations, and we were charged $30. Well, everybody who'd been a prisoner of war hadn't eaten the rations, so we were to get a refund—and I didn't get a refund.

Some of the men decided that since we had been prisoners of war, we should go back to the States. But when they went to see Colonel Taylor to request transfers, he told them he was not about to release officers and men with as much experience as we had and they might as well forget it. We went back to Oran and then to Algiers and got ready for the invasion of Sicily.

CHAPTER 17

"You May Be All Right at the Front, but You're Not So Hot Back Here"

The Record

While Frank Kolb was a prisoner of the Germans, the 1st Division continued to attack and advance in a northeasterly direction until May 13, when the surrender of Axis forces in Tunis brought an end to the fighting in North Africa. Subsequently the 1st Division was sent back to a training camp at Arzew.

In nearby Oran, the 1st Division soldiers found a new enemy: the much despised (by combat veterans, at any rate) rear echelon soldiers belonging to the Army Service Forces (ASF) units stationed in the city. Several days of intermittent street fighting between 1st Division and SOS troops ensued before order could be restored. By then the division had earned the enmity of Major General Omar Bradley, the commander of II Corps. Bradley blamed the 1st Division commander, Major General Terry de la Mesa Allen, for what he judged to be a serious and inexcusable breakdown in discipline; and although he took no immediate action against his subordinate, he would, in due course, make Allen pay a high price for the division's unruly behavior.

In the following account John Finke conveys something of the cocksure irascibility and contempt that 1st Division troops felt toward those who had not been exposed to combat.

John Finke

I returned to the 16th Regiment after an almost seven-week sojourn in the 12th General Hospital and the 1st Replacement Depot, necessitated by a penetrating bullet wound received at El Guettar. It happened on March 28, 1943—my first day in action!—while I was a platoon leader in D Company, 16th Regiment.

On arriving back, I requested transportation to my company, only to be told to report to Colonel Taylor, commander of the 16th, whom I had never met. This news caused me very considerable consternation. I thought, What the hell have I done to merit a visit to the commanding officer of the regiment on my supposedly happy return to my home-away-from-home in D Company?

The reason for the summons could have been a report of our insulting but (as Art Dean, my ex-company commander, and I believed) justifiable failure to salute the base section commander, a Colonel [later multi-starred] Leavey. Colonel Leavey wore what we considered to be a mirage of a stateside uniform: garrison cap, immaculate pinks and greens, gleaming boots and, to the best of my remembrance, glistening and jingling spurs! Art and I were on a pass from the 2nd Convalescent Hospital, dressed in our field ODs and stocking caps, when we ran into the colonel and failed to salute. We were struck almost speechless by the blistering dressing-down we received, which included an insulting reference to our division commander, Major General Terry Allen. Leavey said words to the effect that "You may be all right at the front but you're not so hot back here." This didn't sit so well with two combat-wounded soldiers wearing Purple Heart ribbons on our clean but shabby OD shirts.

Art, who was homeward bound, swore that he would write a personal letter to Terry and also to George Taylor to report the incident and our version of it before he [Dean] left for the land of liberty. I firmly believe that he did so! Since I was sure he would wait until he was safely aboard ship before writing, I still had some slight apprehension about having to explain the facts before the arrival of Art's letter.

(Before Art left we were involved in other less damaging incidents, which included the accosting of an apparent lady of light virtue by a chaplain in uniform. The chaplain was pursuing the lady, who appeared to want nothing to do with him. Art seemed to feel that the chaplain was insulting his cloth. Even though I was certain the lady in question was unaware of her molester's status and couldn't have cared less had she known it, Art felt she needed to be protected from his importuning. I didn't share his concern but I couldn't resist baiting the bastard, because he was so revolting in manner and appearance. Of course, the minute we knights in shining armor intervened, the lady changed her mind, stopped bargaining, and disappeared with the villain.)

Anyway, I was thinking about all this as I sat outside the Old Man's tent waiting to see him. Finally Lieutenant Colonel John Mathews stuck his head out and called me in. I breathed a sigh of relief, for I knew the Kewp, which is what we called Mathews. It was Mathews who had approved my request for transfer to the 16th. So I went in to face my fate.

There, much to my dismay, I was informed by Colonel Taylor that I had been selected to command the regimental headquarters company. We discussed the requirements of the assignment, the problems of HQ Company, and particularly the backing I would get on the job. This was most important to me, since a comparatively junior first lieutenant like myself could expect a lot of more senior people to take advantage of their rank to get special treatment from me. Colonel Taylor left no doubt in my mind that he personally would back me up in running the company my way. I was to phone or see him or Colonel Mathews if I had any trouble.

At this time we were in Arzew planning and preparing for the invasion of Sicily. Shortly thereafter the regiment was deployed to the neighborhood of Algiers from where we were to embark for Sicily. The move was made by land, rail, organic transport, and by sea. The regimental headquarters went by sea on the same ship we would use to invade Sicily—the USS *Samuel Chase*.

On our arrival in temporary billets outside Algiers, we immediately commenced preparing personnel and equipment for loading onto the *Chase* and off-loading in the vicinity of Gela, Sicily. It was a herculean job, but our experience and expertise let us go about it in a minimum of time.

At this point I was still a first lieutenant, commanding regimental headquarters company of the 16th Infantry. But on the fourth of July, 1943, I was promoted to captain. Finally I had caught up with my contemporaries in the regiment who had been wounded but not dropped from the rolls. About ten to twelve officers who had been junior to me until I was evacuated in late March were now again my equals but senior to me as captains by several months.

PART III

Sicily

CHAPTER 18

Gela

The Record

With North Africa secured, the Allies turned their attention to Sicily. The invasion of that island, code-named Operation Husky, would involve two armies: the British Eighth, commanded by General Bernard L. Montgomery, and the newly activated U.S. Seventh, commanded by Lieutenant General George S. Patton. The 1st Division, part of Omar Bradley's II Corps, would land near the small port town of Gela, just west of Cape Passero on the south coast.

The division began preparing for Husky immediately after returning to Algeria following the Axis surrender in Tunisia. Upon completing amphibious training exercises near Arzew and Mers el Kebir in May, the regimental combat teams concentrated outside Algiers between June 8 and June 23. The entire division made a final practice landing at Zeralda on June 24. Elements of the division boarded landing craft on June 26 and departed for Tunis the next day. The rest of the division embarked on July 5 aboard transports for a rendezvous outside Tunis on July 8. From

Tunis, the invasion fleet proceeded to Sicily, battered en route by strong winds, high seas, and heavy rain.

Charles Hangsterfer

After the Tunisian campaign ended, rumor had it that the 1st Infantry Division would return to the States. Then we were told that we would conduct landing maneuvers for Operation Husky. We hadn't even had time to whitewash the rocks in our bivouac area after our return from Tunisia, and now we were scheduled to invade Sicily! A few days later, near Oran, we began to make dry runs, climbing down cargo nets into landing craft.

Everett Booth

We were getting ready to land on Sicily. We boarded this craft called an LCI [landing craft, infantry], which held two hundred troops, or the equivalent of an infantry company. I knew the commander of my ship very well and I went up in the crow's nest with him. Well, I'll tell you, that's the closest I've ever come to being seasick. The ship was long and narrow and would go over at what seemed a ninety-degree angle on one side, and then back at a ninety-degree angle on the other side. Pretty soon I told this navy lieutenant that I was going down to hit the sack, that I couldn't stay up there. In the meantime, all the other troops got very, very sick.

John Finke

Not too many days after I was promoted to captain, we loaded up and departed Algiers for our next landing. At first we went eastward along the North African coast. This was done as much to confuse the enemy as it was to link up with other components of our task force, namely landing craft infantry ships and other sea landing craft that carried the regimental reserve. (The 3rd

Battalion and other tactical and logistical units were not traveling on the assault transports.) I believe we came close to Pantel-
leria, an Italian island which had been almost flattened by massive
air attacks. (It had been used by the enemy to harass convoys
moving through the Mediterranean to Egypt.) We were told we
could see Malta in the far distance as we continued to sail east.

Shortly after dark on the ninth of July we changed course to
the northwest, then due north to approach the coast of Sicily.
During the night we were hit by a storm of gale-force intensity,
which made life difficult for the first-wave troops who were loading their landing craft. As a valuable dividend, however, the storm
made it extraordinarily hard, if not impossible, for enemy aircraft to keep track of us on the way to our landing areas.

Although the seas were still high, the weather started to
improve on the afternoon of the tenth. The outloading was much
facilitated by the easing of rain and high winds. I estimate it was
after 0200 hours by the time we outloaded and started to the
beach.

The Record

*Preceded by airborne drops, the landings at Gela began at 2:34 A.M.
on July 10 with an attached ranger unit leading the way. The 16th
and 26th Regimental Combat Teams followed a few minutes later.
Italian units defending Gela offered only negligible resistance and
were swiftly overcome. The German Luftwaffe, however, was soon
active in the skies overhead, launching numerous raids against the
invasion fleet and the beachhead. In the early evening a Stuka dive
bomber sank LST No. 313, loaded with elements of the 1st Division's
33rd Field Artillery Battalion. On the afternoon of July 11, a large
group of JU 88s attacked the* Robert Rowan, *turning the ship into
a funeral pyre for many of its crew and passengers when detonating
bombs ignited its volatile cargo of munitions and gasoline.*

While the Robert Rowan *burned, the 1st Division beat back a powerful Axis counterattack spearheaded by the elite Hermann Goering Panzer Division. The attack came as the Americans were unloading their antitank guns and artillery from landing craft. The guns were hurriedly brought into action, and these plus the guns of Allied warships standing just offshore were soon pounding the onrushing panzers. Nevertheless, German tanks got to within two thousand yards of the beach before they were repulsed.*

Later that evening twenty-three U.S. transport aircraft carrying troops of the 504th Parachute Infantry Regiment were shot down, with heavy loss of life, by friendly fire from the ships of the Allied invasion fleet.

Tom Lancer

After we landed we went straight into Gela and occupied the town hall. The mayor had departed, of course, but lying on his desk was an Italian translation of *Gone with the Wind*, which he had apparently been reading. I went to the balcony of the town hall and watched the POWs, mostly Italian, some German, being herded by the military police to the beach for evacuation by ship. Their U.S. escorts were just as tired as they were, and they were shuffling along. General Patton arrived. After glaring at them from the balcony for some time, he yelled in his high-pitched voice, "Make it double time. Kick 'em in the ass. Make it double time!" They broke into a ragged shuffle as Patton continued to glare down at them.

Charles Hangsterfer

I landed at Gela with the 16th Infantry's assault team in the first wave. Many of the troops were seasick on the run into the beach. Just before we got there a spotlight from shore focused on our invasion craft and somebody began to shoot at us. Because we knew that the 82nd Airborne was supposed to light fires rather than use a spotlight to guide us to the right beach, we knew the spotlight belonged to the Italians. It was on us for only a short time; the navy shot just one salvo and put the searchlight out. The rest of our boat ride was uneventful. When we landed there on the beach we could still hear the spotlight generator. They didn't knock out the generator—just the searchlight!

The light enemy resistance on shore was quickly overcome, and my company [Headquarters Company, 1st Battalion, 16th Infantry] got safely ashore. At daylight our advance all but halted when we ran into a watermelon patch. After that it was easy to follow the battalion's path of advance by the watermelon rinds scattered along the route.

There wasn't too much activity that night, but our vacation ended quickly the next day. We were attacked by a lot of tanks from the Hermann Goering Division. We spread out all over creation fighting off those tanks. The 37mm antitank guns from HQ Company were useless against them. The only damage they inflicted was to knock a bogie wheel off one of the tanks. However, the gun's muzzle blast could be hazardous to your health. Our battalion CO, S-2, and S-3 were wounded by enemy counterfire when they fired this weapon. The Germans saw the muzzle blast and aimed their guns at it. Our Regimental Cannon Company's 105mm guns and naval gunfire saved us from being overrun by enemy tanks and driven back into the sea.

One thing particularly sticks in my mind. We got up on a high hill overlooking the beach with a view of the armada that had brought us to Sicily. From that position we watched as German planes bombed and strafed the invasion fleet. It was just like the Fourth of July with all the tracers and shells going up. This occurred every half hour; you could have set your watch by it.

At dusk, just after the last tracer was fired at departing German planes, we heard the heavy drone of approaching aircraft. The navy began firing at them, assuming these were German planes. But the planes were ours; they were pulling gliders loaded with follow-up troops from the 82nd Airborne. So our troops were shot down because they were flying over the fleet right after a German raid.

It wasn't the navy's fault. They had been shooting at planes every fifteen minutes. They must have been nervous, and I don't blame them. I know that for us, up on the hill watching, it was nerve-wracking enough. But some thought should have been given to notifying the navy when and where the airborne was flying, as well as keeping abreast of enemy air attacks over the fleet.

Not long after this incident I came across the bodies of some airborne soldiers who had been killed by the navy's friendly fire. Someone had stripped their clothes off and they were just lying there naked on the ground. It was an appalling sight.

Paul Bystrak

I was involved in the logistical planning for the invasion of Sicily. I recall that one of our quartermasters had been given a company of trucks and trailers to be attached to the 1st Quartermaster Company. He couldn't stand empty trucks and trailers going on ship, so he sent them back to the various depots to pick up supplies. All those trucks returned fully loaded. Then he told the lieutenants in the company to study the old manuals to learn how to make ovens out of fifty-five-gallon barrels. Within a short time they were making fresh bread in these ovens and issuing it to the troops. After that we got a call from command headquarters in North Africa to find out what had happened to the flour supply. None of their companies had any flour.

During the invasion one of the LSTs [landing ship, tank] was hit by a German bomb right down the main elevator. The ship blew up and sank all the vehicles and everything else on it. The 18th Infantry S-4 called the G-4 office and said that all the jeeps of one of the battalions were lost on that LST. Of course the LST couldn't have held *all* the battalion's jeeps, but that was his story. He asked that replacement jeeps be sent immediately, claiming that his battalion would be stranded without them. So we wired Algiers and asked for replacements. Algiers wired back and said that we should make an inventory because there were enough jeeps missing in North Africa to equip an entire division. Captain Visel in our G-4 section was asked to go and make inventories in the 18th Infantry. After that, we were able to scale down the requirement for jeeps considerably.

William Campbell

In the invasion of Sicily, my regiment, the 18th Infantry, was a floating reserve attached to an armored division. I was supposed to go in on an LCI with my Service Company. But they had only lieutenants as troop commanders on the Liberty Ships. The general wanted a captain, so I got a job on the *Robert Rowan*. This was a brand-new ship. I thought that being moved from an LCI to a Liberty Ship was like moving into God's pocket. I had a stateroom and everything!

Before leaving North Africa, every crack and cranny on that ship was filled up with five-gallon cans of high-octane gasoline. We also had artillery shells and other ammunition in the hold. Captain Swenson, the commander, had already lost three ships, two in the Pacific. As we got into the Bay of Gela, a 75mm artillery shell was fired at us. There were no hits, but the skipper decided to back out of range. The skipper said to me, "Captain Campbell, she is now yours. This is your ship."

Then the commodore, a navy lieutenant who looked like he always had a good snootful, red-faced and happy, came to me and showed me the maps. He said, "This is your beachhead." The map showed where the beachhead should be—but it wasn't there. I could see that the markers for the landing area were down the beach. I said, "I'll go in with the LCMs and see what the situation is."

Going in on the LCM was like riding in a bushel basket as wide as this room. When I landed, here came Lieutenant Smith, and he said, "Soup"—that was my nickname—"we need antitank guns. There is a tank attack coming in." I'd known something was coming because the destroyers were in close, firing over the sand dunes. Meanwhile, we were attacked by JU 88s.

I counted twenty-four JU 88s, but people say there were more. They came on a level approach, and they appeared to be flying slowly. An incendiary bomb dropped into the number-one hatch on the *Robert Rowan*—with all that high octane gasoline and all that ammunition inside. Soon the ship was smoking and the troops abandoned it. They came down the side of the ship and we picked them up with the LCM. We dropped our ramp to help them aboard. Destroyers also came alongside and dropped nets. We picked up all the men. Then the ship blew up and went to the bottom.

When I got into Gela that night I saw Mike Kelty from the regiment. He told me where the regiment was located. I found this place where there were some German Afrika Korps uniforms. I was all wet, so I put on part of a dry German uniform. Shortly after that the sky darkened and our planes and paratroopers started to come in. Well, they flew over the navy ships—and the navy ships had orders to fire at any planes that flew over them. The air was suddenly full of ack-ack. It was like a shooting gallery. It looked like the planes were just house high, but I didn't see any come down. I don't know how they got through.

The paratroopers dropped in, and there I sat in my German outfit. I said to myself, "I've got to get out of this uniform."

For the rest of the night, the ships were constantly shooting. The best thing for us was to stay under cover. Then it became quiet. The paratroopers just walked around in little bands for a few days after that. I don't know what they were doing, really.

CHAPTER 19

Across Sicily

The Record

After securing the Gela beachhead, U.S. forces drove through the western half of Sicily, capturing Palermo on July 23, and then wheeled east to advance along the northern coast toward Messina. Throughout the campaign the 1st Division was deployed on the right of II Corps in the island's geographical center, fighting its way across mountainous terrain through Niscemi, La Serra, Caltagirone, Caltanisetta, and Enna. Following the capture of Nicosia on July 28, the division advanced to Troina, attacking the town on August 1. Here the 1st Division met its sternest test of the campaign, and it wasn't until August 6 that Troina was cleared of enemy troops.

The following accounts by John Finke, Charles Hangsterfer, and Everett Booth describe the battle of Sicily from the infantryman's perspective, and in doing so reveal much about the nature of small-unit action in World War II.

John Finke

By the time I waded ashore the assault elements had long preceded us, but there was still some small-arms fire falling around
us. A bullet killed my message center chief, one of the finest
sergeants we had.

When we hit the beach and had completed unloading, we
double-timed up into the dunes. My good friend, Old Kewp
[Lieutenant Colonel John H. Mathews], finally asked me to slow
down as he and the men with their loads couldn't keep up with
me. I said we would have to get over the top of the dunes before
we could rest and reorganize. After a very short breather, it was,
"On your feet, move out!" We headed farther inland along a foot
path and came to an area which seemed ideal for the regimental
advance CP [command post]: a smallish olive grove with a slight
rise inland and a trail leading to the beaches. We got the area
into some sort of condition to receive the rest of the HQ just as
they arrived. The Old Man ruled it acceptable for an interim
location. It could be changed as necessary when we had more
information on the tactical situation in general and the location
of the battalions in particular.

The Intelligence and Reconnaissance [I&R] platoon, while
ranging to our front, surprised and captured an almost-new Mercedes command car, complete with a staff officer of the Hermann
Goering Division, his orderly, the driver, and all their baggage—
including a map case with maps marked and annotated. What
luck (and work) for the S-2 section!

I was given the German officer's first-aid kit and musette bag.
Upon checking through his personal belongings to remove
weapons and contraband, I came upon quite a goodly amount of
ladies' underwear and stockings. I kept some to send to a young
lady friend of mine in England. The rest was given to the I&R
troopers to divvy up and do with as they saw fit. We also found

the staff officer's personal correspondence, which was read and returned to him along with all other personal items except military records and money. These personal items were placed in sealed envelopes to accompany the prisoners through the POW evacuation system. The first-aid kit—a heavy leather case with an aluminum liner—I kept as my shaving kit. I used it for some thirty years, until the threads finally gave out and I had to retire it to my very small collection of war souvenirs. The Mercedes command car was appropriated by one of my precursors in command of HQ Company, Captain Steve Ralph. He had been promoted to regimental adjutant well before I took over and was my best friend there.

Some time later that day the CP was visited by General Matthew Ridgway, the airborne commander. Ridgway was looking for news of his troops, who had been badly scattered in their night drops. He was accompanied by a brigadier general, a gofer type from some higher HQ (I believe Omar Bradley's), who tried to enhance his sense of self-importance by substituting a fact-finding mission with a fault-finding mission.

General Ridgway was anxious but kind and polite in his questioning. Not so the gofer. He thought our CP was badly sited, and he was there to criticize Colonel Taylor for choosing the location. Which he did, in what was to my mind an uncalled-for rude manner. It was too much for me. By then I had been seventy-two-plus hours without sleep or food, and I was frankly out of patience for what I considered unwarranted and uninformed criticism of my Old Man from a pettifogging old maid in uniform (which I did not say but maybe implied). So I stepped forward before anyone could stop me and said, "General, if you have any complaints about this location, please don't blame Colonel Taylor. I selected this site based on the latest teaching and training at the infantry school from which I graduated last year, shortly before coming overseas." Or words to that effect. With that, I was abruptly removed from the assemblage by my friends and told to get some sleep. Which I did!

To appreciate what subsequently happened to me that evening, I must tell you that when Colonel Taylor first informed me that I was to command HQ Company, I immediately requested a transfer to a rifle company. And every time thereafter, when I had a personal conversation with him, I always repeated my request. To which he invariably replied, "I put you in HQ Company because I want you there. You are doing a good job. When I am ready to give you a rifle company I'll do so!" Of course he had no intention of letting me go. But then I had my encounter with Bradley's general. That changed his mind in a hurry, for when I awakened later that evening he told me he was ready to grant my request.

Lieutenant Colonel Joe Crawford, commanding the 2nd Battalion, had been wounded and evacuated that afternoon. Captain Bryce Denno, 2nd Battalion executive officer (and later a dear friend), was apparently deemed too young and not quite ready for that command. Most younger officers felt differently, I think; but Lieutenant Colonel Mathews was sent to the 2nd Battalion to take over command. And, glory be, I was to go with him to take over Company F.

Company F's previous commander had been Captain Bill Janney, a very fine young officer who was killed while trying to stop a counterattack by German tanks at Gela. I deeply regretted the loss of Captain Janney, but at the time I was too preoccupied to think of anything except my new command. I didn't realize how busy I would be with a rifle-company strength of four officers and thirty-five enlisted men, plus a provisional platoon of twenty-four paratroopers commanded by a captain who was at least several months (or maybe years) senior to my single week in that grade. However—no sweat!

Not many people were awake when I entered F Company's

Second Lieutenant Ted Antonelli in 1941
(Courtesy of Margaret Antonelli)

Major General Theodore Antonelli at Danang depot, Vietnam, June 1971, when he was Deputy Chief of Staff for Logistics, U.S. Army Vietnam (USARVN). Note the Big Red One patch on his sleeve. (Courtesy of Margaret Antonelli)

Lieutenants Ted Antonelli (seated, right) and Everett Booth (standing, right) with other members of their unit in Oran, Algeria, November 11, 1942 (Courtesy of Margaret Antonelli)

Old buddies at the Antonelli home, December 1991; left to right: Chuck Horner, Ted Antonelli, Steve Ralph, and John Finke (Courtesy of Margaret Antonelli)

Carroll Ed. Beadenkopf and his wife, Loretta, during World War II (Courtesy of Carroll Ed. Beadenkopf)

Carroll Ed. Beadenkopf and Loretta today (Courtesy of Carroll Ed. Beadenkopf)

Everett Booth (left) and John Finke, somewhere in North Africa (Courtesy of Arthur Booth)

Everett Booth with Arab boy in Gafsa, March 1943. This photo appeared in the Hammond Times *above the caption, "Yank and his Brother in Arms."* (Courtesy of Arthur Booth)

Newly inducted Private Everett Booth models duffy hat and fatigue uniform, standard issue to draftees in 1941. (Courtesy of Arthur Booth)

Everett Booth at Omaha Beach in 1984 (Courtesy of Arthur Booth)

Paul Bystrak in France, 1944 (Courtesy of Paul Bystrak)

Paul Bystrak today (Courtesy of Paul Bystrak)

Paul Bystrak and family in Sobotiste, Czechoslovakia, May 1945 (Courtesy of Paul Bystrak)

Fred Dolfi in Grosshau, Germany, February 1945 (Courtesy of Fred Dolfi)

Recent photo of Fred Dolfi visiting the monument to the 1st Division at Camp Blanding, Florida (Courtesy of Fred Dolfi)

Fred Dolfi (right) and an unidentified soldier with "Helen," the jeep he named after his wife (Courtesy of Fred Dolfi)

William Campbell during the war (Courtesy of William Campbell)

John Finke (seated, third from left) and men of his company near Mt. Etna during the Sicily campaign, 1943. They are displaying a captured Italian flag; the truck was also captured from the Italians and used by the company cooks. Finke was wounded near Troina when a bullet pierced his helmet and creased his scalp. Ted Lombarski, wearing an undershirt, kneels at the right. (Courtesy of Thaddeus Lombarski)

John Finke (right, with cane) and Steve Ralph (second from right) converse with two former Wehrmacht officers in front of the 1st Division monument at Omaha Beach, June 4, 1984. (Courtesy of Velma Ralph)

Charles Hangsterfer during the war (Courtesy of Charles Hangsterfer)

Charles Hangsterfer today (Courtesy of Charles Hangsterfer)

*Sidney Haszard on maneuvers in North Carolina with 1st RCN Troop, autumn
1941* (Courtesy of Ann Haszard)

Sidney Haszard in a 1992 photograph
(Courtesy of Ann Haszard)

Frank Kolb during the war (Courtesy of Frank Kolb)

Frank Kolb today (Courtesy of Frank Kolb)

Provost Marshal Major Thomas Lancer (left, front) reads instructions to military policemen at Gela, Sicily, in July 1943, before sending them to the front. (U.S. Army photograph)

Tom Lancer during the war (Courtesy of Thomas Lancer)

Young buddies: Ted Lombarski, shirtless, with headquarters personnel near Gela, Sicily, shortly after the Sicily campaign ended (Courtesy of Thaddeus Lombarski)

Ted Lombarski in 1941, before the 1st Division shipped out to England (Courtesy of Thaddeus Lombarski)

Ted Lombarski in a recent photo (Courtesy of Thaddeus Lombarski)

Steve Ralph (right) reads the Silver Star citation for Major Charles Horner (left) as Major General Terry Allen pins the decoration on Horner's tunic, North Africa, December 1942. (Courtesy of Velma Ralph)

Steve Ralph in England, 1943 (Courtesy of Velma Ralph)

E. V. Sutherland (left) in Karlovy Vary, Czechoslovakia, with a Hero of the Soviet Union and 1st Division buddies, May 24, 1945 (Courtesy of E. V. Sutherland)

Colonel E. V. Sutherland and his wife, Ellie, in 1977
(Courtesy of E. V. Sutherland)

From left: Major General Terry Allen, commander of the 1st Division, and journalists Clark Lee (International News Service) and Don Whitehead (Associated Press) in Cerami, Sicily, August 4, 1943 (U.S. Army photograph)

An advance detail of the 16th Regiment enters Troina, August 6, 1943. (U.S. Army photograph)

Brigadier General Theodore Roosevelt Jr., assistant commander of the 1st Division under Terry Allen, seated on the front bumper of his jeep "Rough Rider." The photograph was taken in Prata, Italy, in January 1944 while Allen was director of liaison to the Canadian Expeditionary Force. (U.S. Army photograph)

Normandy, France: infantrymen take cover behind a hedgerow in the bocage *country near Brione, July of 1944.* (U.S. Army photograph)

Machine-gun crew of the 2nd Battalion, 26th Regiment, involved in mopping-up operations in Aachen, October 15, 1944. (U.S. Army photograph)

Men of I Company, 3rd Battalion, 26th Reg   * for snipers in Schopen,*
Belgium, January 21, 1945. (U.S. Army photograph)

C Company, 2nd Battalion, 16th Regiment, advances on a road near Faymonville, Belgium, during the Ardennes counteroffensive, January 16, 1945. (U.S. Army photograph)

CP and met 1st Sergeant Thaddeus "Ted" Lombarski, a dark-haired, serious-looking young man. I thought "Lum," as we also called him, much too young-looking to be a first sergeant, but he soon convinced me that he was better than the best I could ask for. He briefed me on the status of the company. It was below strength because too many soldiers had not been able to rejoin their units, which had been hit pretty hard while reorganizing after an enemy counterattack. Much worse, however, was the fact that the entire 2nd Platoon was missing, platoon leader and all. We never did see that platoon again. We drew the inevitable conclusion that the lieutenant, whose name I don't remember, must have let himself be captured with most of his men.

My executive officer in F Company was 1st Lieutenant John Kersey, a fine young officer who had one major fault—he fraternized too much with the enlisted men—and they took advantage of it. The next day I met Lieutenants Otto Clemens and Howard Pearre, both fairly recent OCS graduates, who were fine platoon leaders. My NCOs were mostly excellent leaders, although the turnover was too high. We lost Master Sergeant Wages, my top platoon sergeant, before the campaign was over—he was KIA in the attack on Hill 929 outside Troina. Among the other names I remember were Ed Zukowski, Casimir Piso, Fratello, Edward Plona, John Mullins, and Strosni.

We moved out early the next morning with one rifle platoon, one platoon of paratroopers, and the weapons platoon. Lots of battle noises to our front and flanks but very little action in our zone of advance. Around noon we reached the town of Niscemi, our objective for the day, with no casualties. We occupied our assigned positions and put out security to the front and flanks. While we waited for orders, the paratrooper platoon, having requested and received permission to detach themselves, departed with many thanks and expressions of mutual esteem.

I was informed of two things: that we would be given two-

and-a-half-ton trucks to take us to a forward assembly area, where we could rest and feed the troops and maybe spend a night; and that my company strength had risen to approximately eighty soldiers. The additions were men who had originally belonged to our company. They came from other rear units, which had picked them up and returned them to us. There was also a sort of elite group of soldiers who had previously joined other front-line units and fought with them, after which they had insisted on going to the rear and being sent back to us. Most of that group had asked the commanders with whom they fought to give them a chit saying that they had volunteered to fight with so-and-so unit and describing how they had behaved under fire. This became F Company's SOP.

We had only enough transport to carry forty men with equipment, and not enough time to make two round trips. My solution was that the officers and men who were present in the company when I assumed command and those who had been given favorable chits, as noted above, would ride the seven-and-a-half miles to the new assembly area. There they would set up a secure bivouac. All others would march to the assembly area carrying their arms and equipment. The question was raised as to which officer would command the marching troops. I told them that, since I had not fought with the company on the previous day either, it was only fair that I command them on the march.

The march was uneventful, with one exception. We passed a café with a lot of noise going on which didn't sound Italian. So I stopped my column and walked over. I found about forty half-drunk soldiers, NCOs, and one or two officers. I found out their units—mostly regimental special units and various attached non-divisional and some divisional units. A very motley crew. I called them to attention, reminded them that their behavior was against all orders, and told them that I had about forty unhappy soldiers outside who would be only too happy to have them join F Company and see what life in a rifle company was like. All but a very few unattached individuals volunteered to return to wherever it was they were supposed to go under their officers or NCOs. These leaders then volunteered to take the unattached people with them since nobody wanted to join my company.

The rest of the march was routine, and we arrived at our destination in good shape. NCOs who made that march let it be known that, once they realized I was marching with them, they and most of their men felt I had treated them fairly.

That evening we received orders to move about fifteen miles to a new position. The move was on foot through the coastal mountains over very rough, rocky terrain, following foot paths and cart tracks to a main road where we hoped our organic transport and some trucks would meet us. Our maps were primitive, almost illegible copies of outdated maps. After we made contact with the enemy and captured a number of German maps, our own maps improved, with natural terrain features pretty well represented. Even then, however, manmade features such as roads, railroads, bridges, etc.—all as old as the hills we were working our way through—were not very well illustrated.

For this march, then, the battalion had to rely mainly on local guides. Whether the guides were volunteers or had been impressed we didn't know. Contact between march elements was maintained by connecting files, and the responsibility for contact was rear to front. But cross-country marches of this type were not often practiced during our training, and individual soldiers were not made to understand the importance of maintaining unit-to-unit contact. Consequently, that night Company F had a rude awakening when our column was halted for the usual hourly stop. In doing so, we completely lost contact with Company G, which had moved out early and hadn't seen fit to notify us. This happened shortly after we had started down from the ridge we had just crossed. My connecting files were also too busy resting and failed to notify us of the departure of G Company. I took my runner and tried to catch up with the tail elements of G Company. Being pretty green at this sort of thing, I personally assumed responsibility for doing this. I hadn't been with my people long enough to know whom to trust, and though there was a danger of getting into a firefight with our own troops, it seemed worth the risk.

Fortunately this did not happen. However, in rushing about, I forgot that from birth I had been cursed with weak ankles. This came back to me very quickly when I stumbled over a loose rock, took a heavy tumble almost off the edge of the track, and severely sprained my left ankle. The noise alerted one of Company G's tail-end Charlies. He checked us out and so reestablished contact with us. He told me that his company had decided to find a better place a few hundred yards farther along the trail for their rest stop. They had moved on down there but failed to let my people know about it.

My company aid man, Bob Trout, immobilized my ankle and strapped it as tightly as he could. In the meantime the company had to start up and follow the 1st Platoon leader. I couldn't see myself being supported or carried by soldiers who were heavily overburdened as it was, so I followed behind my lead platoon until the next rest stop. Once there, I continued alongside the resting troops until I reached the head of the company column. When the troops moved again I gradually fell back to the end, only to catch up with the head at the next stop.

I repeated this seemingly endless process again and again. It helped neither my morale nor my ankle. Shortly after daylight we finally met the battalion CO, Old Kewp. He had heard of my misfortune and driven back to pick me up in his jeep. He took me to the battalion aid station, where Captain Gus Stola, our battalion surgeon, looked at the ankle and decided to send me right back to the evacuation hospital which had been established near the beach. There I was tested and x-rayed. No fracture was found, so they put the ankle in a light cast and sent me back to the battalion. I was strictly urged *not* to use the ankle at all for at least two weeks or, better still, an entire month.

The doctor who gave these instructions was not one of nature's gentlemen. He was not only arrogant but abysmally stupid to boot. I got the impression that he felt above such a mundane, unimportant job as treating and giving medical advice to a mere rifle company commander. He thought that if I was so dumb as to get a severely sprained ankle, I should not expect him to waste time on the matter. Officers of the infantry ought to be more careful not to become unnecessary burdens on doctors of evacuation hospitals—that was his attitude.

When I returned to the battalion I reported my encounter with the ungentlemanly doctor to Kewp. I asked him to try to get the episode into the after-action report. He and I both knew the Old Man's feelings on such matters, and the Old Man would undoubtedly see to it that the hospital commander was made aware of his subordinate's failings. Meanwhile I had to command my company from my jeep. With a crutch and a cane, I visited and checked on the condition and actions of my troops without undue difficulties.

At this time I must digress on the sad story of the loss of our battalion executive officer, Major Bryce Denno. He was severely wounded, nearly crippled for life. I believe his driver was killed. This was due to an unpardonable lapse or omission by a squad leader from the 1st Engineer Battalion, which was engaged in minesweeping the road we were following to the city of Enna. The engineer troops were taking a well-earned rest in the shade of some trees along the road. The squad leader—whose responsibility it was to leave a guard at their work area, or at least post warning signs to alert vehicles or personnel approaching the danger area—either failed to do so or failed to check that it was done. Whatever, Denno's jeep set off at least one Teller mine. The jeep blew up, throwing both passengers into the air, resulting in serious injuries to Denno and the same or death to the driver. Naturally, being road- and vehicle-bound myself, I was especially careful so as not to encounter a similar fate.

The next day the battalion moved into Enna against little or no resistance. We bivouacked northeast of the city. After I got the troops settled I was ordered into Callascibetta, less than a mile distant as the crow flies but over six miles by road. There were no enemy troops reported in the town, so I took my jeep and driver (who was named Herrington but known as "Herringbone"), an Italian *carabiniere*, and our Canadian liaison officer, who was bored at the CP. The *carabiniere* was reputed to speak English, but I had to resort to my idiomatic German, learned during the five years I spent at the Neues Gymnasium in Bremen, Germany. It worked well and we got along fine as soon as the Canadian and I were able to convince him that we were not Germans in disguise.

On our way up the hill to Callascibetta we kept a sharp lookout, because regardless of what we had been told about the enemy's withdrawing, the terrain was just too perfect as ambush country. When we arrived at the town gate we were met by a delegation of local dignitaries. They escorted us to the city hall, where we were greeted by the mayor with wreaths, homemade American flags, bouquets of flowers presented by pretty young girls, and wine, wine—and again, wine! This was followed by a grand dinner, courses and courses of it. And needless to say, with more *wine*!

A short while after dinner I had to report back to the battalion HQ. It was decided that on the morrow I should move my whole company back into a bivouac area outside Callascibetta in case the Germans decided to harass the population. I was pretty well pissed off at this since I knew that the rest of the battalion had been alerted to prepare to move out very shortly. I wondered why F Company was ordered into a bivouac area. Kewp told me that when he had tried to take us with him, he had been informed that F Company, as the smallest rifle company in the 1st Division, was the easiest one to spare at the time. I regarded this as an insult to the company: we believed we were more than the equal of any other rifle company in the whole damn division. My officers fully agreed with me, but needless to say all but the highest-ranking NCOs were very happy at not having to march again.

As I drove back up to the new company area, I saw a jeep on the side of the road surrounded by German soldiers. The Germans seemed to be trying to pile their weapons into the jeep. When they saw us coming up the hill they lined up along the road and put their hands in the air. The American occupant of the jeep came over to me and said, "Can you help me? I want to get to the town up there and these German fellows want me to accept their surrender. I haven't got any room in the jeep to take their weapons."

He said he was H. R. "Red" Knickerbocker, chief of the United Press office in Berlin until the Nazis had kicked him out and now a war correspondent for UP. I told him I would give him credit for picking up approximately fifteen German soldiers. I would take charge of them and see that they got into the proper hands as soon as possible. He thanked me and asked if it was all right to go up to Callascibetta. I said, "Sure. I've got a crazy Canadian up there who is our liaison from the 1st Canadians. He's OK. But don't buy any weird stories or let him give you any wooden nickels. I'll see you there as soon as I get my people settled."

Then I told the Germans to stack their weapons by the side of the road and start walking toward Enna. I had my radio operator call company HQ and tell them to take charge of the prisoners: as soon as the people at HQ saw them, they were to feed them and provide a small but reliable escort to battalion. The escort was then to report back to the company without wasting any time in Enna or around battalion.

Charles Hangsterfer

To cover their withdrawal the Germans had laid mines everywhere, so when moving through any field, the same precaution was taken as when walking through a field where a herd of cows had been grazing. Using a mine detector ensured a safe and healthy passage.

As we moved farther inland my A&P [Ammunition and Pioneer] platoon was kept busy defusing Teller and personnel mines. As a result of the vast number of mines, many in the battalion received on-the-job training disarming bouncing betties, diabolical devices which, when triggered, would bounce up about four feet in the air and detonate, propelling steel fragments that wounded or killed anyone nearby. The after-action reports revealed that the artillery units sustained most of their casualties from enemy mines.

Sometimes we were fired on by *Nebelwerfers*, multiple rocket launchers with 150mm or 210mm projectiles. The rockets made an eerie banshee shriek in flight and detonated with an earsplitting roar. I had not experienced this weapon in the North African campaign, and the first time I heard it I didn't know what it was. I thought it was some sort of doomsday weapon because of the noise. But the *Nebelwerfers* weren't as dangerous as they sounded, and once the launchers were spotted our artillery quickly knocked them out of action.

Once a lucky shot from one of our 81mm mortars went down the tube of a German mortar that had been firing at us. Right after that more than two hundred enemy soldiers surrendered. We found out that word had spread through their ranks that the

Americans had acquired a secret weapon that could target their mortar tubes with pinpoint accuracy.

Throughout the Sicilian campaign General Patton's MPs were always on patrol looking for soldiers out of uniform. To my dismay they gave tickets to each one of my company cooks for not wearing their helmets. The cooks had been riding along in their kitchen truck when the MPs caught them. I promptly tore the tickets up. A few days later a reply-by-endorsement letter was sent through channels to the battalion adjutant, who was requested to provide information as to what sort of punishment had been dealt to the culprits whose breach of discipline had jeopardized the war effort. It so happened that I was, in addition to the HQ Company CO, the battalion adjutant. It was in that capacity that I somehow managed to "misplace" the letter. A few days later a follow-up letter was hand-delivered to me. To this I replied, "The offenders were restricted to the company area for a period of seven days." Since we were still in combat and on the move, I didn't think this would be cruel and inhumane punishment. Neither did the cooks, especially since I had somehow "forgotten" to tell them that they had been restricted to the area. The case was closed soon thereafter and I heard no more about it.

I will never forget being on a hill outside Caltanissetta. When we got up there, we came across all these folks from the town who were hiding out in the hills, and they wanted to know if we had anything for malaria. All we had was Atabrine and aspirin, so we gave that to them. Then what appeared to be a grandmother, a daughter, and a granddaughter fixed me up with a nice little bed to sleep on—a bunch of straw—in appreciation for the Atabrine I gave them.

After the Sicilian campaign was over we went back to Caltanissetta. We were patrolling the streets. There were brothels in the town that were off-limits to American soldiers, and we had to post MPs in front of those places to keep the men out. Well, I went in to inspect one of the brothels, and who did I run into but the grandmother, the daughter, and the granddaughter—who turned out to be the madam, the housekeeper, and the working crew! They were so happy to see me that they invited me to dinner and everything. We had a grand time even though I didn't speak Italian. I noticed, however, that the daughter was very tired, as if she had spent the entire day engaged in her chosen profession. This seemed strange to me. After all, I had effectively closed down her place of business; she wasn't working, so she had no cause to be tired. Or did she?

I also noticed that none of my company's enlisted men had even tried to frequent Caltanissetta's brothels. My first sergeant told me why when we got back to England. It seems that he had employed the daughter—the same one who had invited me for dinner—in our company area. While she plied her trade, a lookout with a guitar was posted nearby. Upon my approach the lookout would play his guitar extra-loud to warn the first sergeant to get rid of the evidence that anything illegal was taking place. This not only explained why my men weren't seen around the brothels but also why the daughter was so tired at night.

I also remember that when we were near Mount Etna, there was a big cornfield, and we got some fresh corn. There was also a farmer, and we wanted to buy a cow from him, but he wouldn't take our money. He wanted a check. I gave him a check and signed it with the name of another captain. I won't say whose name I used, because the farmer may still be looking for payment for this cow that we "bought."

John Finke

The morning after my encounter with Red Knickerbocker, I was informed that division had ordered my company to guard a very large Italian ammunition dump northeast of Enna. I told division that they were several days late, as we had seen and reported that local civilians were looting the dump of anything they could use to repair their homes and buildings. In particular, I said, they were taking anything wooden, such as ammo boxes; they were just breaking the boxes open and throwing the contents—which included fuses and other easily explodable items—on the ground. I told division that the place was going to go up in smoke any minute, the way the locals were handling that stuff; and if anybody thinks you can stop them now, it'll take a couple of regiments, not a quarter-strength rifle company. I said, "I'll try to keep them out, but it's like an anthill in there and we are not anteaters. They've cut the perimeter fence in dozens of places and I haven't got enough men to station one man at every break in the fence. Let's not be ridiculous. I'm not risking a single soldier inside that madhouse."

Nonetheless we did what we could for just under thirty hours. Then she blew high, wide, and handsome. I'm afraid the locals lost a few people, most of them injured, maybe two killed. The dump burned for about two days. We turned the place over to some ordnance experts who arrived the next morning. We left to rejoin the regiment as soon as they signed off on the whole can of worms.

The next day we rejoined our battalion. I was most happily surprised to find that I had gained a very fine officer, Second Lieutenant Barney Rushe. He had been a platoon sergeant in F Company, and shortly before the 16th Infantry went overseas, he had won what was probably the first Legion of Merit to be awarded to a 1st Division enlisted man for having the best-drilled rifle platoon in the entire U.S. Army. He was then sent to OCS and had recently graduated and requested assignment to Europe to rejoin the 16th Infantry Regiment of the 1st Infantry Division. In Sicily he returned to his old unit, F Company. In addition to Rushe we were also given about twenty soldiers who had been selected by their commanders from companies E and G to build us up to a semblance of strength.

Now the major effort for U.S. troops was to break through the final German defenses in our zone. Then we would move as fast as possible to take Messina, thereby cutting off the escape of German troops trying to use their last port to cross into Italy and continue fighting there. There were definitely no Italian troops trying this. They were content to tie up American units in the western three-quarters of the island by insisting that senior commanders formally visit them to accept their surrenders. It was rumored that a regimental commander of the 9th Infantry Division had broken his leg jumping out of his command car to play his part in one of these ceremonies. His XO, a friend of mine who was later killed at Anzio, was my source for this tidbit.

Everett Booth

The big deal in Sicily, as far as I was concerned, was the city of Troina. My company was given the mission of capturing this city, which was the last outpost the Germans had before our troops moved into Messina. I had Jack Belden, the correspondent for *Time* magazine, with us. As we moved down this road, all of a sudden we were being strafed by our own aircraft—strafed and bombed. Normally an infantry outfit has flags that the men can spread out in front of their unit to tell the air force, "Hey, this is where our line is—don't bomb behind it." But those flags were so big and cumbersome that the men assigned to carry them usually got rid of them. Such was the case here. So we were getting bombed and strafed by these planes, and I issued a command: "Everybody take off your undershirt and place it in front of our positions, so the air force can see where we are. I hope they recognize what we're doing." And the first undershirt to get out in front of the line was Jack Belden's.

The Record

*A dispatch from the front by AP correspondent Don Whitehead, who
tagged along with Booth's platoon on the road to Troina, provides
another eyewitness account of the "undershirt incident."*

. . . Jack Belden, of *Time* and *Life* magazines, and I joined
Lieutenant Everett Booth . . . whose company was scheduled to enter the city first. We walked single file, with riflemen and our flanks in the wheat fields to guard against
snipers.

It was 7:30 A.M. now and we were about a mile from
Troina when our dive bombers roared out of the sun to
unload their cargoes. The city on the big cliff above us was
obscured by smoke and dust.

As the column turned a curve a machine gun and rifle
chattered from the vineyard above. The troops took cover
behind the bank.

"Which way did those shots come from?" Booth asked.

"This way," a soldier said, pointing into the vineyard
toward Troina.

"All right, I'll work my next platoon around on the
flank," Booth said.

We crawled back along the bank and ran across an
exposed place into a shallow irrigation ditch. Rifle bullets
zipped over our heads at intervals as Booth deployed his
men.

Our dive bombers hammered at Troina again, six of
them, and in ten minutes another six.

A few minutes later another flight dived screaming down
in echelon over us.

We watched the first plane roaring toward us. It was fascinating and terrifying at once to see the bombs hurtle from

the belly of the plane. The fins caught the air and the bomb leveled out. It crashed into the vineyard above us near where the sniper had been.

Another dived in and then another. We lay in the ditch holding our breath, making ourselves as small as possible.

"For God's sake," Booth shouted, "don't anyone move."

The plane's machine guns were chattering as they raked the road which a few minutes before was enemy territory. Then they disappeared over the ridge.

"Every man take off his undershirt," Booth cried. "We'll lay them on the ridge over us, and dammit, hurry!"

We stripped off our undershirts, most of them gray from days of wear with no chance to wash them.

"They'll have to be whiter than this or they can't be seen," someone quipped.

Second Lt. Claus Anderson of Kenosha, Wis., grinned. "Didn't I say we were getting close air support?"

We gave our shirts to Sgt. Vincent Burns of Woodhaven, N.Y., and he carried them up the slope and laid them before us. We lay back in the trench when we heard the drone of planes again.

"They might have been Heinies flying our planes," someone cracked. "My friends, blankety-blank-blank. I hate war."

"Burns," said Booth, "when we push on be sure and pick up all the undershirts."

"I just want mine," a muffled voice said. "I just washed it."

"Sure," Booth said sarcastically, "we'll send them all to the laundry and have them ready for the next dance."

Everett Booth

My company took over Troina. Everything was in good order, and then someone came looking for me. Well, you know where he found me? He found me in the local barbershop. It had been a long time since I'd had a good haircut. I was getting a haircut from a local Sicilian. How about that?

Following this we went back into a rest area, waiting to see what was going to happen next, and I had a little problem with one of my enlisted men, a fellow who happened to be from Chicago. So it wound up that I invited him to go behind the hill. I took my brass off my collars and said, "OK, let's go to it." He said, "Oh, Lieutenant, put your bars back on." At a later date each company commander was requested to assign two or three soldiers to be sent over to a unit going into Italy, to a division that was short of troops. I told the first sergeant my selection was this fellow who had given me trouble. The next morning, the first sergeant comes up to me and says, "Lieutenant, whatsisname wants to talk with you." I said, "Fine, let him come in." He comes in and says, "I don't blame you a bit for assigning me to the out-fit making the invasion of Italy. I understand. I hope some day we'll be able to meet in Chicago and have a drink together." Well, this never happened. I lost track of the gentleman. I wish I'd had the opportunity to see him again, but maybe he never made it through Italy.

The Record

Chicago Sun *correspondent Red Knickerbocker was with Everett Booth and his company when they entered Troina. He subsequently wrote the following account of that episode, which appeared in the* Sun *under the title "East Chicagoan Leads Capture of Sicily Town."*

. . . In order to cover their withdrawal, the Germans early yesterday morning counterattacked in such force that it appeared they were stronger than ever. As we followed the troops into the shattered town past many bodies of Germans lying where they had fallen we came up with the famous I Company of one of the most celebrated American divisions, Maj. Gen. Terry Allen's Fighting First.

Its leader and the first man into Troina was 1st Lt. Everett L. Booth [of] . . . East Chicago. This imperturbable young man, having completed a swift survey of the town and disposed his forces, was having a shave on the square beneath the town's principal church which, having served as an observation post for the enemy, had been somewhat bruised. . . .

Lt. Booth said, "It's an old custom for I Company to be the first. We were first at Enna, first at Nicosia and first here. For my part I found the Germans did a tough job holding out the way they did. But it got too hot for them.

"Our artillery had lots to do with it and also our machine guns. We had two heavy machine guns posted where they raked the enemy unmercifully and they couldn't get at us. I wasn't surprised that they finally had to withdraw but I was surprised yesterday when they counterattacked.

"It was evidently to make us think they were going to try to hold many more days.

"When they attacked they went all-out and showed not much sign of being tired. They all were armed with automatic weapons and once they got within two hundred yards of our lines. We drove them back with mortars, artillery, machine-gun fire and hand grenades. Our platoon leader, Sgt. Michael Foti of New York, threw twenty-two grenades himself. . . ."

John Finke

The linchpin for the final German defensive line on the north-western slope of Mount Etna was the heavily defended town of Troina. This was now the primary objective of the 1st Division. All attacks had been repulsed for several days by stubborn, well dug-in defenders, members of remnants of elite Panzer grenadier units. The 26th Infantry, which had been leading the advance, was stopped or at least slowed down, and it was now the turn of the 16th. The 2nd Battalion was to move up close to the Germans under cover of darkness and attack at dawn.

Companies E and F were both under strength as a result of fighting many small-unit actions against an enemy who gave ground slowly and stubbornly while trying to inflict maximum casualties on our troops. An apparent reluctance by E Company's commander—a certain lieutenant whose name I will not mention—to attack aggressively meant that I had to command both units, with E Company attached to me.

The two companies moved out in column with F leading and E following some distance to the rear. The so-called improved road we were following seemed to have petered out, and we were now following a cart track that led steeply uphill but was easy to follow. We had previously captured some enemy-owned horses as well as three mules, which we now used to transport ammunition, the rifle platoon BARs, and the Weapons Platoon mortars and machine guns. These were following at a distance of about five hundred yards. Another four to five hundred yards farther back was E Company, followed (I found out later) by a battalion wire party with a telephone. The wire party had come along behind E Company, and the company's commander did not see fit to tell me that he had a telephone.

At first light I was with my leading elements coming onto a gentle rise about two to three hundred feet high and then rising more steeply to what was obviously the crest of the ridge. As dawn broke we came under fire from there. I saw two German soldiers double-timing in step toward us, carrying what appeared to be a light machine gun. They jumped into what looked like a prepared position and commenced firing. We were caught in the open and there was nothing to do but attack immediately from a march column.

There was a large rock formation just to our left and I directed company HQ to take positions behind it. I did this so that I could point out to the platoons where I wanted them to deploy and advance on the enemy. I sent the 1st Platoon to the right of the formation and the 3rd Platoon to the left. I then followed the 3rd Platoon, and as soon as we cleared the rocks I moved up with my small command group into the interval between platoons, more or less forming a connection between them. We had no 2nd Platoon, as there were not enough soldiers to form two full-strength platoons, much less three.

While this was happening the men with the animals transporting our supporting weapons blundered along without fully realizing the danger. Within one or two minutes the German machine gun had taken full advantage of these unexpected and, to them undoubtedly God-given, targets. They fired on and killed all the animals and made casualties of their escort. Our attack resolved itself into a pure rifle assault without any supporting weapons. The grass was very high around us, so I got up on one knee to see what was to the immediate front. As I looked to my left, I felt a blow on my helmet. It was as though I had been hit with something much heavier and harder than a baseball bat. I felt very woozy and suddenly had blood streaming into my eyes and all over my face and the front of my uniform. I believe that I initially fell forward onto my face and maybe was out for a moment or two.

I soon got to my feet, having first ascertained that I was alive and, second, that I was able to move. In the meantime we had apparently driven the German outpost unit back. We started to organize the position so that we could check our situation with regard to losses and the status of our ammunition supply. A truly astonishing—or maybe miraculous—fact was then reported to me. Two German soldiers with red crosses on their uniforms had held up their arms and stopped the firing for long enough to cross over to our side and help take care of their wounded. When their comrades withdrew they stayed with us to help with our casualties.

While our ammunition supply was still enough to move farther without worrying about running out in an emergency, our personnel situation was, as always seemed to happen, very serious. A quick count showed nine KIA, with two others wounded so severely that we weren't likely to be able to evacuate them in time to save them. Our WIA included myself and First Lieutenant Pearre, who was able to evacuate himself. Most of the other wounded were able to withdraw on their own or with the assistance of other more lightly wounded men. The two German aid men, who had shown no pronounced desire to follow their withdrawing comrades, were also of inestimable help. I of course had neither the desire nor any excuse to absent myself from my company, so there was no question about my status. I stayed. All I had was a diminishing headache and some fairly considerable loss of blood, as scalp wounds always make you bleed like a stuck pig.

I had used a small amount of the water in my canteen to wash off most of the blood around my eyes, and was eating my favorite K ration (breakfast ham and eggs) preparatory to making an inspection of the troops on the line. All at once I heard shouting. I looked up and saw my executive officer, Lieutenant Kersey, who had been discussing our situation with me a few minutes earlier, running toward the front line and waving his arms. I then saw both Kersey and Clemens and some of our noncoms trying to physically restrain our remaining enlisted men from running to the rear before my first sergeant or myself could intervene and try to stop them. As Clemens passed me, he shouted "Counterattack!" while still trying to physically stop the men.

I could see no sense in chasing after the company. I got my first sergeant, my mail clerk, Corporal John Mullins, Sergeant Martin, and (a little later) a PFC of Italian descent who had decided not to run. The PFC picked up a rifle and some ammunition dropped by the other men and was firing as fast as he could up the hill at the Germans whether he could see them or not.

We started an orderly withdrawal down the mountainside, covering each other with fire as we withdrew. It appeared that the Germans were not very interested in exploiting the success of their surprise counterattack, but they followed us carefully. Much to my regret the troops who had preceded us set off some enemy mines in their headlong stampede. These caused more casualties, which included one American KIA and several wounded. But what hurt us survivors the most was the death of both our chivalrous German aid men, who were somehow killed during the action. Before they were killed, many of our soldiers had asked me if we could take them along with us for the duration. I had been forced to say no to this idea but considered it a fitting tribute to their brave, life-saving efforts.

I had been unable to check on Company E elements as I had planned to do before the disaster, and having further been unable to find any trace of them during the withdrawal, it now became my duty to find out what had happened and why. First of all, as soon as I heard about the wire party that was with the company, I almost exploded. Their telephone would have enabled us to call in supporting mortar and artillery fire to not only defend our position but also to give us support during our attack. It would have prevented many casualties and unnecessary deaths.

The next troubling question was, What had happened to E Company? That company had been less than one thousand yards away from us while we were involved in an intense and prolonged firefight. Yet E Company's commander had made absolutely no attempt to assist his direct commanding officer (me) or to find out if there was any mission for his men to perform. Why not? This question could have only one answer: the pusillanimous nature of the company commander had, to a degree, infected his officers and men. Having heard the company commander often airing his opinions about the futility of the current campaign and his doubts about our ability to win the war, I was convinced that this was the case. His doubts must have caused similar doubts to arise in the minds of the men he commanded.

The worst thing about all of this, I thought, was the complete lack of interest E Company's commander had demonstrated with regard to the fate of his comrades and supposed friends.

When we got to the foot of the ridge we found a very crestfallen F Company under the control of two very angry officers and several angry NCOs. It was plain to all that I was in a towering rage. Because the troops felt a certain amount of guilt about the stampede, they feared that my rage was directed at them. In my opinion, what they did was inexcusable. But after all, they had suffered heavy casualties; many had lost close friends and/or revered leaders on whom they depended and whom they admired. I was relatively new to them, but I was their Old Man. To see me with blood dripping from my face so that I was practically unrecognizable had certainly not been conducive to helping them feel confident and at ease about their future.

As soon as I got an inkling of what was in their minds I made an effort to reassure them. Not that I allowed them to believe or assume that all was forgiven, or that a soldier could run away whenever he wanted to. But I kept my rage under control, because after all it was not directed at them. It was being husbanded for the coming confrontation with E Company's commander.

I had fully resolved to shoot him like a mad dog. I had no compunction in announcing my decision to the battalion staff members, who met with me to discuss the incident. Then I was given an order from Colonel Mathews to report to him immediately. Kewp told me, "It's no use looking for your proposed victim. He's gone up to regimental headquarters to face the Old Man. They want you up there too—after you've cleaned up."

I replied, "Balls to any clean-up! I want that bastard tried for cowardice."

Kewp said, "Suit yourself. But calm down!"

Leaving Johnnie Kersey in charge to feed and bed the troops, I headed for RHQ. Colonel Taylor was not available, but good old Steve Ralph was. After getting "Herringbone" (my driver) fed, Steve gave me some good whiskey, then filled me up with some good HQ chow. Later we talked in Steve's small-wall tent where he had an extra cot set up. After a while Colonel Taylor joined us. He said, "E Company's CO is gone. And if he weren't, we couldn't try him on your testimony alone anyhow. I want you to stay here tomorrow so Charley Tegtmeier [the regimental surgeon] can look you over."

The next day found me sitting on a nice veranda at the villa that housed the RHQ, having coffee and relaxing after lunch. I had a large bandage on my head; it looked like a turban and I couldn't wear a tin pot over it. While some of the staff and I were chewing the fat, we heard incoming artillery fire that landed fairly close to us. Suddenly, the Old Man and I were the only ones left on the lovely veranda. The rounds were close, but not close enough to make us move.

After a little while, just as I was getting drowsy, in walked Teddy Roosevelt, our assistant division commander. He said hello to Colonel Taylor and then turned and looked at me with some surprise. "Hell, Finke," he said, "They sure picked the wrong place to shoot a Dutchman, didn't they?" and roared with laughter. As did we all.

That did it. I had been feeling a little worried about the small fragments of the helmet liner that had lodged underneath my scalp and were giving me a bit of trouble and about what I should do to avoid infection. Enough of all that. I turned to the Old Man and told him that I felt fully recovered and asked permission to leave immediately to get back to my own command, F Company. Permission was granted, and I left as soon as my jeep and driver were found. It took just a few minutes. I rejoined the company in our new area shortly afterwards.

I arrived none too soon. Both evening mess and another very unpleasant mess were waiting. Messes don't go away, but chow does, so I asked my men to let me eat first and then be briefed about our troubles. No way. The problem was urgent, so we discussed it while we ate the evening meal. The problem: the battalion chaplain, a great big Polish Catholic priest whose name escapes me, had not picked up our dead soldiers, giving another excuse each time the battalion adjutant tried to pin him down as to when he would do this.

This situation had created a very serious morale problem in the company. Our comrades had been killed on the third of August. It was now the seventh of August and cadavers did not keep very well in the Sicilian summer heat. There was also the real probability of the corpses being despoiled by impoverished peasants, who were coming back into the area and trying to recoup losses caused by retreating enemy soldiers plundering and living off the land.

I realized that nothing could be done about the bodies until daylight the next day. I decided that, in the meantime, I would speak with Father Deary, our revered regimental chaplain, who knew the priest in question and might have some influence on him. I thought that if the good Father Deary couldn't help us, I would have a chat with the delinquent priest himself and, if necessary, let some of his Polish parishioners who had lost their friends in battle see if they couldn't bring him to a different point of view.

Later that evening I met with Father "DP"—short for "delinquent priest"—at battalion headquarters. He said he would not go up to the battlefield because there were enemy mines there. I told him there were no mines. He said that he knew there were and would not go up there, period.

I decided that First Sergeant Thaddeus Lombarski and a couple of volunteers selected by Lum would accompany me up the mountain to the field of death and battle. We were prohibited from taking out any corpses or from removing their dog tags. But we could try to search through their clothing and find and read their ID tags.

When we got to the battle area the stench was so awfully strong and thick around the bodies that there was no difficulty finding them. Where not covered by the remains of their uniforms, they were covered with a carpet of maggots that made it look as though the corpses were alive and twitching. They were so bloated that we were lucky they hadn't all burst the uniforms and scattered their belongings through the deep grass. A soldier had to go to each body, force his fingers into the folds of the neck, and try to find the dog tag chains; then he would pull out a tag and copy the name and serial number.

That was as far as we could go with the ID tags. They had to be left on the bodies until each was officially identified and buried. We were able to reach into the uniform pockets and extract all personal belongings, which we wrapped up in whatever was available and took back to the company for the friends of each dead man to send to his family. There were about ten or twelve bodies there. Lombarski, the two volunteers, our two drivers, and myself all had to pitch in and do what had to be done for as long as we could stand it.

That evening we all sat together at our mess table not talking, not eating, not drinking, just trying to forget the horrible miasma surrounding us and almost making *us* feel like cadavers. Ripe ones at that. There weren't any good hot showers to stand under, just buckets of lukewarm water and little cakes of soap, which, if you dropped or squeezed out of your hand, you lost forever. You couldn't get the smell of the dead out of your hair, and all you could do with your clothes was burn them. The only thing we had that helped at all was some good Italian red wine. We called it Dago Red even though it wasn't. Finally Ed Wozenski— "Big Woz"—my very good friend and the commander of G Company, walked in. By that time Father Deary, Big Woz, and I were the last ones up and around. Ed broke out a bottle of whiskey or brandy—or some stronger stuff—which we finished well after midnight, when I was finally able to go to bed and sleep. I guess I drank most of the liquor, because later the padre and Ed told me that in the future I should be more considerate of my friends and let them have a little of the booze, too.

Taking care of our KIA caused me to miss Terry Allen's farewell visit to the regiment. But it was a job that had to be done. Afterwards, D Company commander Dick Harris, whom Terry Allen had chosen to take back home with him as his reinstated aide-de-camp, dropped by to say good-bye to me. We had a friendship dating back to my first arrival in the 16th, when Terry allowed him to return to D Company to get some combat experience as a platoon leader. I asked him if he would take my bullet-holed (in and out) helmet home to leave with my mother so that she could give it to my son as a war souvenir. He had to get Terry Allen's permission, which of course was granted. Terry always told me that he had personally brought that damn helmet home for me.

About two days later, Tony Prucnal, then the regimental S-1, called to tell me that Father DP had said he would be in the 2nd Battalion area to say mass and wanted to do so at F Company. I told Tony, "Keep that bastard away from F Company!" Tony said, "John, why should I do that? After all, he is our battalion chaplain." I replied, "Because he's a dirty, yellow son-of-a-bitch, and if he comes around F Company, I'll shoot him." Tony asked, "Why, John, why?" I replied, "Because if I don't shoot him, one of my best noncoms will. And I don't want any of my fine soldiers put on trial for murdering that scum! So if I have to, I'll do it myself."

That was the end of that conversation.

That evening I was told that Father DP had been transferred to the umpty-umpt station hospital. So I had done him a great favor after all. I had done us a much greater one, however. We were rid of a festering sore.

The next day I was still in command of E and F Company remnants. The regiment was assembling to the south of Troina, on the south side of the Messina highway. It seems to me now that combined E and F Companies were left behind in place for almost a week. The area formerly occupied by regimental units was being reoccupied by artillery units—not only 1st Division Artillery and 9th Division Artillery but II Corps and Seventh Army Artillery units as well. It was most exhilarating to hear the guns fired. A little hard on our ears but, wow, what power! How great to feel that this attack might result in the end of the present campaign. On the other hand, I wondered why we were not rejoining the regiment. Was it possible that our two units were in purdah, or being quarantined, because we had run away from the Germans? These thoughts were in my mind only and not communicated to anyone else, not even to Old Kewp or Big Ed or the padre, when they dropped in to say hello. Had the Old Man dropped by, I would have asked him. But him only. It was a sobering thought though.

E Company's First Sergeant Imperato came to me, reporting that he and all of the noncommissioned officers and most, if not all, of the men were deeply ashamed of the company's perfor-mance on the third of August. He wanted to know whether there was any way to get the former company commander to face a court-martial to try and convict him for what he had done to them. I said that if they were willing to testify, I would make a further attempt to have him brought before a court-martial. I made this attempt but was unequivocally rebuffed at all levels of command within the regiment.

That was, for all intents and purposes, the end of the Sicil-ian campaign. Our artillery continued to support the attack. The rest of the division settled down to replace personnel, arms and equipment, and all manner of supplies. And the troops settled down to a well-earned rest period. But our rest was not to last very long.

CHAPTER 20

Sanctimonious Old Bastard

The Record

*The fall of Troina closed out Terry Allen's tenure as 1st Division
commander. On August 7, Allen as well as the assistant division
commander, Brigadier General Theodore Roosevelt, were replaced
by Major General Clarence R. Huebner and Colonel Willard G.
Wyman. The decision to remove Allen and Roosevelt was made by
Omar Bradley, who had disapproved of their idiosyncratic command
style and the effect it was having on the division—notwithstanding
the division's record of achievement. "Under Allen," Bradley wrote
in his memoirs,* A Soldier's Story, *"the 1st Division had become
increasingly temperamental, disdainful of both regulations and senior
commands. It thought itself exempted from the need for discipline
by virtue of its months on the line. And it believed itself to be the
only division carrying its fair share of the war. . . . To save Allen
both from himself and from his brilliant record and to save the
division from the heady effects of too much success, I decided to
separate them."*

But there was more to it than that. It seems that Bradley had conceived a personal dislike for Allen that could be traced back to North Africa and beyond. The reason for Bradley's enmity is something of a mystery. "Terrible Terry," as he was fondly known to his troops, was a colorful and charismatic figure who had gained a deserved reputation as a bold tactician, a hard fighter, and a natural leader. An ex-cavalryman, he was the virtual personification of a distinct type of American soldier: the individualistic, rough-and-ready commander who rejects by-the-book orthodoxy and tolerates a certain degree of unconventional behavior in his men—and, significantly, in himself as well—so long as all concerned get the job done. If he sometimes drank heavily, used profane language, and was insubordinate to his superiors, it was also true that he produced victories. Not surprisingly, he was immensely popular with his troops, who had developed an esprit de corps and a matching competence in battle that was the envy of other division commanders. But Bradley deplored Allen's attitudes and behavior, the more so as they evidently rubbed off on his men. He viewed Allen as a loose cannon who needed to be brought under control. But the dynamic, independent-minded Allen resisted control, so Bradley gave him the boot. It was a controversial move, but Bradley did not hesitate to make it. Nor did he hesitate to sack Roosevelt, a kindred spirit of Allen's with the same maverick proclivities.

Almost immediately upon assuming command, the division's new leader, Huebner, began to impose his own regimen on the troops. What this entailed was training, and lots of it. It also meant lots of close-order drill and other activities of the sort collectively known as "chicken shit" in the GI lexicon. Charles Hangsterfer recalled that Huebner directed his reserve units to conduct rifle marksmanship training while the battle for Sicily was still in progress and that a rifle range was improvised behind Mount Etna for that purpose. Not surprisingly, these measures thoroughly rankled the seasoned veterans of the Big Red One, who had grown accustomed to Terry Allen's rather laissez-faire approach to soldiering. But they got used to

Huebner, who was, in his own way, as good at his job as Allen was and who eventually proved to be quite popular with his men.

Continuing his account, John Finke offers another perspective on the whole affair, one where Bradley comes across as someone quite different from the decent and reasonable man portrayed in his memoirs.

John Finke

When our old friends and comrades of the 9th Infantry Division, under the command of Major General Manton Eddy, executed the passage of our lines with their usual and admired efficiency, it marked the end of an era for the 1st Infantry Division. That was the end of the Allen and Roosevelt era—or, better yet, the "Terry and Teddy" era. It had begun with the preparation for, and the execution of, the invasion of Oran; the nearly eight-hundred-mile deployment on the battlefields of Tunisia; the almost heartbreaking, piecemeal commitment of the division to combat in that area; and, due to Terry's unflagging fight to command an undivided division, it culminated in a major contribution to the Allied victory at Tunis. It continued through the planning, preparation, and successful amphibious assault on the south shores of Sicily at Gela. And it concluded when a superbly trained and led, battle-tested, and *victorious* division said a fond farewell to its famed leaders, who had led it to its fame and thereby gained their own.

The Sicily campaign also marked the last time the 1st Division fought an enemy force comprising German and Italian troops. [Italy surrendered unconditionally to the Allies on September 3, 1943.] We all agreed that, in general, we had gone up against a reasonably chivalrous foe, one that had recognized the Geneva Convention as an instrument for governing military conduct on both sides of the conflict and who had pretty much followed the rules it set forth for waging war.

(It is interesting to note that my second cousin, who was then a major general in the German army, took a far dimmer view of his own side. Before the war, when I last saw him, he was a jolly and kindly horse cavalry captain. He came from Darmstadt and represented the continuation of a long and honorable family tradition of military service. By the autumn of 1943, however, he was thoroughly disgusted with Hitler, the whole civilian Nazi government, and especially the Waffen SS. He was a member of the Wehrmacht, the regular army, and had served with Rommel's Afrika Korps in the Western Desert. His negative feelings about the SS were typical of men in his position. I shared his opinion of that supposedly elite organization—I found its fighting units to be overrated, as they had a tendency to lose their discipline as soon as they met with any setbacks. My cousin's disaffection with the Nazi regime may have extended to marginal involvement in the July 20, 1944, assassination plot. I am not sure about this. He was never arrested, but he was under a cloud simply because he was a Wehrmacht general. He was certainly sympathetic to the plotters' aims. Being a career officer with a strong sense of duty, he had loyally obeyed his superiors through most of the war, but not long after the attempt on Hitler's life he requested hospitalization for treatment of an old wound. He was subsequently granted retirement for medical reasons. His voluntary separation from the army must have convinced the Nazis that he had no part in any Wehrmacht-sponsored effort to overthrow the government and was therefore not a worthy object of their suspicion. He was thus able to avoid the fate of many more prominent, active-duty officers—such as Rommel—who were implicated in the anti-Hitler conspiracy.)

The rest of our stay on Sicily was under a new commander, Major General Clarence R. Huebner. At first Huebner's regime appeared to the troops to be harsh and dull in its approach to the training they now had to undergo. No attempt was made to build on the foundation of their magnificent small-unit victories—actions in which their comrades had died while the remaining troops had bled and sweated to ensure that those losses were not in vain. The troops should have received training that capitalized on the hard-earned lessons that were fresh in their memories and needed to be engraved in their minds. What they got instead was training in rifle marksmanship and close-order drill! They also were given instruction in military courtesy by jock-strap PFCs. The latter were to be saluted by officers, NCOs, and enlisted men, who were then critiqued by those self-same PFCs as to their carriage, the way they held their arms and hands, and how they held their heads and looked at the joker who was their so-called instructor.

This was an insult and degrading to Huebner's whole command—and this from a senior major general who had a reputation as a World War I hero and as a troop commander. Later, however, General Huebner showed himself to be a gentlemanly, kind man who appreciated his troops and was, in reality, a fine commander. I can never be convinced that he was such a mean, despicable, and self-serving person as to try to degrade those whom he expected to follow his orders to their possible deaths.

In my opinion the removal of Terry Allen from command of the 1st Division was *not* undertaken at the behest or on the advice of General George S. Patton, an old friend and drinking-and-cussing buddy of Terry Allen. Patton was in no way Terry's enemy, as he is often said to have been. Nor was Patton a jealous rival, either on the polo field or as a commander on the field of battle. Such rumors were spread by persons who had reason to dislike one or the other. It was far more likely that the only man who envied and detested Terry was that "sanctimonious old bastard, Omar Bradley"—which was the way Terry described him to me. I might add that I had personal experience of Bradley—which I won't go into—that confirmed Terry's opinion. In any event Bradley finally got the media to take him at his self-evaluation: as a saintly old man without a mean bone in his body.

The Record

On August 17 U.S. troops entered Messina, there to link up with British forces that had been driving up along Sicily's east coast. The city fell without a fight, as the bulk of German forces had by then fled across the Strait of Messina into Italy. The invasion of Italy would come soon, but the 1st Division would not be part of it. Instead the division was sent back to England to begin training for the main event of the war in Western Europe—but not before General Patton was made to perform his rituals of atonement for the infamous slapping incident, an episode whose particulars are so well known that they need not be recounted here. Suffice to say that it landed him in considerable hot water with his superiors, civilian as well as military, and nearly cost him his career. Charles Hangsterfer was present for one of Patton's expiatory performances, which proved typical of the general in that it left somewhat other than the intended impression on his listeners.

Charles Hangsterfer

After the battle in Sicily was over, the entire 1st Division was assembled to hear an address by General Patton. I didn't know in advance why he was addressing us, and he used so much profanity that it wasn't clear to me what he was talking about. On the march back to our battalion area, one of the men in my company remarked, "That fucking fucker of a general swears too fucking much."

Much later I learned that Patton had hit one of the soldiers from the division and had been ordered to apologize for his action. So his address was meant to be an apology, but the thrust of it was lost in all the profanity. In retrospect it occurred to me that I could have applied for separation from the service using this as an excuse: I could not tolerate vulgar and obscene language. But then I would have missed the exciting boat ride to Omaha Beach on D-Day.

PART IV

D-Day

CHAPTER 21

"They Just Wanted to Get the War Over and Go Home"

The Record

Transports carrying the 1st Division departed Augusta, Sicily, at the end of October 1943, arriving in Liverpool on November 3. Immediately upon debarking, the greater part of the division proceeded to cantonments in Dorset County in southern England (some elements went to Scotland), where the troops spent most of the next five months training and refitting for the invasion of Normandy, code-named Operation Overlord.

Charles Hangsterfer

On our return to England we took all our insignia off so nobody would know who we were. We were moved to the south coast to various little towns—Weymouth, Bridgeport, Lyme Regis—and there we started to practice landing maneuvers for the invasion of Europe.

One time during our stay in Lyme Regis, a night exercise was scheduled. I looked in the field manual to review the duties of an adjutant and discovered that part of the job description was to look after the morale of the troops. I decided that my morale also needed looking after since, after all, I was one of the troops. My buddy "Pop" Dion (the CO of D Company) and I were dating American nurses who were stationed at a nearby U.S. Army hospital. I realized that going on this night maneuver meant that Pop would not be able to see his sweetheart (later his wife), Nell, nor would I be able to visit my friend Alyene. So I gave my jeep driver a map with the location of the battalion command post marked on it and told him to pick up the two nurses. But under no circumstances was he to show them our position on the map unless they got hopelessly lost. What we intended, of course, was for the nurses to read the map and figure out for themselves where the CP was located.

That was what they did, and it wasn't long before they showed up at the command post. Nell and Alyene were still there when the battalion commander unexpectedly walked in. I quickly explained to the colonel that the nurses were on a reconnaissance to learn our location in case we required any emergency medical assistance. He asked me if I was going to be the dummy in a demonstration of mouth-to-mouth resuscitation. I have often wondered what he meant by that.

When we practiced amphibious landings, we went through it all just as if we were landing in Normandy. First we loaded up everything and went to a marshaling area where we got on trucks; then we went down to Weymouth to load aboard ship. We landed at Slapton Sands, which was supposed to have terrain identical to Normandy's. After that the trucks picked us up to go back to Lyme Regis.

The people of Slapton Sands went through all sorts of trials and tribulations while we were there. They had to vacate their homes, many of them centuries old, so we could practice. One time while it was raining I was running by one of these houses with my HQ group; the house was boarded up but had a door open, so we went in. Someone saw me go in there with my group and wrote a report on it. I was subsequently accused of unauthorized use of a house. I wondered what they were going to do with me. My defense was to tell them that if I'm not smart enough to come in out of the rain, they don't need me as a soldier. "Send me home," I said. "That can be my punishment. Just send me home."

At Lyme Regis we knew that something big was going to come up because General Montgomery came around to talk to us. We were in formation and figured he was going to inspect us like reviewing officers usually do. Instead he said, "Come on, men. Come over here." Then he got up on top of a jeep and gave us some kind of a big pep talk. But our guys never needed any pep talk. They just wanted to get the war over and go home. That was all.

I remember General Bradley. He was ground force commander for the Twelfth Army Group, and he was in charge of us. He gave a little pep talk for the officers in the 16th Regiment. I listened to him and heard him say he would give anything if he could be in the first wave going ashore with us, but he was the commander so he had to stay back. I figured if he was going to give anything I would sell him my seat for $20. I almost asked him if he wanted to buy it, but I didn't.

Sidney Haszard

After Sicily we spent a lot of time in Scotland on the Duke of Argyle's estate, where we lived in quonset huts the British had built. The huts had cold cement floors and were heated by two very small stoves. During this period we often went to the coast to practice getting off landing craft, and we always got our clothes soaked in these exercises. When we returned to our cold huts, we needed to get a good strong fire going right away in order to dry out our wet clothes; however, we had a very small ration of coal, which was insufficient for the task. After some discussion we arrived at a democratic solution. Every day we would each give up a board from our bunks to get a quick hot blaze going. The stoves burned up a lot of wood, and we used the pinewood boards on the beds, three or four at a time, breaking the boards up to make a fire. Finally everybody was down to about three boards, then two boards, and finally no boards. After that we slept on pine boughs we gathered from the duke's forest. The duke wasn't exactly happy about this.

The food situation was no better. So we threw grenades into the duke's streams and came up with trout. Sometimes we killed fish by electric shock, cranking our field telephones to build up a charge, then sticking the exposed ends of the hot wires into the water. We also went hunting in the duke's forest, and as a result the deer population got scarcer. The Americans didn't play the game as the duke would have preferred but, as the Brits liked to say, these things happen in wartime situations.

Paul Bystrak

Bystrak was also stationed in Scotland for a short time. He subsequently received orders transferring him to southern England to help plan the invasion of Europe.

On the way down from Edinburgh, the MPs came on the train looking for me. I thought, Oh my God, what did I do? They said, "You have to get your stuff and come off the train with us." They wouldn't tell me why. They took me in a car to a secret British underground complex, where I helped develop a plan for the invasion of Europe. The invasion was to be carried out by the 1st and 9th Divisions, and the plan called for us to be in Berlin in two weeks! Evidently we were counting on the German army to help us get there.

We actually laid out the plan and movement orders directing which regiment would go first, which would follow, etc. We stayed there for several weeks working on that plan, working on the logistics necessary to support it. Obviously the plan came to nothing, and eventually I was sent back to my old unit in the 1st Division. I stayed with the unit for a few months and then moved down to Plymouth and the underground command post there, where we began planning the Normandy invasion. Colonel Eymer and I did the logistic planning for the 1st Division attack force.

One of the things they asked us was how many vehicles and how many landing craft the force would need. Someone was always asking for this information, so I prepared a chart. Across the top of the chart I put the different units and their complement of vehicles, weapons, guns, and the like. And in the margin I put down the different units that would be involved on day one, day two, day three, etc. I worked out the table of allowances and decided which vehicles ought to be taken. Colonel Eymer was really proud of that chart. Every time they had a staff meeting he would take out the chart and show the generals how far we had progressed in the planning.

One day we finally got a form developed, top secret, that all units had to fill out to show what they wanted. I decided to erase all the information off my chart and start posting the actual requests. After I had done that, the colonel came in and asked for the chart. He had a big group down from Eisenhower's headquarters and he wanted to show it to them. I asked him if he couldn't wait a day or two, and he said, "I want it now." I said, "Oh, Colonel, can't you wait just a little while?" He said, "No. What's the matter with you?" I finally told him that I had erased all the information. He ordered me to never destroy, erase, or tear up a piece of paper while I was in planning headquarters. That worked for a while. I took every piece of scrap paper to him until he realized that this was a little ridiculous.

Everett Booth

My company was assigned to the village of Abbottsbury, a town so small that I had more people in my company than the mayor had in his town. In fact, I assumed the job of mayor and was nicknamed the "Mayor of Abbottsbury." While we were there we underwent intensive training with landing maneuvers in preparation for the Normandy Invasion. We went on thirty-mile forced marches and set up relations with the British Army. I personally set up the perimeter defense for the southern coast of England and coordinated my efforts with the British Home Guard.

During this period we met a lot of the British people. We got along very well with them and were often invited into their homes. Christmas of 1943, we were guests in their homes and they treated us like their own. Friday nights were devoted to attending one of the local pubs and eating the traditional fish and chips, which were great.

I was the commander of Company K for a time in England. Because we were stationed in Abbottsbury, we were too far away from our regimental headquarters to use their recreational facilities. So our enlisted men usually went to the coastal city of Weymouth, a few kilometers and a short train ride away, for R&R. Weymouth just happened to be home base for the 18th Infantry. And, as it happened, one night two of my enlisted men were caught pissing in the doorway of the Weymouth Electrical Company. The MPs grabbed them and, you know, in a situation like that, there was all kinds of fuss. The regimental commander of the 18th raised heck with my regimental commander of the 16th. Of course my commander had to do something about it, so he relieved me of command of K Company. I was assigned as executive officer of M Company. I felt very bad about the situation. But when the gentleman who took over command of K Company landed during the invasion of Normandy, he was killed on the beach. Now if that isn't fate, I don't know what is.

The Record

On March 23, 1944, the 1st Division was alerted to be ready to move on short notice to its invasion marshaling areas.

Everett Booth

The training went on and on and on. Then one bright night we moved into an assembly area in preparation for loading on the ships. We left the area in deuce-and-a-half trucks. As we rolled through these little towns all the villagers were out waving good-bye to us. They surely knew what was coming off and where we were going.

Charles Hangsterfer

One time as we were loading up for what we thought would be another practice landing, we were told to get all our laundry back and pack everything. So we knew this was it. When we got into the marshaling area and they issued us some invasion currencies, we knew the day had arrived. We were going to make the landing.

The Record

The movement to the marshaling areas occurred between May 7 and May 11. At the end of the month the division went to the port towns of Portland, Weymouth, and Poole for embarkation, completing the loading process by June 3. Originally scheduled for June 5, the invasion was postponed until the next day because of inclement weather.

Everett Booth

We loaded on military transports in Weymouth on the night of June 5, 1944, and sailed out into the English Channel in the early-morning darkness of June 6. As we entered the Channel, I saw that ships dotted the waters for as far as the eye could see. Off the Normandy beach we showed no lights. We were wearing our regular combat uniform, which was woolens with a steel pot. Somewhere around midnight my company and I, each man with his hands on the shoulders of the man in front of him—and no conversation—followed a guard through the maze of the innards of the ship to where our LCI was located. We loaded and were lowered to the water. We followed the lead boat, which circled around until it was time to approach the beach.

CHAPTER 22

"Being in That First Wave Was Like Committing Suicide"

The Record

Two American army corps were to take part in the Normandy invasion: VII Corps, which would land at Utah Beach in the Varreville vicinity on the southeast coast of the Cotentin Peninsula; and V Corps, which would land at Omaha Beach on the north coast of Calvados near Saint Laurent-sur-Mer, between Port-en-Bessin and the Vire River. To the east, the British XXX Corps and I Corps, consisting of British and Canadian forces augmented by various Allied units, were to seize three beaches code-named Gold, Juno, and Sword.

The assault by V Corps was to be spearheaded by two regiments landing abreast, the 116th Regiment of the 29th Division (attached to the 1st Division for that day only) and the 16th Regiment of the 1st Division. The 116th was to land on the right (west) part of the beach in the sectors designated Charlie, Dog Green, Dog White, Dog Red, and Easy Green; while the 16th was to go ashore on the left (east) in the sectors designated Easy Red, Fox Green, and Fox Red. Each regiment would conduct the initial assault with two battalions landing abreast in columns of companies, with the 3rd Battalion companies coming in behind them. In all, nine companies plus attached ranger units were to land in the first wave.

After securing the beach, the division and its attached units were to advance up the bluffs overlooking the beach and inland to the fields beyond. At the end of D-Day the division was to have penetrated to a depth of five to six miles.

The landings began at 6:30 A.M. and were in serious trouble right from the start.

Everett Booth

At this point we were pretty much in the hands of the navy. My M Company, a heavy weapons company of the 3rd Battalion, 16th Infantry, had machine guns and 81mm mortars. Our plan of attack was that I Company would be on the left and K Company on the right, with M Company following I Company. But the navy landed I Company about five miles away from the landing spot and dropped them on nice sand. I Company's commander got out and said, "Heck, this is the wrong beach." So they got back on board their landing craft and went out to find the right beach. In the meantime the navy substituted M Company for I Company in the landing scheme.

Charles Hangsterfer

Hangsterfer was in Headquarters Company of the 1st Battalion, 16th Infantry.

During the landing it would be my job as battalion adjutant and HQ Company CO to call out the boat numbers so the troops could proceed to their embarkation stations next to the boats they were assigned to. The troops would climb aboard the LCVPs [landing craft, vehicles and personnel], which would then be lowered into the water to circle the ship until all landing craft in the wave were loaded. Then we would head to the beach.

I had watched a lot of these maneuvers from the rowboats in the Gunpowder River by Edgewood Arsenal, Maryland. Some of the soldiers were not good sailors and they got seasick while the LCVP circled. I never get seasick, but I get sick when I see somebody else sick. So I was real happy to have this job loading the boats, because I would be the last one on. I would call out the boat numbers and then run down and get on board my LCVP. As soon as my LCVP joined the others, they'd stop going around in circles and head for shore. It was strange then, because the adrenaline pumped so much that as soon as you got near shore, the seasickness stopped. I figure adrenaline is some kind of cure for seasickness.

When we were on board the ship, there were messages to be read to the troops from General Eisenhower, Churchill, and President Roosevelt. Well, I am not much of a radio announcer. I could call out boat numbers well enough, but when it came to reading out all these big words . . . I was never very good at reading aloud. Fortunately there was a radio announcer who was going to give a shot-by-shot account of the invasion, and he was on board our ship, the *Samuel Chase*. John McVane was his name. I got him to read the messages to the troops over the loudspeaker system. All the troops thought I was the one reading. Some of the soldiers later complimented me: "You have such a good radio voice." I never told them that it was John McVane instead of me.

This reminds me that earlier I was in a hotel in Scotland. My nickname is "Hank." So some guy said, "That's Hank Greenberg." (Hank Greenberg was a famous baseball player.) The guy came over and asked for my autograph. I signed it Hank Greenberg. Then they found out who I really was. They were awfully disappointed. I really didn't want to disappoint them originally, but I guess I did.

Well anyway, here we were off Normandy, and all the LCVPs had been lowered into the water and we were heading for shore. I remember that it wasn't raining and I didn't hear the roar of navy gunfire or our planes bombing the beach. We passed some LCVPs from the first wave headed in the opposite direction, returning to their ships from Omaha Beach. Though the skies were overcast, the whole scene reminded me of a sunny Sunday afternoon boat ride on Chesapeake Bay, where you would wave to people in the other boats and they would wave back at you. And so I thought, My goodness, it's a real nice day. Now, we were supposed to have landed the previous day, but the invasion was called off because of bad weather. But before it was called off, they had given us a steak dinner with ice cream, just like they would give a convicted murderer his last meal on the evening of his execution. On the evening of June fifth they gave us another steak dinner for what might be our last day on earth. Oh my. But it was such a nice day that I couldn't imagine that anybody would want to shoot anybody.

When we got close to shore, however, they were shooting at us! I had thought that the navy was going to be firing their big guns, knocking out all the pillboxes. And before that, the air force was supposed to bomb the beach. We used to practice moving around and in and out of bomb craters, but there weren't any bomb craters. And the combat engineers were supposed to land before dawn to take away all the underwater obstacles on the beach, but the obstacles were still there. My friend Al Smith was in the same LCVP I was, and we could see that some of the LCVPs were hitting these mines and blowing up. And I'm shouting over the roar of the boat's engine, "Open the ramp!" and he's shouting, "Keep the ramp up!"

I didn't know why he gave that order. I didn't question it, however. But on the fortieth anniversary of the landing, when we were touring Omaha Beach, I finally asked him, "Why did you do that?" He told me that machine-gun bullets had been hitting the front of the ramp, and he was not about to let it down.

Anyway, here I am looking toward the beach, and I'm seeing these boats blowing up. We finally got off, but the Germans did put machine-gun bullets in my LCVP. Some of the fellows were wounded, and I had to help get them off the boat.

The Record

Prior to D-Day, Omaha Beach was known to be a formidable objective, but even so, the difficulties encountered there went far beyond what Allied planners had anticipated. It was no secret that the German defenses, which consisted of an elaborate system of pillboxes, gun emplacements, and connecting trenches, were situated behind the beach on a line of bluffs that rose to a height of 100 to 170 feet—an ideal place from which to oppose a seaborne onslaught. Accordingly, they were subjected to intensive air and naval bombardment in advance of the landings. Despite all the metal and explosives thrown in their direction, however, they were not reduced by any appreciable degree. A low cloud cover obscured the target area from Allied aircraft and caused them to bomb wide of their targets. Preliminary gunfire and rocket support provided by a host of warships proved too inaccurate and too short in duration to do significant damage to German fortifications and beach obstacles.

The failure of Allied air and naval forces to blast a hole through Hitler's Atlantic Wall was compounded by the fact that many of the men on the other side of that barrier belonged to the German 352nd Infantry Division, a battle-hardened outfit that had seen action on the Russian front. Allied intelligence had previously thought that the Americans would be going up against an inferior "Ost" (east)

Division composed mostly of non-German troops (mainly Poles and Russians) who were more or less dragooned into the service of the Third Reich; the additional presence of soldiers who could be counted among the Wehrmacht's very best was not discovered until a few days before the invasion, when it was really too late to do anything about it.

As if all this weren't bad enough, a strong northeast wind had whipped up waves averaging from three to four feet high in the landing zone, and the rough water combined with the tidal current to wreak havoc on the approach to the beach. Armor support for the infantry was to have been provided by specially designed amphibious tanks, but most of these foundered on the run into the beach, as did many of the DUKWs carrying the division's artillery and ammunition. A number of troop landing craft were also swamped, while the majority of those that stayed afloat were driven leftward by the force of wind, wave, and current. In the ensuing confusion, the complex two-battalion assault plan quickly broke down. Companies I and L of the 3rd Battalion, which were to have landed in the first wave on Fox Green, went ashore late and too far to the east on Fox Red. As a result the 16th Infantry's initial assault was conducted solely by Companies E and F of the 2nd Battalion, with boat sections from these units landing alongside the 116th's E Company, which was also out of position, on Easy Red between Saint Laurent and Colleville-sur-Mer and on Fox Green in front of Colleville-sur-Mer.

The assault troops debarked from their landing craft at distances of one to two hundred yards from the shoreline, jumping off the ramps into rough water that was neck-deep in places and boiling with bullet and shrapnel splashes and shell bursts. After slogging through the surf to the water's edge, the troops had another two hundred yards of open sand to cross before reaching the dubious shelter of a sea wall or shingle bank. All the while they were subjected to withering artillery, mortar, and small-arms fire from German positions on the bluffs. Casualties were heavy as a result.

Ted Lombarski

Lombarski was a sergeant in F Company.

We were the first wave to hit the beach, Companies E and F of the 16th Infantry. Almost all the tanks that had gone in before us were sunk. The tank crews had a rough time, and so did the navy personnel who drove us in on the LCVPs. As we went in we knew that the air force had dropped their bombs too far inland and that the navy shelling had done likewise. The first wave went through hell that day, and we have all heard enough said about that.

Can you picture the Germans waiting for us? They only had to fire on the LCVPs as we landed. There were so many bullets zeroing in on the first wave that it was impossible to cross the beach. Being in that first wave was like committing suicide. Yet some of us did cross that beach and reach the shale. Here we had protection from small-arms fire. In front of the shale were mines, barbed wire, and Germans raining bullets all over. All this plus mortars, antitank guns, and artillery—all zeroed in on the beach. If you exposed yourself, you were dead. We were brave and we had a job to do, but we weren't stupid. If you exposed yourself you were a casualty, and dead soldiers don't help anyone.

I'll say it again: E and F Companies were on a virtual suicide mission. It's a miracle any of us survived.

Fred Dolfi

Dolfi was also a sergeant in F Company.

I was on an LCVP that carried vehicles loaded with ammunition and a lot of essential supplies. The beach was well fortified with concrete and train rails that made it impossible to get the landing craft close to shore, and the waves were coming in so hard they could wipe you out. I drove my jeep off the LCVP and it got hit by a wave and sank. I couldn't swim, but fortunately I had two lifebelts, one already inflated and the other as a reserve.

On the beach I got on a tank but couldn't get it started because it was all flooded. When I came down off it, I was hit pretty hard. I took two pieces of shrapnel, one in my spine, and I was knocked completely out. I couldn't raise up. That was the morning of June 6 at about six-thirty.

Everett Booth

We landed on Omaha Beach at about 0700. They didn't get us very close to the sandy beach, I'll tell you. I think they wanted to get rid of us as soon as they could. So they dropped their ramps and we ran off into water about chest high. We were met with machine-gun bullets hitting all over the water. I received a superficial wound in my arm when I was a little more than waist deep. We pushed through the water and finally, after maneuvering around Teller mines and various obstacles, we reached the beach.

At this point, I had no idea of the number of casualties to my unit. The enemy was riddling the beach with machine-gun fire. My men and I took off as fast as we could across the beach toward an area of high ground. I can't recall any conversations with my men from the point of loading the landing craft until we reached high ground. We were all too concerned with getting our butts out of the water to some safety on the beach.

CHAPTER 23

"It Was a Pretty Good Killing Zone in There"

The Record

The second group of assault waves began landing at 7:00 A.M. only to find that the invasion was apparently stalled on the shoreline. Movement off the beach was occurring within the hour, however, and by mid-morning small groups were advancing up the bluffs. But the Germans still had the advantage and were resisting fiercely, so much so that when the 18th Infantry started to come ashore on Easy Red shortly after 10:00 A.M., the ownership of Omaha Beach was still undecided.

William Campbell

I went into Normandy with 18th Regiment headquarters. I had a couple of LCMs going in with equipment. We started in around 9 A.M. The beach was loaded with fire; the beach was hot. Some of our equipment had drowned near the beach, and we had to get it out of the water. As we moved it up onto the beach a 150mm shell hit nearby and knocked me out for a while. I should have been taken back to England, but I didn't think I was hurt that badly. There was sand in my ears, but I didn't know I was bleeding from the ears—I didn't notice anything. I was tagged for evacuation, but I took the tag off and kept going.

We loaded up and moved off the beach, but we didn't get far. There was a big tank trap right up front of where the cemetery is now. Troops could get around the trap but you couldn't get any vehicles up there. It wasn't until about seven o'clock that night, when the engineers neutralized the trap, that we were able to start moving things off the beach.

In the meantime we did manage to get up under the cliff, where we found some protection from German artillery. Nevertheless, the artillery kept pounding us until one or two in the afternoon. It was a pretty good killing zone in there. But the fire was especially heavy on the beach.

Charles Hangsterfer

We made it to the beach. There was a big swamp on the inland side of the beach where my LCVP had landed; it was just in front of the slope going to the top of a steep bluff. There had been so much rain the day before that it had filled this little gully, and we had to wade through in water up to our waists—or higher for the short-legged guys. At breakfast they had given us an apple and an orange in a paper bag, but I lost the orange while going through that swamp. So as soon as we got on dry land again, I decided to eat the apple right then and there. I wasn't about to lose that apple like I had lost my orange. I sat down on the beach with Al Smith, and he had a bottle of booze, of all things. He gave me a drink of his booze and I gave him a piece of my apple.

After I finished eating I went back through the swamp to the landing area, where I rounded up members of the company who were coming in on other boats. Easy Red beach was where the

16th was supposed to land, but I found that part of the 29th Division's 116th Infantry was there also. They had landed on the wrong beach. The 116th were setting up mortars and were going to fire. I asked, "What are you going to fire at?" The guy setting the tubes up said, "I don't know. I got to do something." So I said, "Well don't do it here because our 16th Regiment troops are up on the top of that hill. Don't go shooting up there." I knew I had to go back up, and I didn't want him shooting me. I told him, "Go shoot down on your own beach."

Then I went up the hill to the top, where the war of the hedgerows started.

The Record

At a little after 1:30 P.M. Lieutenant General Bradley, commanding American forces from the cruiser Augusta, *received a welcome radio message: "Troops formerly pinned on beaches Easy Red, Easy Green, Fox Red advancing up heights behind beaches." But this was already old news; by then, elements of the 1st and 29th Divisions had penetrated the enemy defense line at several points, with the 2nd Battalion of the 16th Infantry pushing inland beyond the bluffs to cut the coastal road that ran roughly parallel to the shore.*

Ted Lombarski

My unit lost every officer on the beach except the CO, Captain John Finke, who was wounded near Colleville-sur-Mer and evacuated. For the rest of the day I was the head man of Company F. There weren't too many to lead, however. Ten of us made it up the bluff and afforded some protection for Major Hicks's 2nd Battalion CP. We formed an outpost on the left side of the road leading to Colleville-sur-Mer—me and ten men, survivors of F company.

Everett Booth

The conditions on the beach were not conducive to setting up our heavy machine guns and 81mm mortars. So we worked ourselves along the beach, hoping to tie in with any other units that had moved inland. Sometime later that morning, the navy brought I Company to its assigned landing area. By then the tide was up and the landing craft risked hitting the enemy's Teller mines, which were stacked atop poles planted in the tidal flats. When we had landed, the tide was low and the mines were no problem because they were above water. But when I Company came in, the mines were submerged and one of the company's landing craft hit a mine. The mine exploded and many of the men were terribly burned all over their bodies. It was a terrible sight.

We continued on forward off the beach and found an area where we could work our way through to high ground. We moved past a German pillbox that had been manned by machine guns and small artillery earlier in the day. Then we moved into the town of Colleville-sur-Mer and set up our defense there. The next morning I saw our battalion medical officer, who treated my bullet wound. It wasn't necessary for me to leave my unit for any further treatment at the hospital. The rest of that day was spent mopping up enemy forces in and around the town.

CHAPTER 24

"These Things Do Happen in Wartime"

The Record

The 1st Battalion of the 26th Infantry began landing at about 6 P.M. on Fox Green; Major General Huebner and the 1st Division's command group came ashore an hour later on Easy Red. By this time the 3rd Battalion of the 16th Infantry had taken up a blocking position astride the coastal highway at Le Grand Hameau.

Paul Bystrak

Bystrak was a chief warrant officer in the division's G-4 section.

On D-Day I was on board the command ship with General Huebner and his staff. Early in the morning before sunrise I went out on deck and watched the airplanes coming over from England and dropping their bombs. The ships started their attacks with their long guns and blasted the beaches. Something that was different about General Huebner compared to General Allen was that, in the invasions we made with Allen, we always landed before dawn. That was an old cavalry type of tactic. General Huebner insisted—actually, I don't know whether it was him or someone of higher rank—on landing in daylight so he would know what was going on. So the landings on Omaha Beach started at daybreak.

Shortly after the landings began, the reports started coming into headquarters about how bad things were on Omaha. One story is that General Huebner got a call on the radio from Colonel Taylor, commander of the 16th Regiment, reporting that things were going very badly. When General Huebner asked how many troops were left in the 16th, Colonel Taylor said, "Just a minute, I will count them." Which meant that the 16th, which had started the operation with three thousand men, had suffered so many casualties that its CO could easily count the number of combat effectives left to him!

Even so, around noon General Huebner decided things couldn't be that bad. He said, "Let's all go take a look." He had the whole staff board landing craft. All the officers went with him on one landing craft, and I took all the enlisted men from division headquarters on another.

We started toward the shore, heading for Omaha Beach. I don't know much about maps and topography, but I did have a map with me. I looked at it and I looked at the shoreline. We were supposed to be going to the right of a certain cleft in the hills but, I realized, we were going to the left. I told the navy man running the craft, "I think we are supposed to be going to the right." He said, "On board a navy craft the senior navy person is the commanding officer. I am running the boat. I know where I am going."

We arrived at Juno Beach, where the Canadian Army was landing. The Canadians wouldn't let us come ashore; they had enough troubles of their own. The officer on the beach came over and demanded, "Who are you? Where are you from?" We told him we were the 1st Division. He said, "We don't want you here. Get out of here." So we started back out. Then for some reason the landing craft broke down and started sinking. As we drifted toward the beach, some of the Germans fired at us with rifles. I told the men to throw away their weapons, radios, and everything. I kept the G-4 briefcases with the logistics documents, but everything else we threw overboard. The navy man finally shot flares and eventually got someone's attention. We stayed afloat until another landing craft came over to pick us up.

They took us to an LST that had been stranded on a sandbar and put us there for the night. The next morning we landed on Omaha Beach. By this time they were preparing to declare the division HQ's enlisted men and myself missing in action. I walked over to the division command post. Brigadier General Wyman and Colonel Eymer both happened to be in the G-4 area when I came in. I said to Colonel Eymer, "Colonel, I managed to bring all your reports in." He said, "Well, it is about time." But General Wyman said, "We are very glad to see that you and all the men made it."

While going to the beaches we saw bodies floating in the water. The platoon of graves registration people were sort of frightened—they were hiding in foxholes and the bodies were floating in the waves, so we had to push our way through bodies to get to the beach. It was terrible.

Tom Lancer

Lancer commanded the division's Military Police Platoon on D-Day.

In England, before the landings commenced, I watched my men go aboard different ships. One of them, a big coal miner from

Scranton, Pennsylvania, had once been somewhat delinquent by sleeping on duty. I had gone easy on him because he had a good record. As he went by me, he was carrying a bazooka on his shoulder and he gave me the rifle salute with the bazooka, which is very unusual. He said, "I will get a tank for the major," using the third person, which was quite common in the old army. He was the first man out of his landing craft. When the ramp went down he jumped off and was instantly killed by machine-gun fire.

When I landed, my landing craft's ramp would not go down, so we had to climb over the gunwales. We dropped into the water, which was up to my neck. I saw a little soldier next to me go right under. I grabbed him by the harness on his pack and held his head above the water and walked him into the beach. I didn't realize it at the time, but in the course of wading in to the shore I lost my college class ring. It was my only casualty.

Sidney Haszard

I went into Normandy with the 2nd Battalion, 26th Infantry. Our biggest problem on Omaha Beach was the navy. We came in on LCTs in rough seas; our landing craft didn't want to go where *we* wanted to go, so we forced them in and got a bit closer. But we were still dropped a long way from shore. When we got off, we took a few steps and then went down under water. Our first sergeant turned around, took a fifty-caliber machine gun and pointed it at the control officer and told him: "Raise the ramps, back off, and try again."

I'll never forget Paul Skogsberg splashing around, saving guys from drowning. We had dead guys floating in the water. Four days later, when we came back down to the beach to get our vehicles, I saw their corpses. They had been put in trucks. It was awful—all those men killed by drowning, all purple, stacked like cordwood on trucks.

The Record

While the 26th Infantry was landing, the 1st Battalion of the 16th Infantry, Charles Hangsterfer's unit, was fighting in the fields beyond the coast road between Colleville-sur-Mer and Saint Laurent.

Charles Hangsterfer

I got back up on the top of the hill, where we ran into these hedgerows. On the way we captured a German. We asked him where his headquarters was, and he showed us the location on a map. We had a naval gunfire officer with us, and we thought we might as well use him. He said he wanted a fire mission and that he could direct fire on the German HQ.

The navy officer gave a call back to his ship, and soon a salvo was on the way. We could hear the shells going out, and it sounded so good to hear outgoing shells rather than the ones coming in. We said, "Do it again. Fire for effect." But the ship wouldn't. The naval gunfire officer wanted to see the effect for himself. He got up on top of the hedgerows, but he could see only a hundred or so yards to the next hedgerow. There was nothing to see but hedgerow and trees, and the navy wouldn't fire unless they could have observed fire.

The Record

As the day waned, the 2nd and 3rd Battalions of the 26th Infantry advanced inland across the coastal road between Saint Laurent and Colleville, while the 1st Battalion moved in an easterly direction to take up positions in front of Caubourg.

Sidney Haszard

Our platoon moved off the beach and went to provide security to the left flank. We ran into a German reconnaissance outfit.

We knocked out one light vehicle and withdrew. Then we took up a position at a crossroads and got into a kind of safe area. I was designated to go back and see who was behind us. I saw what I thought was a German tank, which I identified by the muzzle break on its gun. I tried to knock it out with a bazooka, a great mistake. I didn't know anything about bazookas—I was learning how to use it on the job, in combat. I was really sweating. I fired at the tank and hit the right front side. The next thing I heard was: "Blimey, now we've hit a land mine." It was a British tank, not a German, and I had killed or wounded the radio operator. I snuck out of there. We later apologized to the British, and their commander said, "These things do happen in wartime." The British weren't upset at all. This was the first Allied tank we had ever seen with a muzzle break on its gun. I had thought I was battling a Kraut, not a Britisher.

CHAPTER 25

Aftermath

William Campbell

I was out of the combat zone that night. By then I couldn't hear a thing. I was deaf and my head was cut, so they sent me to a hospital on the beach the next day. Then they put me on a hospital ship which took me back to England. I stayed in England until July 24 or 25, returning to Normandy just before the big breakout at Saint Lô.

Fred Dolfi

I lay on the beach, wounded, until about six at night. Then they had German prisoners pick us up, put us on litters, and carry us over to an American ship, the *Thurston*. The doctors asked me what was wrong and I told them. They took shrapnel out of my left leg, my arm, and my shoulder. I also had two pieces along my spine, and they took one of these out but left the other one in. Then I was sent to the 55th General Hospital in Malvern, England, where I was operated on again. They thought I was in pretty bad shape because of that remaining piece of shrapnel so close to the spine. It's still there, although it has since moved three inches down from where it hit me.

While I was in the hospital, representatives from the American Red Cross, fine people, called on me. They asked if I had any relatives close by. I told them I had a brother at the B-17 Flying Fortress base in Norwich, England. I gave them the address and within a few hours my oldest brother came down. He was with me for seven days. My youngest brother was in the 222nd Chemical Outfit, and he was also brought over for seven days. It was really wonderful.

Charles Hangsterfer

Somewhere along the line, when I was on the beach, a mortar shell exploded near me, and I got hit in the knees with all these stones. It hurt like the dickens, but I persevered with it for about six days. Then I got evacuated back to England. At a hospital they found I had a bad case of housemaid's knee—bruises and contusions. Then I was sent back to France.

But first I had to go to a replacement depot. I boarded a ship, but this time I landed on Utah Beach. My orders were to report to the 30th Division. I saw a 1st Division vehicle, and I said to the driver, "Give me a ride." He took me to the 16th Infantry. So instead of going to the 30th, I went AWOL. I arrived back at the 16th Infantry just as preparations were being made for Operation Cobra, the breakout at Saint Lô.

The Record

Casualties for V Corps on D-Day numbered about twenty-five hundred killed, wounded, and missing, with the two assaulting regimental combat teams (the 16th and 116th) losing about one thousand each. Danger Forward, *a history of the 1st Division, reports:*

At the end of D-Day, the assault on Omaha Beach had succeeded, but the going had been harder than expected. Penetrations made in the morning by relatively weak assault groups had lacked the force to carry far inland. Delay in reducing the strong points at the draws had slowed landings of reinforcements, artillery, and supplies. Stubborn enemy resistance, both at strong points and inland, had held the advance to a strip of ground hardly more than a mile and a half deep in the Colleville area, and considerably less than that west of Saint Laurent. Barely large enough to be called a foothold, this strip was well inside the planned beachhead maintenance area. Behind the forward positions, cut-off enemy groups were still resisting. The whole landing area continued under enemy artillery fire from inland. (Society of the First Division. Danger Forward. *Nashville: Battery Press, 1980, page 189.)*

Yet for all that, the Americans were firmly in possession of Omaha Beach. The other beaches, Utah, Gold, Sword, and Juno, were also secure. In all, over 150,000 Allied troops had gotten ashore by nightfall; and though it was not apparent at the time, the Germans were incapable of driving them back into the sea, much less containing them in their seaside lodgements. The campaign to liberate France had begun, and the 1st Division was destined to play an important role in it.

Part V

Normandy to Czechoslovakia

CHAPTER 26

The Bodies That Moved

The Record

After D-Day the fighting shifted to Normandy's bocage country, where the Allies found the going slow and bloody through the rest of June and most of July. In the final week of July, however, the Allies broke out of Normandy and the pace of events quickened dramatically. In August, Allied armies raced across France, subjecting the Germans to the same kind of blitz campaigns that the enemy had used to conquer much of Europe three years previously.

Blitzkrieg (lightning war) is commonly associated with fast-moving armored divisions, but in the summer of 1944, Allied infantry divisions showed that they also could move very fast and far under the right circumstances. During a three-day period in the last week of August, for instance, use of motorized transport and the rapid disintegration of German forces enabled the 1st Division to advance ninety-six miles across northern France. This movement occurred August 23–26, on a route that took the division through Alençon and Mamers to Courville-sur-Eure. Nor did movement end there, but instead resumed the very next day, with the division

*advancing east another fifty-five miles to bivouacs in the Étampes
vicinity.*

*At the beginning of September the division was in the Mons
area, but on September 7 it swung away from Mons and headed for
Liège. By September 11, the division was across the Meuse River and
driving toward the German frontier and the enemy's Siegfried Line
defenses. It seemed to many that the Germans were just about
finished and that the war might be over before the year was out. But
it was not to be. The Germans still had a lot of fight left in them, as
they proved in the months ahead.*

Everett Booth

One incident I remember from this time is what we called "the
bodies that moved" or "the dead that weren't there." I was the
commander of K Company, and we went out to set up an outpost in front of the new position we had been assigned to. One
of the fellas who went to the outpost came back and said, "Sir,
there's a couple of dead Germans out there." I said, "Well, we
don't want them lying around out there; bring 'em in, we'll set
'em near the CP and have the first-aid people take care of them."

This was done. The next morning, the battalion aid people
came by to pick up these dead Germans—and they weren't there!
We got out, looked all over the place, and wondered what the heck
happened. I talked to the men who brought them in. They said,
"Gee, Captain, we had them in a wheelbarrow, their heads were
bouncing and hitting the wheel and we thought for sure they
were dead!" Well, apparently they weren't. Hence we became the
laughingstock of the company. It was really a funny situation and
I had a hard time living it down for quite a while. Lieutenant
Walker, who was a battalion S-2, wrote a poem about it which
was published in the *London Times*. The poem is called "Lessons
Learned," and it goes like this:

If you need a zombie see Captain Booth,
And he'll tell you it's the honest truth
That two Krauts killed by Company K
Are running around our lines today.
It was early in the morn, at the very first light
When K's two dead Krauts decided on flight.
They had been killed at five, but then at dawn
When they looked again—the dead were gone!
They called battalion to say there were four
Who had tried to come through our lines once more:
One captured, one wounded in the head,
And two that were supposed to be very much dead.
But these are the two who were killed by K
Now around our lines do romp and play;
Apparently they move about with ease
And do pretty much as they darn well please.
They roam around and where they go
I don't suppose we'll ever know.
Imagine if you will, the deep chagrin
Of the man who had to push them in
As they lay in a wheelbarrow, cold and still
Up the deep snow-covered hill
And now who wonders if at best
A zombie isn't a very poor guest.
He'd checked their pulse before he started
And believed that from this life they had parted;
He says we need a lot more schooling
To realize just when they're fooling.
Our manuals are good, but fail to tell
What to do with these creatures from hell,
Now what to do when and if
A Kraut is dead but not a stiff.
We sincerely hope that never again
Will our lines be patrolled by two dead men.

Another story I recall has to do with my battalion commander, Lieutenant Colonel Chuck Horner. He used to have an expression; he used to say "Batshit!" and consequently got the nickname "Batshit Horner." Now, Horner and I didn't always see eye to eye, but generally, being a good officer, I did my job. We were in one attack where my company, K, was on the left, I Company was on the right, and L Company was bringing up the reserve. The plan of attack was that when I Company reached its objective, L Company was supposed to work through us (K Company) to the next high ground on the left. This was the plan as we started out. Now, my company was fighting most of the day, and we finally arrived at our objective. Bob Cutler, who was the L Company commander, came up to me and said, "Well, go ahead Albie, take that next objective." I said, "What do you mean? The plan was for L Company to pass through K and take that objective themselves." "Well," Cutler says, "The colonel [Horner] changed his mind and you're supposed to continue the attack."

This upset me quite a bit since I wanted to look out for my own troops who had been fighting all day, while Cutler's gang had just been walking behind us. We had a telephone hookup following behind us all the time, and I had the communications man bring the phone up to me. I got Colonel Horner on the line and started blowing my stack. I reminded him of our plan of attack and maybe I got a little noisy; it got to the point where Horner couldn't stand it any longer and he said, "Booth! Stand at attention!" I don't know if there's any other man in the army who would stand at attention over the telephone, but I did. And I continued the attack as ordered, of course—being a good soldier.

CHAPTER 27

Aachen

The Record

The attack on the Siegfried Line began on September 12, with elements of the 3rd Armored Division breaking through three days later. On September 15, the 16th Infantry cut the roads leading southeast out of Aachen and continued to advance to the northeast, occupying a position in the Siegfried Line by nightfall. The division completed a movement to encircle Aachen by October 10 and launched a direct attack into the city on October 12.

Aachen (Aix-la-Chapelle) was the first large city on German soil to come under attack by Allied ground forces. It was the ancient seat of Frankish kings, and the Franks were a Germanic people. The mighty Charlemagne, founder of the Holy Roman Empire—the First Reich—had made it his capital. To die-hard Nazis of the Third Reich it was a sacred place. For that reason it had great symbolic value to Allies and Germans alike, which weighed heavily in their considerations regarding its fate. Though its strategic importance was debatable from a purely military standpoint, the Allies were determined to have it. The Germans were equally determined to resist its capture.

Hitler wanted it defended to the last man and countermanded a decision by the garrison commander to yield without a fight. The commander was replaced and the defenders were ordered to stand their ground. They were expected to emulate the doomed soldiers at Stalingrad, and they did. The battle for Aachen immediately degenerated into a bitter struggle that went from street to street and house to house. It lasted nearly three weeks. "Your fight for the ancient imperial city is being followed with admiration and breathless expectancy," the German Seventh Army commander told the garrison. "You are fighting for the honor of the Nationalistic German Army."

The garrison finally surrendered on October 21. German honor had been satisfied, but the city was destroyed in the process.

Everett Booth

We approached the city of Aachen on October 13, 1944. It was the first German city to fall into the hands of Allied troops. As I understand it, the German unit that was originally supposed to hold Aachen had moved out, but as we were building up for our attack, another unit moved in and gave us a fierce battle. They didn't want to give up the city, though most of it was destroyed and turned into rubble from artillery and aerial bombardments.

The 18th Regiment was the unit of the 1st Division assigned to capture the city. My company, which was part of the 16th Regiment, had to cover an area outside the city which we referred to as Crucifix Hill because there was a wooden crucifix on top of it that could be seen for many miles.

We had quite a few pillboxes in our area. I had my headquarters in one pillbox and most of the platoons had pillboxes also. One platoon of K Company, however, was in combat outposts out in front of our defensive perimeter. About two o'clock in the morning I'm sacked out in my pillbox having a pretty good night's sleep, when my telephone rings. The caller is this lieutenant, the commander of the platoon that has the outposts. He says, "Captain, my outpost unit came in and they won't go back out." Well, I tried to tell him that it's his responsibility to send his outpost unit back where they belong, and he says, "Sorry, Captain, I can't handle it." I said, "OK," and hung up the phone. I started to put my boots on and said, "Come on, Malardy, we've got a little trip to take." Malardy was my runner and a terrific guy. Though he was only a PFC, he was still a dependable fella, one at my heels at all times when we were on the move.

Malardy got his boots on and we headed out to this platoon's headquarters. I don't know how we found the platoon CP, it was so dark that night. But we did find it, and as I walked, the sergeant of the squad that had refused to go back out saw me. He grabbed his steel pot, stuck it on his head, and said to his men, "Come on, guys." He took his squad to the outpost, and that was the end of that problem. He wasn't going to give me any argument because he knew I wouldn't ask them to go out if I wouldn't go out too.

The Record

Following the capture of Aachen, the Americans persuaded Franz Oppenhoff, a prominent local attorney, to assume the position of Bürgermeister for the city. Oppenhoff did so reluctantly and in fear that the Nazis would seek his death for collaborating with the Allies. Subsequent events proved his fears well founded. In January 1945 SS chief Heinrich Himmler ordered his assassination. It was duly carried out on the night of March 25 by three operatives belonging to the nascent (and ultimately abortive) guerrilla organization known as the Werewolves. The killers slipped undetected across the front lines into the city and shot Oppenhoff in the hallway of his home, escaping into the countryside before his body was found the next morning. Tom Lancer, the first military governor of Aachen, explains how the

Germans were able to murder such an important person right under the noses of the occupying American troops.

Tom Lancer

I raised the American flag over Aachen on the twenty-second of October, 1944. I found a building with a flagpole—I thought it was the library, but it was actually the city archives—and I raised the flag there. By then Aachen was dead. Hitler had ordered the German army to defend the city block by block and house by house, and it was devastated. Before we took Aachen, the city had a population of one hundred thousand. But there was almost no one there when we arrived, just a few people scattered around.

At that time I had gone from being the provost marshal to assistant chief of staff, G-5, in charge of what was officially called Military Government and Civil Affairs. We tried to find a German to be the burgomaster of Aachen under the military government. We finally found a lawyer who very reluctantly agreed to take the job. I knew he would be a marked man, so I detailed a couple of MPs to guard him. He was guarded twenty-four hours a day as long as the 1st Division was there.

We moved out of the Aachen area in December. My successor in office as military governor was Lieutenant Colonel Carmichael, who had been lieutenant governor of Alabama at one time. He had been given a military commission but had very little military training. I told him he should protect the burgomaster because he was a marked man. Carmichael assured me he would. But there was some slippage. Under Carmichael, the burgomaster was guarded only during the daytime, whereas we had guarded him around the clock. And so, one night in January 1945, some SS men were sent across the line and went to the burgomaster's home. When he came to the door they shot and killed him. This was the only case of political assassination in Germany that I recall.

CHAPTER 28

Hürtgen Forest and the Ardennes

The Record

Following the capture of Aachen, the 1st Division moved southeast of the city to the Hürtgen Forest, with the aim of crossing the Roer River north of Düren and advancing to Cologne. Immediate objectives were the town of Gressenich and the Hamich-Nothberg ridge. On November 16 division elements attacked Gressenich; others advanced to Hamich and north and northeast along the line of Weh Creek and into the forest east of Schevenhutte. The battle for the Hürtgen Forest was underway.

The Hürtgen was not a natural forest. It was man-made, planted specifically as a defensive barrier. To the dismay of Americans who fought there, it fulfilled that role all too well. "The Hürtgen Forest was as deadly, as miserable, as unrewarding and as relentless a battle as the 1st Division ever engaged in," observes Danger Forward *(p. 286). "The woods were treacherous; the mud was thick and slimy. The roads were practically nonexistent and the weather*

*became worse and worse. . . . Casualties on both sides were heavy—
each house, each hill, each hole in the ground was fought for, and
gains were reckoned in yards—not the miles of the race through
France and Belgium."*

Frank Kolb

The worst time I experienced in World War II was in the Hürtgen Forest. I was in a reserve company and I came out of there
with twenty-plus men. I was the only officer not wounded or
killed. The whole thing was useless. We never did anything there.
We hardly even made contact with the enemy. Instead we were
cut down by tree-bursts of German artillery as we were moving
up. On other occasions, in other battles, we had lost men, but at
least then it seemed as if we were accomplishing something. But
to me the Hürtgen was just a dead loss. I don't know—maybe the
battle there contributed to the big picture.

Up to that time we had a good unit with plenty of seasoned
people. By D-Day, for instance, all our wounded from Sicily had
rejoined the unit. Everyone was well trained and we were a fighting machine. In the Hürtgen there were replacements coming in,
but we were getting a bunch of retreads. In one bunch we got
sergeants and corporals from coast artillery with technical grades.
The only thing I knew to do was give them a choice. I told them
that if they wanted to try the rank and could cut it, I'd let them
keep it. But if they couldn't cut it, I would bust them back to
privates.

After the Hürtgen we were getting green replacements, men
who hadn't fought before. We had to more or less manhandle the
company. The lieutenants and the sergeants were just pushing
and shoving everybody, trying to get them to go in the right
direction. Before that, you told your people what had to be done,
and everybody did his bit. You could depend on the men on your
right and left.

If we could get the replacements on the line and get them through two or three days of combat, they would be all right, but many of them cracked before that. I don't think there was anything wrong with the men; we were just putting them on the line before they were ready. We had one truckload of them who got hit coming up. None of them could make it after that because they were too demoralized.

One night after crossing the Roer River, I had a window blow in on me. I got a Purple Heart for it. But the main thing was, it shocked me or something, and I couldn't walk. It was as if I was paralyzed. I was taken back to the battalion aid station, where the doctor said there wasn't anything really wrong with me; all I needed was rest. So they sent me back to the regimental rest area. You could stay a certain number of days there and then you would be sent back. But even before my time was up I got orders to report back. By then we had reached the Rhine.

Everett Booth

In the battle of the Hürtgen Forest there was a large castle, the Schloss Laufenberg, in a heavily wooded area. The castle proved to be a key position for the Germans: it kept us at bay for several days. I ended up there with Cutler of L Company. Company I was pretty badly shot up and had more or less disbanded for lack of any commanding officer. Also there was no one from battalion headquarters up there, and our communications were slim as well. So we were getting close to this castle and the fighting became pretty rough. Cutler comes over to me and says, "Hey Albie, I've got that million-dollar wound. I'll see you later." And he took off. That left old Albie Booth, the only officer in the battalion, up there to handle the situation.

We moved toward the castle and got hit by an artillery barrage. As the barrage hit the trees it created tree-bursts, spraying shrapnel all over. Malardy and I found a hole and jumped into it.

In the next instant a fragment from one of the shells, a big piece of steel, embedded itself into the wall of the hole two inches above my shoulder. Malardy exclaimed, "Hey, Captain, look at that!" But I said, "Don't look at it! Ignore it! Forget about it!"

We took the castle shortly after that. I have to give a certain Sergeant Roby a lot of credit for our success here. He took his squad around one side of the castle and did all the dirty work. The Germans ran off and we were able to continue our advance. I feel that taking this castle was the key to our breaking out of the Hürtgen Forest.

Ted Lombarski

In the Hürtgen Forest the Germans tried to take our position at night. But they couldn't because we had too much stuff going out at them. We fired like hell all night and the next morning there were a lot of dead Germans out there. But not all of them were dead. Some of them were still alive, and these laid low until it became daylight. Then they got scared and jumped up. When they jumped up we had them cold out there in the open field, and we shot them down. Even when we advanced there were a couple who jumped up, and we got them also. I don't know how many we shot and killed, but we held our position.

I was wounded in that engagement. Sometime during the night I was hit in the right eye by a small piece of shrapnel from a German hand grenade. The wound affected my vision—it also hurt!—and I was evacuated the following day. I was sent to a hospital in Paris, where I was treated and released about a week later.

The Record

The division pushed on through the Hürtgen Forest toward the Roer River, capturing Luchem on December 4. After that date the fighting began to slacken, and on December 7, the 1st Division was relieved by the 9th Infantry Division. Most 1st Division units were sent to the vicinity of Henri Chapelle, Belgium, southwest of Aachen; however, the 16th Infantry was quartered in the Monschau area.

The division's respite was cut short by a massive German counterstroke in the Ardennes region on December 16. The attack, which developed into what is commonly known as the Battle of the Bulge, was directed against the northern portion of the broad front held by the VIII Corps, between Monschau in the north and Echternach in the south. The enemy objective was to cut off the Allied supply port at Antwerp, Belgium, and capture the huge American supply dumps in the Liège, Verviers, and Eupen areas. The 1st Division was just north of Eupen when the Germans attacked.

Sidney Haszard

I remember the Hürtgen Forest as a very gloomy place because of the weather. It was always damp and wet, and sometimes it snowed. But on December 14, 1944, we were relieved and sent to Vaals in Holland. We stayed in a school there until the Battle of the Bulge began just two days later, on December 16. On the morning of December 16 I was carrying my bedroll out of the school to my jeep or armored car—I forget which—when I heard the worst noise I ever heard in my life. We saw an airplane going down the road, straight down the road at treetop level. We didn't know what it was at first but then discovered it was one of the first jet planes, a German plane. Today we are used to jets, but then it was very scary because it was something unknown. I hadn't heard about jets at that time.

Ted Lombarski

My company was in a town not far from Liège when I caught up with them again. The men were billeted in private homes and were to have their first big break since D-Day. Then the next day the Germans made their breakthrough in the Ardennes. We were loaded onto trucks and brought up to a town the Germans had taken. It was our job to drive them out.

We attacked in the morning, and it was snowing so hard you could barely see your hand in front of your face. This was to our advantage because we were on the German positions before they spotted us. We just overran them without any problem.

In that same attack we came to a patch of woods with a road running along the other side of it. We went down about halfway through the woods and decided to take a look out on the road. We spotted a German tank sitting there. We were behind that tank in a beautiful position to get a good shot at its rear. You don't get opportunities like that often. So I went back to my platoon and got my bazooka man, and we both went out to the road. He fired and missed. The tank turned around and fired. It killed my bazooka man but missed me. I was lucky again.

I returned to my platoon and we advanced deeper into the woods, capturing two Germans. At this point I decided to try to locate Lieutenant Jamrus's 2nd Platoon. I left my men and walked a short distance. I saw several soldiers dressed in white about two hundred feet in front of me. We were all dressed in white, so I thought they were ours. I yelled, "Is that the 2nd Platoon?" They turned toward me and said something in German. I did not think it was a good idea to start shooting, so I turned and nonchalantly walked away. Miraculously, they did not fire. A few minutes later I went back to this spot with a squad from my platoon. But by the time we got there, the Germans were gone.

There was a lot more fighting after that, of course. We went on patrols, we conducted attacks, we were shelled by artillery more times than I can remember. It's as if many of the events and incidents from that winter have been erased from my mind. For example, I have no memory of Christmas during the Battle of the Bulge. In retrospect it seems to me that I really don't care to remember.

CHAPTER 29

Prisoner of War

The Record

On December 17, the 26th Infantry was sent down from the Eupen area to Camp Elsenborn on the northern flank of the German breakthrough to contain the enemy drive and prevent it from spreading north. The first elements of the 26th Infantry reached Camp Elsenborn early in the morning on December 17 and occupied Butgenbach just ahead of the 12th SS Panzer Division, which was advancing toward the town from Bullingen. The 16th Infantry, meanwhile, was on its way down from its bivouac area in the vicinity of Verviers to take up positions north of Weismes. The 18th Infantry remained just south of Eupen to deal with enemy paratroopers.

Between December 17 and December 22 the Germans launched several attacks down the Bullingen-Butgenbach-Weismes road. But none achieved the hoped-for breakthrough to the supply dumps at Spa and Verviers, and after December 22, enemy offensive activity in the area abated. A stalemate ensued during which both antagonists were severely hampered by heavy snow and subfreezing temperatures. The Americans counterattacked on January 15, 1945, with the 1st Divi-

*sion being assigned the towns of Faymonville and Schoppen as its
initial objectives.*

Carroll Ed. Beadenkopf

*A native of Baltimore, Maryland, Carroll Ed. Beadenkopf was a late-
comer to the war. He was not too late, however, to find himself thrust
squarely in the path of the last great German offensive in the West.
Initially assigned to a training unit on the border of France and Belgium, he was subsequently sent to F Company of the 16th Infantry when
the Germans attacked in the Ardennes. He was soon involved in the
fighting around Faymonville—but, as we shall see, for only a little while.*

I was inducted into the army on June 21, 1944, at Camp Meade,
Maryland. I was then sent to Fort Blanding, Florida, for seventeen weeks of basic training with the 218th Replacement Training Battalion.

On October 28, 1944, I received orders to report to the Army
Ground Force Depot No. 1 at Camp Meade for assignment overseas. On November 13 I arrived at Camp Kilmer, New Jersey, and
went aboard a British ship named the *Canavoran Castle*. At dawn
the ship headed out into the Atlantic as part of a large convoy.
A few days later I was lying in my bunk when we heard a loud
scraping and screeching sound that ran the length of the hull, as
if the ship had struck or rammed a large object. The ship's alarms
sounded and I jumped out of my bunk, which was the top bunk
in a tier of three. As soon as I hit the deck I put on my shoes
and life jacket and tested the light on the jacket. After that I just
stood there waiting for further orders along with the rest of the
men in my compartment. Some men came down from topside
and told us we had rammed a German sub and that the convoy
was under attack. We remained where we were on standby alert
for a few hours. Nothing happened. Finally the all-clear sounded
and the convoy proceeded to England without incident, arriving

at Southampton on December 5, 1944. We unloaded, marched down the dock, and immediately boarded a ship named the *Empire Javelin* that took us to Le Havre, France.

I was stationed on the border when the Germans launched their offensive in the Ardennes on December 16. That same day a bunch of us were issued one clip of ammunition for our rifles, loaded into trucks, and moved to a front-line outfit. On the way up to the front it was a mess. The Belgian people didn't know what was happening. They didn't know which flag to wave, American or German. Roads were jammed with men and equipment coming back to regroup, and the retreating troops hollered to tell us what was ahead. We went through the cities of Liège and Eupen, and arrived in the 1st Division sector at night. A colonel, who was standing in his jeep with his flashlight turned on, put me in Company F, 16th Regiment of the 1st Division. I was told to sleep in an empty house. The next morning a sergeant would be there to take me to my squad.

The squad had seven men: squad leader, assistant squad leader, BAR man, grease-gun man, and three riflemen. I was given two hand grenades, two bandoliers, and one cartridge belt of M-1 ammunition. Company F occupied four positions arranged in a square; our squad's first position was the company command post, a house heated by coal briquettes in a potbelly stove.

I had to pull four hours of guard duty at the CP that night, eight P.M. to twelve A.M. I was ordered to stop all vehicles and personnel and check their ID cards. I was alone on that road in front of the CP. The weather was bad; it was snowing and very cold. While I was on guard, a German reconnaissance plane flew over and dropped two flares that lit up the whole area. I backed up against the house and stood there without moving until the flares went out. Every once in a while I would hear a door open in the distance and see someone stand near the doorway and smoke a cigarette. It was very scary.

When my guard duty was over, I went inside and slept. The next day at dusk the squad moved to another position. We pulled guard and stayed on alert until dusk the next day and then moved to another position. On my fourth day we were back at the CP to clean up, shave, and write letters home. If they could get any beer they brought it to us at the CP.

On the line in our foxholes, however, we were fed one hot meal a day. To get it, you had to creep and crawl about a block to the jeep that brought it up. You would get your mess gear filled, get your coffee, and take it all back to your foxhole. Then the next soldier would get his. If you didn't want the hot food, you could get C rations.

In addition to snow, high winds, and zero temperatures, the Germans subjected us to harassing fire every day and night with their artillery, mortars, and tanks, just to keep our nerves on edge. The German buzz bombs didn't do us any good either. Due to the bad weather many of the buzz bombs fired at Liège, Eupen, Brussels, and Antwerp came down in our lines.

I went on my first patrol on December 28, 1944. It was a five-man patrol consisting of a squad leader, one BAR man, one man with a grease gun, and two riflemen. We moved out through our lines at dusk with a telephone, a coil of telephone wire, and a blanket. We passed the soldiers in the listening post, went maybe four blocks farther, and set up our outpost. This was on a horse-cart road with high hedges on both sides. I spread the blanket on the side of the road, hooked up the telephone, and reported to company headquarters. Me and another rifleman took the first watch. We picked a break in the hedges fifteen feet from where the rest of the squad sat. The other rifleman took the field side and I had the roadside. The weather was cold; it was foggy and the snow was about two feet deep. The soldier with me kept clapping his hands and stomping his feet to keep warm, and it really bothered me.

Finally our watch was up. The two automatic-weapons men took over our position, and we started back to sit with the squad leader. Suddenly we heard the sound of footsteps crunching in the snow, moving toward us from the position we had just left. As we looked down the road to see who was making the noise, there was a loud blast of automatic fire and I saw two bodies fly about eight feet in the air and lie still in the snow.

We didn't know at first who went down in that machine-gun blast, and we didn't try to find out. The squad leader pulled the phone loose and ordered me and the other soldier to get out of there. We ran up the road toward our line. I expected to be shot in the back. I outran the other men and stopped to wait until they caught up with me. I said to the squad leader, "How about ducking into the hedge and picking the Krauts off if they come after us?" He said to keep going until we got through to our lines.

I got through first and jumped into a weapons carrier. A few seconds later I climbed out of the vehicle and lay in the snow behind it. I was joined by our machine gunner. We were lying there together when up through the barbed wire came two soldiers pushing a third soldier with his hands on his head. It was Hayward and Orgast with a German prisoner, and they were good and mad at us because of the way we took off.

Hayward and Orgast took their prisoner back for interrogation; then the three of us were sent back to the outpost to pick up the telephone, the phone wire, and the blanket. When we got there, I took the phone and Hayward and Orgast buried the two dead Germans we found there. It turned out that these were the men who had been killed in that blast of automatic-weapons fire. They buried them with snow behind the hedges and covered their blood with snow. I called the CP and told them we were coming in. We gathered our blanket, rolled up the wire, and headed back. The dead Germans had a Schmeisser machine pistol and a flare pistol, which we also took.

The sound of all that gunfire had alerted our sector. The men in the listening post later said that we sounded like a pack of wild horses as we ran up the road, what with the way we were gasping for breath in the cold air.

Ironically, the German prisoner told the interrogators that they had been coming into our lines to surrender when his two buddies were killed.

We went back to the same routine of holding positions and stopping German probes and advances in our sector. One day they trucked us to Eupen for new clothes, a bath, and delousing. Many of the guys got loaded on a drink called Calvados.

Before dawn on January 15, the outfit packed up and moved out of the position we were holding. We marched a short distance to a town and stayed in basements until daybreak. The Germans had been driven from this town and it was our company's job to take the next town. We lined up against the houses and, on orders, the attack was on. Hayward and I were at the point. The day was clear and cold, with snow in heavy drifts. We moved out into the open countryside where the going was tough and exhausting. We had to take a farmhouse. As we neared it we could hear from inside the crying and moaning of the sick, the wounded, the elderly, and the children. Hayward kicked the door open and went in, and I stood in the doorway. The people inside were begging for the medics. An officer took over the house, and Hayward and I were off again, running across the open field.

After about a half hour of running, we lay down in the snow to rest. I looked back to see where our troops were. About three hundred feet behind us I saw a long skirmish line of our troops advancing across the field toward us. About one hundred feet in front of us was a wooded area. As we lay there in the snow two German soldiers—they looked like tank men to me—came walking out of the woods, headed in our direction. They didn't see us—our helmets were covered with white cloth that came down below the neck, so we blended with the snow. They got within thirty feet of us when Hayward told me to wave them in. But when I waved they turned and ran instead.

Hayward had the grease gun and he could have gotten them quick. But he wanted me to make my first kill. I began firing from the prone position and missed. The rifle was frozen and didn't eject the cartridge casing. After ejecting it and putting in another round, the rifle was warm and ready to fire. The two Germans were running side by side, and I fired at one without really looking down the sight. I missed him; then I fired at the other one and missed. Finally, I got into a sitting position, took aim, and fired again. One went down; the other made it back into the woods. I had fired eight rounds to get that one German. I ejected the clip and put in a new one. I got up and charged through the woods after the other German. But he had discarded his coat so that he could move faster, and we lost him.

We continued through the woods to the other side where there was an open field. We took count and there were seven of us in our group. We started to dig foxholes in the woods. Some of our men didn't have shovels. I had mine and was digging through about two feet of snow and about six inches of frozen ground when a German tank began firing at us with its 88mm cannon. I gave my shovel to the other guys. I remember we were soaking wet with perspiration from all the exertion, and our clothes had started to freeze on us. Then we saw the tank, which was dug in with its turret and 88mm cannon at ground level, about three hundred yards away.

The tank fired into the trees above us, sending shrapnel all around. I had my head in the foxhole with my ass up. I heard this piece of shrapnel singing and whirling around above my butt. I looked up—saw it and heard it humming. It had lost its speed and plopped into the snow next to me. I dug it out after it had cooled. It looked like a cutting off a machinist's lathe.

The tank kept firing point-blank for what seemed like hours. It was evening and the company still hadn't caught up with us. Hayward and an assistant squad leader decided to go back and find out why. Hayward told me and the rest of the men to be ready to move out fast when they returned. It was getting dark when I saw them coming through the woods. I waved and tried to get over to them, but they couldn't see me because of all the blown-down trees. They couldn't find us. I also had a hard time finding the other foxholes in the dark. By the time I did, the two men had vanished. We were left once again: just five riflemen and no noncom in charge.

I had a feeling that most the men in my squad were recent replacements like me. It was a moonlit night, and we were cold, scared, and suffering from hypothermia. We knew we had to do something to get out of there or we would freeze to death. We got together to make a plan in the field outside the woods where we had dug in. We knew the password for the day and decided to use it if we ran into a problem. But that was as far as we got. We didn't have time to plan for what would happen in the next few minutes.

There was this sound of crunching boots in the snow. It was going from left to right. We stood still and silent as this large patrol of about seventeen men passed by us fifteen feet out in the field. One of our men called out the password. The leader of the patrol answered with the German word *Achtung*. We went down in the snow and could see the Germans level their machine pistols and rifles right at our faces. Our men who were closest to them began to surrender by hollering *"Kamerade!"* [surrender] over and over. Their voices were quivering with fear, exhaustion, and hypothermia. Finally, we all surrendered with our hands up.

The Germans ordered us to drop our rifles and remove our hand grenades. I couldn't pull the bows on my grenades to release them because my fingers were numb. A German was threatening me with his gun so one of our men pulled my bows and let the grenades fall in the snow. The Germans lined us against the fallen trees and paraded in front of us with their machine pistols like they were going to shoot us. We knew they had shot American prisoners at Malmédy in Belgium, and we thought they would do the same to us. But finally they decided to make us prisoners instead. They took us to their CP, which was in an underground bunker. We climbed down a manhole to a room where an officer questioned us.

When the questioning was finished, the officer said the war was over for us and we would be sent to Germany. We left the bunker and began the journey. We went without food for three days. At night we were locked in barns and cellars, and during the day we were marched toward Germany. I wasn't wounded or injured, so I was put on various work details. When the toilet barrels where we stayed were full, me and another prisoner would carry them to the Germans' gardens and dump them. The shit would splash on our clothes, arms, and everywhere. The German people in the towns would stand there watching and laughing at our humiliating predicament.

One night I was taken to a railroad terminal to unload bales of hay from boxcars. In one town I was given a makeshift shovel with a tree branch for a handle and ordered to retrieve the body of one of our dead airmen. He was frozen beneath the ice in a nearby gully. But the ice was eight inches thick and I couldn't break it to get him out.

On another night I was locked in a room with the wounded and sick. The room was on the second floor of a barn, and it was crowded with prisoners lying on the straw-covered floor. I was next to this guy who began to moan and had a hard time breathing. Later that night I didn't hear any more sounds but noticed an odor coming from him. The next morning we found that he had died during the night. I knew he was having trouble, but there wasn't much I could do to help him. A lot of the men had aches and pains, and you couldn't touch or move them without making more problems.

That morning I called through a window in the door to the guard, "Comrade *kaput*." He opened the door and ordered me to get the dead man down to ground level. I had an airborne soldier help me bring him down. This airborne soldier had a shrapnel wound in his forehead. It looked as if the shrapnel wasn't in the bone but just under the skin.

I don't know how many days it took before we finally reached a prisoner-of-war camp in Germany. I don't know the name or number of the camp or the date I got there. The only way to get this information would be to find a POW camp that was destroyed by bombs during an air raid at night, possibly in February 1945.

When the raid started I was lying in the straw on the floor of our hut. There was no room to walk because so many prisoners were sleeping on the floor. The men near the toilet bucket had it the worst. The bucket had overflowed and they had got shit all over them.

I heard planes flying over and saw a red flare. Incendiary bombs began to land in the camp, spraying phosphorus everywhere. Then came the sound of the big bombs swishing down, like a steam locomotive. The windows and the door blew out. I was lying with my head on my shoes, fully dressed, with my wool cap on my head. I could still hear the planes, and incendiary bombs were falling all around us. I grabbed my shoes and my helmet and ran over the men on the floor and through the doorway. Just as I made it outside the next big bomb exploded, blowing my cap off. I ran to the shelter, which was not far from my building. I was maybe the first man in the shelter, and as other bombs fell, the dirt came in through the vents.

The bombing lasted just a few minutes and then the planes were gone. As I looked out the opposite end of the shelter I saw big fires. Other prisoners began to come into the shelter. But I put on my shoes, got myself together, and went outside. I looked around the camp and saw that it was destroyed. Prisoners were walking about in a daze, not knowing where they were or where to go or what to do. The fences were down and the guards were gone. We were alone and didn't know what to do. I was cold, so I picked up a foreign army coat I found lying on the ground. (There were foreign prisoners in this camp.) After the air raid everybody was roaming all over the place trying to find something they could use. I went back to my building, which had been blown down, and climbed under the gables of the collapsed roof and went to sleep.

At daybreak the Germans came back and tried to get things in order. They ordered those of us who had taken anything during the raid to step forward and put the stolen item on the ground. We were warned that we would be shot if we were later found with any stolen items in our possession. I took the foreign coat off, put it on a pile, and got back in line. So I wasn't shot, but I was punished just the same: the coat was full of lice, and I got them bad.

CHAPTER 30

"*Panzerwagen*, Hell!"

The Record

By January 28 the Bulge had been eliminated and the 1st Division was attacking east toward the German border, seizing Murringen, Hunningen, and Honsfeld on January 30. The next day the division took the high ground northwest of the Holzwarcke River. By February 3 elements of the division had once again penetrated the Siegfried Line. On February 5, three days after capturing Hollerath, the division was relieved by the 99th Infantry Division.

On February 8, the 1st Division (less Combat Team 16), moved to the forward assembly area to take over the defense of the Unter-maubach-Bergstein-Grosshau sector. The division crossed the Roer River on February 25 and advanced rapidly to the Rhine. Between March 1 and March 3 it fought for and captured Erp, and on March 8 it entered Bonn—too late, as it happened, to prevent the Germans from blowing up the city's bridge across the Rhine. Bonn's garrison formally surrendered to the division on March 9.

Everett Booth

My favorite story about the war concerns the capture of Bonn. I was battalion S-3, the Plans and Training Officer, of the 3rd Battalion, 16th Infantry, under Colonel Edward Wydzenski. We had moved into a position outside Bonn. There had been another unit in that position for a few days, but they moved us in there. They wanted to use the 1st Division, this being a major assault. We waited a couple of days until the regimental headquarters called us up to advise us that the 3rd Battalion was to capture the northern half of the city and the 2nd Battalion would take the southern half. We got into our jeep, and big Ed Wydzenski says to me, "Well, when we get back to our CP, let's sit down and plan our attack. We'll call our company commanders in and review the plan with them to see what they think." I said, "Ed, I *know* what we're going to do." Ed said, "Oh?" I explained my plan to him. Ed didn't buy it, saying, "I don't know about that, but we'll call the company commanders in and talk about it." We did, and all the company commanders thought it was a great idea. You have to remember that I had been a company commander for a long time. Most of these fellows were closely associated with me and had a lot of confidence in my thinking.

We pulled off the attack as I had planned it. We moved into the city, all the way to the Rhine River. We did not have a single casualty and we took about five thousand German prisoners. Let me explain my plan of attack.

First, when you have a major attack, usually you call on artillery fire (called "prepared fires") to blast the heck out of your targets, to weaken your enemy's defenses. Second, you push forward, firing, with a lot of tank support. Now, my plan of attack was to have no prepared artillery fires. The reason for that was that the enemy knew we were out there; we had been there for some time, and as soon as they heard artillery fire, they would know to get ready. So at 0100 on March 8 we moved out with no artillery fire and went right down the city's main drag.

Another important feature of our attack was the new type of tank we used. The tank, a Sherman, very much resembled a German tank because it had a 76mm gun with a muzzle break. (Our older-model Sherman tanks had 75mm guns without muzzle breaks.) We started down the street very quietly in columns of companies, with Company L out front and the new tanks in support. The first German we encountered was a guard on the road. His comment, to our company commander who came walking up, was "*Was ist das Panzerwagen?*" ["What kind of tank is that?"] The company commander's runner stuck his bayonet in the German's side and said, "*Panzerwagen*, hell!" and iced him. [Editor's note: The enemy soldier probably used the word *Panzerkampfwagen* ("armored fighting vehicle"), which is the correct term as well as the term a German would most likely have used in this situation.]

The company went into a building on the corner of the road and down into the basement. There was a bunch of Germans in the basement, all sound asleep. The company took them prisoner and continued on through the city in that manner. We got many prisoners and didn't have a single casualty, of which I am most proud.

CHAPTER 31

Rhine Crossing

The Record

At the end of February, with American forces nearing the Rhine, the Germans began to demolish the bridges spanning that wide river. All but one were destroyed. At Remagen the massive Ludendorff railway bridge remained miraculously intact.

Everett Booth

Our next mission after Bonn was to cross the Rhine at Remagen to the bridgehead that had been established on the east bank. One of our armored units, Combat Command B, 9th Armored Division, had arrived at the Rhine River on March 7, the day before we took Bonn. It got control of the Ludendorff Bridge at Remagen as the Germans were preparing to blow it. They got some tanks across; now they needed infantry troops, so they called on us. There was danger of the bridge collapsing—sections of it were already destroyed or weakened—but we got to the bridge and crossed it on March 16, one day before it collapsed.

Tom Lancer

Just as he had in Aachen, Lancer raised the Stars and Stripes over Bonn after American troops captured that city. And, just as in Aachen, he also became Bonn's first military governor. But he held that post for only a few days. When the 1st Division moved south to participate in the Rhine crossing at Remagen, however, Lancer went with it.

I remember crossing the Rhine on March 17, Saint Patrick's Day. We went across on a pontoon bridge because the Remagen bridge was being worked on. When I got to the 1st Division's new CP in Unkel, they said, "Did you see it? Did you see it?" "See what?" I asked. They said, "Did you see the bridge go down?" The bridge had collapsed, taking a company of engineers with it, on March 17. But I had not seen it go.

Frank Kolb

When I got back to my company after being wounded, there was a platoon of black soldiers assigned to the 16th Regiment. I learned that the army had decided it wanted to find out how black soldiers would do in a regular unit. My executive officer was from Alabama and I was from Kentucky. I guess because we were from the South, somebody somewhere decided that we should get them. The platoon was supposed to have a white officer and a white sergeant, but it had lost both men, so I assigned an officer and a sergeant from the company. Then I told the rest of the men in my company that we were not going to have any trouble. I told them that the black soldiers were going to be in the mess line and everything else, and that I just didn't want any problems at all.

So we crossed the Rhine, and the blacks fought as well as anybody else, and they bled just as red. They weren't any better or any worse than anybody else. I had them until I left the company. I think there were several black units assigned to other divisions. The best thing about having them in my company was that it gave me a fourth rifle platoon, so I had more strength than the other companies. And because they had been together for a while, they functioned pretty well as a unit.

CHAPTER 32

"We're in This Thing Together"

The Record

Between March 16 and March 24, the 1st Division worked to enlarge the Rhine bridgehead and defend it against numerous German counterattacks. The division attacked on March 24. By March 25 the bridgehead was secure, and the way was open for the First Army to drive in force across the Rhine into the heart of Germany.

After March 27, the 1st Division advanced swiftly into Germany's interior. On April 8 it crossed the Weser River and advanced toward the Harz Mountains, reaching the western slope on April 11. This move precipitated the collapse of enemy forces in the region. On April 18 the division was driving into the enemy's rear areas, taking the high ground overlooking Blankberg and Thale on April 19. By April 20 all significant German forces in the 1st Division's area of operations had been destroyed and organized resistance had ceased.

The beginning of May found the 1st Division in Czechoslovakia, where it became embroiled in combat with a scratch force known as Division Benicke, made up of men from an officer candidate school at Milowitz. The 1st Division attacked this force on May 5, five days after Adolf Hitler committed suicide in Berlin. The division cleared the Drenice area and then advanced down the road from Cheb to Falkenau on May 6, seizing several towns en route and liberating the Falkenau concentration camp. At the time of the German surrender, the 16th, 18th, and 26th Infantry Regimental Combat Teams, in conjunction with Combat Command A of the 9th Armored Division, were attacking toward Karlsbad.

At 8:15 A.M. on May 8 the division received an order to cease firing at once and halt in place. Later that day, the division accepted the unconditional surrenders of Division Benicke as well as the eighteen thousand troops of the German XII Corps (Seventh Army) in the Chemnitz-Marienbad vicinity. The war with Germany was over. As the following accounts reveal, however, the Cold War had already started.

Everett Booth

Our next step was the Harz Mountains. There wasn't too much activity in the mountains, which was a beautiful area, like a resort. We found the German navy holed up there, and we always liked to kid each other by saying that the 1st Division captured the German navy in the Harz Mountains.

From the Harz Mountains we continued to Czechoslovakia. Our battalion was assigned to an area just outside Cheb. We were supposed to stop there because the Czech border was for the Russians. Well, I was a little antsy—I wanted to see what Czechoslovakia looked like; I wanted to meet the Russians. So I picked up our battalion medic and another gentleman whose name I forget, and the three of us, together with our driver, went into Cheb.

As we entered the city all the Czechs were waving American flags and talking to us. They were so happy to see us. But this dog-gone medic, he didn't use his noodle too well. He told the Czechs that the Russians were coming. We finally got out of the main part of the city, toward the outskirts, headed toward the Russian lines. We came to a little creek and sure enough, there were two Russian doggies on guard at the creek. As we approached them in our jeep, their eyes opened up, and they said, *"Americano? Americano?"* And we said, *"Da, da."* They were also happy to see us.

We got out of the vehicle and proceeded toward these two doggies, and this officer came out from the bushes someplace. He wore glasses about an inch thick, and he raised his hand and said, "You shall not pass!" I said, "What do you mean? We're in this thing together, we're allies." But he said again, "You shall not pass!" So I said, "Okay, we'll take off." We got in the jeep and drove back through town. This time there were red Soviet flags hanging out the windows, and people were running in and out of stores buying more red flags. So we drove back to our headquarters.

Later on, my battalion commander, Colonel Ed Wydzenski, went over to Czechoslovakia to visit the Russian regiment that occupied this area. The Russians stuck him out in the parking lot with his entourage and put them under guard so they couldn't move. It was a silly situation, but it was finally resolved.

While the colonel was with the Russians, I had two German generals come into the headquarters and, being the senior officer on duty, I accepted their surrender. They saluted me, but I didn't feel that it was proper to return their salutes, so I didn't.

One night, Ed invited the Russians over for dinner at our headquarters, which was in a nice hotel. Well, the Russians came over and each one of the officers had a bodyguard. And the bodyguard sat next to the officer at the dinner table, with a subma-chine gun between his legs. You could see by this how much they trusted us.

Tom Lancer

The thing I remember most about Czechoslovakia is that the Czechs all asked us, "Will the American army stay here now or will it not?" We replied, "Oh, no, you are now liberated. We are going back to Germany." They said, "Oh, we wish the Americans would stay." They knew they were going to be taken over by the Soviets.

CHAPTER 33

"I Always Stood at Attention as the Body Went By"

Carroll Ed. Beadenkopf

In stark contrast to the 1st Division's triumphant advance across Germany and into Czechoslovakia, Beadenkopf remained a prisoner of the Germans right up to the final days of the war.

The Germans moved us to another camp. Then we marched from this camp to a city not far from it, eating whatever we could find on the roadside along the way. The city was on the Rhine River. There was a large bridge over the Rhine, and while I was walking across it, a German woman shoved a loaf of rye bread down my jacket. At the end of the bridge there was a sign that said "Siegburg." The city had a railroad yard where we were loaded into boxcars like cattle.

On the journey that followed we were locked in the cars and left on sidings for hours, during which time we were subjected to more air attacks. Needless to say, sanitary conditions were very bad in those boxcars.

We finally reached another prison camp in a town called Limburg. At Limburg I was interrogated several times, and each time the questioning was interrupted by an air raid that was aimed at the rail terminal and tracks near the camp. At this camp I received a prisoner of war number: M-Stammloger XIIA No. 099943.

I don't know how long I was there, but it wasn't very long before we learned that American forces were heading in our direction. So we were moved again. The Germans gave us one Red Cross food package to be shared by two prisoners. The package was supposed to last two to three days until we reached the next camp at Bad Orb. I split the package with another prisoner, who ate his portion or swapped it for cigarettes. He was without food most of the trip. I gave my cigarettes away and had food for the whole trip to Bad Orb because I saved my food and ate sparingly.

Bad Orb, German Stalag IXB, was in the mountains. We walked up a winding road leading from a town at the bottom of a mountain to the camp at the top. It was quite a few miles and the trip was exhausting. We all had leg cramps and some of the men literally crawled on their hands and knees, but somehow they made it. We spent the night in a large barnlike building, and I thought the Germans were going to get rid of us by setting fire to it. In spite of our fears, however, we soon fell asleep because we were so exhausted.

Nothing happened during the night. The next day we were assigned to huts in the American section of the camp. We had potbelly coal stoves in the huts, and you could put your food on the stoves to cook it or keep it warm. In the group I shared my hut with, there were six or more deaths. I went on one burial detail, and the body was covered with a blanket and placed on a two-wheel cart with wood handles in front and back to push and guide the cart. I had the back handles and another soldier took the front. We pushed the cart through a different sector of the camp, with most of the prisoners standing at attention as we passed by. The burial grounds were just outside the camp, in a clearing in the woods. Russian prisoners dug the holes. There were a Catholic and a Protestant chaplain to handle the services; they were prisoners too. There were other burials, but I wasn't directly involved in them. However, I always stood at attention on the road as the body went by.

The kitchen for the prisoners was in a building on the main road that ran through the camp. The building had a tower which made it look different from the barracks. Our meals consisted of soup, potatoes, greens, and cabbage. Whenever a horse got killed in the fields nearby, the cooks used the horse meat to flavor the soup for that day. The Germans also gave us cheese that had a green mold on it. We ate it and it tasted good with the sour-dough rye bread we got.

The Germans gave us a loaf of this bread to be shared by six prisoners. I had a GI spoon that was sharpened on one side to be used as a knife. It was a very big job to cut the bread into six pieces that satisfied everyone. The only way it could be done was to rotate the pieces. One day two men would get the ends, which were the smallest pieces; two men would get the pieces next to the ends, which were a little bigger; and two men would get the pieces in the middle, which were the biggest. By rotating which pieces each man got, everybody was satisfied. Another food that some of the prisoners liked was cat meat. I didn't know we were eating cats until I heard one of them let out a yowl when the cooks caught it.

I saw American prisoners who were from the South or the country collecting and picking greens in the camp area. It turned out they were picking dandelion leaves. I picked them too. We put them in our helmets and poured hot soup over them. That way, we would each have a larger portion of soup.

Dysentery, pneumonia, wounds, and lack of food were the main ailments amongst us. I never got dysentery, but I lost about thirty pounds. The guards made things worse for us by making our roll calls several hours long. We would line up five deep and they would begin the count. If one of us was missing, the Germans would start the count again. This would go on for hours in all kinds of weather. The ground was thawing, wet, muddy, and very sloppy. It got to where we stayed in line and did whatever we had to do, going to the toilet right in the mud until the count was over with.

In the barracks the bunks were doubled up and stacked three high, so there were six bunks in each group. The Germans assigned two men to a bunk, and there was no mattress—just rough boards and a blanket. We slept head to foot. Lice were bad and they would drop from the top bunk to the floor.

The soldier who shared my bunk was a Private Wesley Coates from Cave City, Kentucky. He had been in the Golden Lions [106th] Division, which had taken the main attack from the Germans in the Bulge. He was wounded and captured in December when his outfit was overrun. He told me how it happened. He was shot while surrendering—shot at close range while holding a white piece of cloth with his hands up. The bullet went through his chest and came out his back. Wes told the Germans that he was wounded, but they didn't do anything to help him. He was made to push the German jeeps and other vehicles that got stuck in the drifts. During all his prisoner life he was never given medical help. Wesley's coat showed where the bullet went in and came out. I looked at his chest and back, and it seemed to me that the wound did not bleed too much. The wound was just small purple holes and had healed. But Wesley always looked very tired and weak. I don't know where Cave City is, but Wesley reminded me of a young country boy; his eyes showed that he had gone through a very bad time. I'll never forget Wesley's face as long as I live.

We got into a daily routine at Bad Orb, which consisted mainly of trying to stay alive until we were liberated. We knew the war was coming toward us because of the air activity. In all that time the only dispute I had with Wes was over the piece of bread I saved every day. I would eat my soup and half my ration of bread; the other half I saved until the next day. By doing that I had accumulated about ten extra slices of bread. I kept them in my scarf by opening one end and using it as a bag. I had no idea that the others had noticed what I was doing.

Wes slept with his head at the wall and he used my bag of bread as a pillow. There were no lights on at night in the barracks, so it was very dark. One night someone walked past my head and snatched my bread from under Wesley's head and disappeared into the dark before I could move. When I found out what had happened I got real mad. I thought about the sacrifice I had made to save that food, and I got upset and blamed Wesley for not trying to prevent the thief from stealing it. After a while, though, I got to reasoning that there was nothing he or I could have done. Wes was too ill to have done anything and I had been asleep. So our friendship continued until we were liberated and came home.

We could tell the fighting was coming toward us by the air bombing and flashes off in the distance. Also the French prisoners who worked and did details outside the compound were acting like they knew something was going to happen soon. On the morning of April 1 we woke up to find that the older guards had been replaced by young boys, and a white flag was flying over the kitchen tower. Air activity was getting heavy, so the prisoners used lime from the latrine to mark our camp with large POW letters on the ground. Some of the planes would fly over and waggle their wings in recognition. A few B-17s flew over with two motors out, trying to make it home. It was here that I saw my first jet plane; it was German. It was strange seeing a plane fly without a propeller. It was noisy and flew fast.

The day we were liberated I could hear and see the tanks and American soldiers coming toward our camp, up the road and through the woods. The Germans surrendered, and the tanks and troops from the 44th Division took over the camp. The prisoners went wild with excitement and joy. Sections of the fence were torn down. The prisoners went into the guards' barracks, looting and looking for souvenirs; some made it to the towns the troops had just taken and looted houses. I went into the headquarters building, where I found a crystal radio earphone set and some military insignias. I was going back to my hut when gunfire broke out close by. I hid behind a three-foot-high wall waiting for it to stop. When an American officer came down the road, I came out of hiding. He asked where I was from. I told him that I was from the prison camp. He told me to get back there because the woods and the surrounding area were not yet cleared of Germans.

The Red Cross came in and the army moved out. I don't know how many days we stayed at Bad Orb after being liberated. They moved us by truck to a place called Gelnhausen. We were examined by medics who took our name, rank, and serial number; the name of our division, regiment, and company; and the date of our capture. I slept in a field hospital tent until a C-47 was flown in to take us out. On the C-47, I sat fourth behind the pilot. I became air sick and had to use the slop bucket. I must have made the other passengers sick, because it wasn't long before most of them were upchucking too.

The plane trips out of Germany, Belgium, and France were a little bumpy. The worst feeling came when the plane hit a downdraft as it flew out over the English Channel. It felt as if my stomach was going to come out of my mouth. The plane made a turn back to France and landed. We were loaded into trucks, and the roads were bumpy too. Each bump caused bad pains in my stomach. I lay on the floor of the truck and held my stomach to keep it from bouncing and to ease the pain.

We finally reached a RAMP [Recovered American Military Personnel] camp in Le Havre. I don't know how long I stayed at the camp. We were well fed and cared for there: they cleaned us up, gave us new clothes, and got us ready to be sent back to the United States. We went aboard a troop ship, the SS *Argentina*, which was bringing back the first group of thirteen hundred American prisoners of war from the European theater. That was May 15, 1945.

CHAPTER 34

Journeys Home

Paul Bystrak

In the first days of May 1945, when the 1st Division was in Czechoslovakia, there was an uprising against the Germans in Prague. Things got so bad that higher headquarters finally authorized the 1st Division to go ahead with the 3rd Armored Division and try to get into the city before it got any worse. Various units started toward Prague but were soon stopped because the war was about to end.

I was at division headquarters in Cheb, so I knew that the war was going to end on May 8. I arranged a party with some of the city officials and the division staff. We had bathtubs full of wine and champagne, lots of food from the quartermaster, and tables all set up. The radio came on and the war was announced at an end. The Czechoslovak officials all began crying and hugging and then started singing their national anthems. Some of this was touching, but a bit of it was humorous.

The Czechoslovaks had two anthems, the Moravian and the Slovak. The Slovak anthem is rather swingy, and when they started singing it, our division surgeon started singing "Don't

Fence Me In." I finally had to go over and tell him to stop, that this was serious stuff.

While the party was going on I went to see Colonel Eymer. I asked him if I could go find my grandparents in the village of Sobotiste, where I was born. Since the village was located at the eastern end of Czechoslovakia, in Russian territory, he told me that, obviously, he had no real authority to let me go. He said, however, that I could go "somewhere" for three days—but he was not authorizing anything. Then I went to see Colonel Lancer, our military government officer, and asked if he could prepare me a phony pass. Colonel Lancer prepared a pass with a bunch of rubber stamps and some misleading statements authorizing me to visit Sobotiste.

I got my command car and went to the quartermaster. I filled the car up with all the rations and gasoline and oil that we could carry. My driver and a Czech sergeant came with me. I got the Czech sergeant in a trade: I gave some shirts to one of his officers and the officer gave me the sergeant in return.

We reached the Soviet demarcation line, where Russian soldiers stopped us. They tried to figure out what my pass said, but it obviously didn't make any sense to them. They wanted to call for an officer. I said, "Just a minute." I gave each of them a carton of cigarettes. They bowed and let us go on.

We drove all the way to Sobotiste. There I found my grandparents, and all my relatives too. There must have been fifty or sixty of them. Everybody was still alive, even the grandparents who had raised me. I asked to have a picture taken with everyone. But I had no camera, and the photographer in the village had only enough film for one photograph. He said that he would try to get as much of the family into this one picture as he could. He couldn't develop the photograph before I left, so I made arrangements for him to send it to a certain colonel in the Czech army who would send it on to me. Nine months later a copy of the photograph finally caught up with me in America.

We stayed with my family for two days, drinking way beyond capacity. Apparently my dad must also have had a few drinks in his day, because everywhere I went people said, "Your father could drink an entire liter of beer." I figured if he could drink a liter, I could drink one too. Because of all the drinking I don't remember too much who I met. The day we were supposed to leave, I said I wanted to see my Aunt Pauline. Everyone said, "Why do you want to see Aunt Pauline?" I told them that, before leaving, I wanted to see everybody in my family. They told me she had come all the way down the mountain the night before to see me and didn't I remember talking to her?

I dropped the subject after that.

One of the villagers wanted to go to Prague, so I took him along with us on the way back to Cheb. Before we left the village I had the driver estimate as nearly as he could how much gas and oil we would need for the trip. I left the rest with my Uncle Pete. In 1974 my wife and I visited my birthplace and met with my relatives. One of my male cousins told me that I had been his hero. It seemed that shortly after I left Sobotiste he picked up a German grenade. It exploded and tore up his upper arm and shoulder. With the gasoline I had left behind, my Uncle Pete was able to start his motorcycle. He took my cousin to a hospital and saved his life. The arm and shoulder were also saved, although it looked like skin stretched over bone.

Anyway, we started back, and outside Brno, in Moravia, the command car went dead. The driver and I were still under the influence; the driver could hardly stand up, but as long as he was driving—which meant that he was sitting down—he was okay. He got out and looked at the car, patted it, and said, "Dodge car." Then he started taking the carburetor apart and laying pieces out all over. I thought, "Oh my God, we are going to be picked up by the Russians. We will never get out of here." Amazingly enough though, the driver put the carburetor back together and the car worked just fine.

After going through Prague we were stopped by Russian officers near a stalled civilian vehicle they had taken from some Czech officials. We started talking and they asked if we could help them. They thought I was a Czechoslovak officer or something. They didn't recognize the American uniform. They started to get kind of pushy with us, and I began to worry that we were going to have to walk back to Cheb. I thought, They are going to take my command car because they outrank me. We started talking and finally they realized that I wasn't a Czech. They asked, "What army are you from?" I said, "The American army." They became like children. They couldn't give me enough souvenirs. One of them gave me a cigarette lighter, and I don't even smoke. He said, "You know how many German officers I had to kill before I found one who had a cigarette lighter?" So I took it, along with souvenir money and that type of thing, and we drank all the slivovitz I had brought from the village.

Meanwhile, to my surprise, my driver was able to get their car started. So we parted as friends. They wanted me to go with them to their bivouac area. I said, "No, my general is waiting— I am a day late. But you show me where you are on the map and I'll come back—we'll have a party tomorrow night." So they gave me a map with their location, for which they could probably have been shot, and I promised I would return. Obviously I did not intend to keep my promise.

We got back to Cheb. By then the division had moved to its occupation area down in Germany, and I went there to join it. We were stationed near Ansbach.

I remember when the war ended, the 1st Division had captured a whole German army. General Andrus [Major General

Clift Andrus, who assumed command of the 1st Division on December 11, 1944] was of German extraction. The Germans asked that all prisoners captured after May 6 be returned to them. General Andrus is reported to have said, "If they want them they will have to fight me for them." Then he called the staff together and said, "I want to demobilize the whole army, the whole German army under our control, and send them home." We didn't know whether that was procedure, but we had the Germans set up their own separation point, under our control, and we loaded them into all kinds of vehicles. Our biggest problem was finding vehicles to get them back to their homes.

I stayed in Ansbach until October 1945. I finally had to leave, and the reason was that all the MPs were changing. You see, each time I was picked up somewhere for some infraction and brought to the provost marshal, it became more difficult for him to find reasons for letting me go. Finally, Major Regan, the commander of the MP platoon, said, "Why don't you go home? I can't find any more reasons to keep releasing you." So I went home.

Sidney Haszard

When the war ended I was assigned to conduct a control point just east of Cheb in Czechoslovakia that handled German army units returning from Russia. We set up a collection spot for German POWs on an airfield and arranged for them to administer themselves under American supervision. These Germans were good-looking men—although they were part of a defeated army, they were still a proud collection of soldiers. You could see their pride in the way they carried themselves.

It was a touching thing to see a military column moving along four abreast at a brisk pace. But it was especially touching to see the walking wounded, many on crutches with only one leg, trying to keep up and asking no favors. That is a sight one does not easily forget.

Frank Kolb

I think I sort of liked the Germans. I wasn't mad at them or anybody else, but I had a job to do. We may have had others who were fighting for different reasons, but basically I think most of us thought we were mainly doing it as a job and trying to do it as well as we could. Fighting the Germans was what we were being paid to do, and the sooner we got it over with, the sooner we could go home. I will tell you, though, that I had no feeling that the war would ever be over, really. For me it lasted only two years, but I was only twenty-two years old, and that was darned near 10 percent of my life. For example, back then the period from Thanksgiving to Christmas seemed a lifetime. But now the same period is like just one night.

Tom Lancer

After the war the division CP was established in Ansbach in northern Bavaria. We were there the entire summer of 1945. In the autumn the division headquarters moved to Kitzingen, in northern Bavaria. From there I went home for the first time in three-and-a-half years, back to Madison, Connecticut, for Christmas 1945.

After forty-five days of R&R, I came back to the 1st Division. We moved from Kitzingen to Regensburg, and I stayed with the 1st Division until November 1946, when I returned to the States for another assignment. It was my last connection with the 1st Division.

One person I especially want to mention was a French officer, Captain Jacques Giard, whom I met in the latter part of the war. He came from Solesmes Nord in France. In civilian life before the war he owned a sugar beet factory, but in 1940 he was on active duty as a captain in the horse artillery. He was taken prisoner when the Germans invaded France. After the French capitulation, he was released by the Germans and returned to making sugar. When we landed in France in 1944 he put on his old uniform, got on his horse, and started riding at night. He knew the area very well. He stayed off the main roads and went cross-country. When it came close to dawn he would wake up a farmer, turn his horse loose with the farmer's horse, and sleep in the cellar or the hayloft until the way was clear to continue. Finally he got up to the front line and got himself into a deep cellar until the American army overran his position. When he appeared, he had a tough time convincing the Americans that he was not a spy. He was then assigned as a liaison officer to various outfits and wound up with the 1st Division. I still keep in touch with him, and my wife and I have often visited him in his home. He is a very fine gentleman and now is one of the leading sugar manufacturers of France.

CHAPTER 35

Conclusion: "Do You Want to Be a Good Soldier?"

Everett Booth

As soon as VE Day was declared, we started sending troops back home. Two officers of the 1st Division, myself and Captain Marendino, were the first officers to leave our regiment after the war was over. Our regimental commander had a piano player on his staff, and we had quite a few dinners. The piano player always played a lot of songs. They had a party for us the night before we left, and I went up to the piano player and asked him if he remembered a certain tune. He said, "Oh yes, I do." The tune is one that I used to sing with a fella by the name of O'Brian, who was the captain of our cannon company. We always had a ball any time we got a break and could grab a couple of beers someplace; we would have a little party, and he and I would do a skit and sing this song. The name of the song is "They're Moving Father's Bones to Lay a Sewer." It's an English ballad

O'Brian and I picked up while we were in England. This is how it goes:

> Oh, they're moving father's bones to lay a sewer.
> They're doing it at considerable expense.
> Oh, they're shifting his remains
> To lay in ten-inch drains,
> To satisfy some posh new residents.
> Cor blimey!
>
> Now what's the use of having a religion
> If when you're dead your troubles never cease?
> If some high society bird
> Wants a pipeline for his turd,
> They'll never leave your blooming bones in peace.
> Cor blimey!
>
> Now father in his day was not a quitter,
> And I don't believe that he's a quitter now.
> All dressed up in his sheet,
> He will haunt that
> shithouse seat
> And never let them crap till he'll allow.
> Cor blimey!
>
> Won't there be some blooming constipation?
> Won't the toffs all swear and rant and rave?
> But they'll get what they deserve
> To have the bloomin' nerve
> To bugger up a British workman's grave.
> Cor blimey!

At our going-away party I got up and made an announcement that I was going to sing this number in memory of our old friend, a fella we called Obie. Then I sang the song and mimicked the little skit O'Brian and I used to do. When I was finished, I got a good round of applause. But the regimental commander stood up and said, "Let's forget the dead! Think of the living!"

That was about it for the evening. The next morning, who else was on the bus with us but Father Lawrence Deary, the Catholic chaplain. Being a chaplain, he resented what the colonel had said about forgetting the dead. He had gone up to the colonel and told him, "Forget it! I'm going back to the States with Albie and Marendino."

We went to a staging area in France and boarded a ship that took us to New York harbor. From there I went to Indianapolis. At the separation center in Indianapolis, I reported to the adjutant general's office. He looked at my 201 file, looked up at me, and said I had the greatest number of points [which were accumulated through various campaigns and commendations] that had come through the center until that time. Then he said, "Do you want to be a good soldier and fight the Japs, or do you want to be discharged from the service?" *Ha!* After three years and eight battle campaigns, including three invasions, what do you think I told him?

Apothegm

Charles Hangsterfer

In the years since the war many people have asked me if I was ever scared or frightened during combat. I always answer the question by telling them a story about my operation for colon cancer. After the surgery I had to have barium x-rays taken, and the attending nurse, knowing that about a foot of my colon had been removed, commented, "Hank, it doesn't seem as if you've lost any of your bowel." To which I replied, "I kept a tight anus"— actually I used a less formal term—"for nearly three years while I was in combat. Keeping such a tight hold on my bowels must have stretched them an extra foot."

Men of the First

Theodore Antonelli was born in New Haven, Connecticut, in 1920. He graduated from the University of Connecticut in 1941 and was commissioned a second lieutenant in the infantry reserve in June of that year. He began active duty in July 1941 with the 16th Infantry Division at Fort Devens, Massachusetts, serving with that regiment as a platoon leader and, later, company commander until wounded in action in North Africa. After a period of hospitalization he was assigned to VI Corps and participated in the amphibious landings at Salerno and Anzio. In 1947 he accepted a commission in the regular army and was assigned to the Transportation Corps. He served in duty stations around the world as a transportation and logistics specialist before retiring in September 1978 as a major general. Antonelli passed away on November 17, 1993, at Walter Reed Army Medical Center.

Carroll Ed. Beadenkopf was born in Baltimore, Maryland, in 1919. Upon his release from a German prisoner-of-war camp in May 1945, he was given ninety days leave with a ten-day rehabilitation leave at the St. Moritz Hotel in Miami Beach. From there he went to Fort Hood, Texas, for a short tour with a mortar battalion, during which the war with Japan ended. After additional postings in California, Georgia, and Montana, he was honorably discharged from the army on December 10, 1945, at Fort Douglas, Utah. He returned to his prewar job with the B&O Railroad at the Mount Clare Shops in Baltimore and became lead man of the sheet metal gang. He stayed with the B&O for twenty years, then went to work as the sheet metal foreman with the Baltimore Department of Public Schools and the Department of General Services until he retired in 1981.

Beadenkopf had been with the 1st Division for only thirty days (from December 16, 1944, until January 15, 1945) when he was captured and reported missing in action. He actually spent more time under German military authority than he did with the Big Red One. But the fact that his papers list him as a member of the 16th Infantry when he mustered out of the army, coupled with the pride he feels at having been associated with the division during one of its most difficult battles, leave him no doubt as to where his soldierly loyalties lie: "I considered myself a 1st Divisioner from the day I joined it until the day I was discharged. And I always will be."

Everett Booth was born and raised in East Chicago, Indiana. Drafted into the army on April 11, 1941, he was assigned to the 16th Infantry in June 1942. He remained with that regiment throughout the war. After the war he returned to East Chicago to work for General American Transportation Corporation, his prewar employer. He also became active in the army reserve program, retiring as a lieutenant colonel in May 1970. He left General American in 1967 to take a sales position with an engineering firm, where he worked until his retirement in 1981. In the 1970s he became involved with the Society of the First Division, attending their annual reunions. He and his wife, Johanna, had planned

to return to Europe for the first time since the war for ceremonies held in commemoration of the fortieth anniversary of
D-Day in 1984, but Johanna died in 1982. He made the trip
instead with his son Arthur. "It was," says Arthur, "a memorable
trip for both father and son." Booth died in 1990 of complications from emphysema.

Paul Bystrak left the 1st Division in October 1945 and married his childhood sweetheart in December of that year. He stayed
in the army after the war ended, serving at duty stations in the
United States, Europe, and Japan before retiring as a major in
November 1963. From 1963 to 1984 he worked in the Defense
and Space Center, Westinghouse Electric Corporation. He also
earned a B.S. from the University of Maryland and an M.S. from
George Washington University. He and his wife are currently
"enjoying retirement, travel, and gardening, etc.," in Odenton,
Maryland. He lists his birthplace of Sobotiste, Slovakia, as one
of their favorite and most frequently visited travel destinations.

William "Soup" Campbell was born in Newport, Rhode
Island, in 1913. He served in the 18th Infantry from his induc-
tion in December 1939 through September 1945, then went on
to pursue an army career that spanned nearly thirty years. Upon
retiring as colonel in July 1968, he went to work for Sperry Sys-
tems Management, now known as Unisys, on Long Island, New
York. He retired from Sperry in 1978 and now lives in the Mar-
riott Fairfax Military Retirement Community in Fort Belvoir,
Virginia.

When Campbell thinks about his comrades from the Big Red
One, the face that always comes to mind is that of Archie
Cameron, also a member of the World's Fair detachment in the
summer of 1940. "I shall always remember Archie Cameron, who
was well known and liked by all, and his popularity continued

throughout his all-too-short life," Campbell recalls. "We served together in the 18th Infantry of the 1st Division from 1939 until he lost his life trying to save a fallen comrade in France. Archie 'The Snake' was big-hearted, full of fun, and he loved life.

"While we were back in England in 1944 after the North African and Sicilian campaigns, preparing for our next show, I visited Snake, who was hospitalized for hepatitis. As I was leaving he said, 'Here, Soup, take my ring. I'm not going on the next one. It will fit you better, and it has taken me through some tough ones.' So we exchanged rings, and that was the last time I ever saw him. However, he was discharged from the hospital and took his company across the Normandy Beach on D-Day. I was hit the same day and evacuated to a hospital in England.

"On or about July 24, 1944, Archie was on reconnaissance with his battalion commander, who was struck down by machine-gun fire. Archie, again to help a friend, was trying to carry him to safety when he was struck down by the same machine gun and killed. Sometime later I received a letter from Archie's mother indicating that she had received his personal effects, and that the class ring had my name in it. I must say that she worded the letter most delicately, and I did my best to reply in kind, but there is no easy way to confirm to a mother that she has lost her son. After returning home in September 1945, I visited his wonderful parents and we exchanged class rings.

"At the Officers of the First Division Annual Dinner, which bridges three wars, we always drink a toast to the division's dead, and I always hear a few voices saying softly, 'the Snake.'"

Frederick Dolfi was born in Connerville, Ohio, in 1918. He was living in Dillonvale, Ohio, when he was drafted on March 5, 1941, "with draft number 214, serial number 30501173." Assigned to F Company, 2nd Battalion of the 16th Infantry, he served with that unit as a transportation corporal for most of the war. He was a member of the 1st Division's advance detachment to England in July 1942 and a participant in the North African and Sicilian campaigns. Wounded on Omaha Beach, he spent fifty-two days recovering in the 55th General Hospital in Malvern, England, and rejoined the division in time for the capture of Bonn and the drive through Germany and into Czechoslovakia. He was honorably discharged from the army on June 16, 1945, and now lives in Rayland, Ohio.

"I served in three initial invasions, eight major campaigns, and spent three Christmases away from home," Dolfi proudly notes, "all total four years, three months, and twelve days. When I was discharged from the Big Red One, I came to a separation center camp at Atterbury, Indiana, on June 16, 1945. My lovely girlfriend waited for me from 1938 until 1945. My jeep was named Helen after her. On July 21, 1945, we were married.

"I got myself work in a steel plant on a rolling tandem mill. Worked there from 1945 up to 1980, retiring after thirty-five years. I have one son who served with the army in Vietnam. This coming July 21 [1994] my wife and I will have been married fifty golden years.

"My health has gone to pieces—triple bypasses, problems with the carotid arteries, blockage of six veins on the left side of my heart, prostate and bladder infections. Old soldiers really don't die, they just fade away.

"D-Day is every day.

"Speaking of World War II, F Company was the best of all. Members of the company still visit us: John Finke and his wife, Blythe, Lum Lombarski, and Ed Zukowski. Also Bob Trout, Albert Cimperman, William Pacek, Bill Greasing, among others.

"I fought in thirteen different countries and believe you me, the cause of Old Glory was just. God bless us all."

John Finke was born in Vicksburg, Mississippi, in April 1911. In 1921 he and his older brother moved with their German-born mother to her home city of Bremen, Germany, where the boys were enrolled in the Neues Gymnasium. At the end of 1926 Finke transferred to a one-year course in a Bremen business school and was apprenticed to an import-export firm upon graduation. Six months later in 1928, his parents, fearing a Nazi takeover of the Bremen city government, sent the boys back to America. They lived in New York City until mid-1935, then moved to Saginaw, Michigan.

Finke left Saginaw in December 1940 to enter the army at Fort Custer, Michigan, where he was assigned to the 2nd Battalion of the 2nd Infantry Regiment, 57th Division. After attending the Infantry School at Fort Benning, Georgia, he completed training as a military policeman and served as assistant provost marshal at Indiantown Gap and Tidworth Barracks. He joined the 1st Division in December 1942 and served in the North African and Sicilian campaigns. On D-Day he commanded F Company of the 16th Infantry in the first wave of assault troops to land on Omaha Beach. He was with the division through the end of the war to mid-1946, and again from 1950 to 1953.

He retired from the army in August 1964 as a lieutenant colonel. He was employed for a while by the Allied Chemical Corporation, then traveled widely in Europe and the United States. After living in Snedens Landing on the Hudson River for twenty-five years and in California on the Point Reyes National Seashore in Inverness for six years, he and Blythe, his wife of thirty-six years, now reside in the Fairfax Military Retirement Community at Fort Belvoir, Virginia.

Charles "Hank" Hangsterfer, after recovering from wounds suffered on D-Day, returned to the 16th Infantry in July

1944, just prior to the Saint Lô breakout. He served as Regimental Headquarters Company commander and communications officer up to the battle of Falaise Gap, and as Headquarters Company commander and battalion S-1 through the Hürtgen Forest campaign and the opening stages of the Battle of the Bulge. He left the 1st Division in December 1944 and retired from active service in March 1945. For the next thirty years he served in the U.S. Army reserve, retiring in 1971 as a colonel. Born (on October 31, 1918) and raised in Philadelphia, Hangsterfer now resides with his wife in nearby Drexel Hill, Pennsylvania.

"The day I left the army on October 31, 1945 (my birthday!), I married Geneva Campbell, a lieutenant in the Army Nurse Corps," he says. "I met her in January 1942, the first day she came on duty at Fort Devens, Massachusetts. She went to the South Pacific in May 1942, so we did not see each other for over three years. We were married in California and honeymooned all across the country back to my parents' home in Philadelphia. I got a job as manager of a chain-link fence company and stayed with the company until they went out of business in 1978. A friendly competitor said I was too young to retire and I have been working for his company to this very day.

"If you are going to be one, be a Big Red One. No mission too difficult, no sacrifice too great, duty first!"

Sidney "Hap" Haszard, born on August 7, 1922, was a native of Natick, Massachusetts. He served in 1st Division reconnaissance units throughout World War II, beginning with the landing in North Africa and continuing through Sicily and Europe. He held the ranks of scout corporal, heavy section sergeant, and platoon sergeant before receiving a battlefield commission and assignment as a reconnaissance platoon leader toward the end of the war. He stayed in the army after the war ended, eventually logging more than thirty-five years of active service.

His formal military education included the Armor Officer Advanced Course (AOAC), the Command and General Staff College, and the Army War College. His postwar service involved numerous command and staff assignments in cavalry units. He served as a platoon leader and troop commander in the 2nd ACR on the Czechoslovakian border. As a squadron commander, he organized, trained, and deployed 3rd Squadron, 5th Cavalry Regiment to Vietnam, where he was also a division and corps plans officer and commander of the 3rd Brigade of the 3rd Armored Division. He subsequently served as an instructor for the AOAC and as deputy assistant commandant of the Armor School.

Haszard retired from the army as a colonel and moved with his wife, Ann, to Fiddlers Green, a farm in Hudson, Kentucky, thirty miles southeast of Fort Knox. He frequently spoke before AOAC classes at Fort Knox, usually on the topic of reconnaissance work during World War II. He passed away in January 1995, shortly after reviewing the final draft of his story as it appears in this book.

Frank Kolb, born in 1923, is a native of Paducah, Kentucky. He graduated from Columbia Military Academy in 1941 and was called to active duty out of Purdue University on July 30, 1942. He served with the 1st Division from November 1942 to May 16, 1945. Married in June 1945, he was discharged from the army with the rank of captain the following September. He returned to Purdue University and received a degree in pharmacy in 1948. He is now retired and lives with his wife, Susan, in Mayfield, Kentucky.

Thomas Lancer was born in 1907 in New York City. He served with the 1st Division throughout the war until November 1946. Postwar service included assignments as provost marshal in Munich and Berlin during the Soviet blockade of that city, command of the army's Military Police School at Fort Gordon,

Georgia, and assignments as provost marshal of the Fifth Army in Korea and the First Army. He also attended the Armed Forces Staff College and the Industrial College of the Armed Forces. He retired in 1970 with the rank of colonel, and went to work in Washington, D.C., as a government appeal agent for the draft board until selective service was abolished. He and his wife, Ann, now divide their time between homes in Madison, Connecticut, and Fort Belvoir, Virginia.

"When I think of the 1st Division," he says, "I always recall *Henry V* and his words to the troops before the battle of Agincourt: 'We few, we happy few, we band of brothers.'"

Thaddeus "Ted" Lombarski was born in Avoca, Pennsylvania, in 1917, and raised in Greenville, Long Island. He enlisted in the army on March 29, 1939, at 39 Whitehall Street in New York City, and was assigned to F Company of the 16th Infantry, then stationed on Governor's Island. Except for a summer stint with the 1st Division's World's Fair detachment in 1940, he remained with F Company throughout his army tour. He was in the first wave that landed at Arzew during Operation Torch and fought in the entire North African campaign, receiving a promotion to first sergeant near Mateur. When the Allies invaded Sicily, he was in the first wave of the Gela landings and subsequently received a Silver Star for his actions in the battle of Troina. On D-Day he was once again in the first wave of the Big Red One's assault force when it landed at Omaha Beach.

In October 1944, Lombarski received a battlefield commission to second lieutenant near Eilendorf, Germany, and became a platoon leader. Reflecting on that promotion, he notes, "My chances of survival were not very good. But the Lord was on my side again. After many close calls I was sent home just before we reached the Rhine River. I got out of the army on points on June 4, 1945, at Fort Dix, New Jersey." He was then a first lieutenant.

After leaving the army, "I tried to reacquaint myself with my wife, Ruth, and my son, who was born while I was in North Africa. Having no skills, I found it hard to find a good job."

Lombarski and his family moved to Wyndach, Long Island, and he eventually hired on with the Grumman Aircraft Corporation, where he worked for the next thirty years. He and Ruth have been married for fifty-two years, and in that time their family has grown to include three sons, one daughter, and nine grandchildren.

More than fifty years after leaving the army, Lombarski and his wife keep in touch with his wartime comrades by faithfully attending the 1st Division's annual reunions. His memories of the war are still very strong, and so too are his feelings for the Big Red One, especially with regard to its role in the Normandy invasion.

"Of course we all know many military units helped to make the D-Day landings a success," he says, "and they deserve all due praise and glory for their achievements. But no unit had a harder task or suffered more than E and F Companies of the 16th Infantry. And some of us had gone already through the same thing on a smaller scale in Africa and Sicily. That's why I think we were a unique group and deserve some recognition.

"I was proud to be a soldier in the 1st Division, proud to be part of F Company, and proud of all we did to help win the war."

Steve Ralph was born on September 25, 1911, in Phoenix, New York. He entered the army on July 16, 1941, and was assigned to the 16th Infantry, serving with that regiment until he was honorably discharged on February 5, 1946. He returned to active service on February 25, 1947, and retired from the army as a colonel on July 31, 1966. From 1966 through 1972 he was a director of administration for an electronics firm, and a real estate broker from 1972 through 1975. He died in February 1993. He is survived by his wife, Velma, and three children. Velma Ralph recalls, "My husband and I met during World War II in Lyme Regis, England. He was with the 1st Division and I was a lieutenant in the U.S. Army Nurse Corps. He was my hero! He was extremely supportive of the 1st Division and an active member of the Society of the First Division until his death."

Following his 1942 duty tour in Libya and Egypt, **E. V. Sutherland**, returned to North Africa in May 1943 as a casual officer stationed in Oran, awaiting assignment to a unit. In June 1943 he rejoined the 1st Division as assistant G-3, a post he held through the Sicilian campaign. In December 1943 he was assigned as executive officer of the 26th Infantry, and from the end of the Hürtgen Forest campaign through the first five days of the Battle of the Bulge, he served as temporary commander of the 26th while the regimental CO was in England. He again assumed temporary command during the final weeks of the war, then commanded the 1st Battalion of the 26th in Anspach, Germany, for a month immediately following the German surrender. He reassumed full command of the regiment shortly thereafter.

His postwar service included a variety of assignments that took him from Paraguay to Phnom Penh, and from the Pentagon to West Point, with many stops in between. In 1961 he joined the faculty at West Point and was subsequently named head of the English department. He served in that capacity until May 1977, when he retired with the rank of brigadier general. A native of Philadelphia, he now lives in Amagansett, Massachusetts.

"I was very lucky, as a young man in the Great Depression, to receive an appointment to the United States Military Academy," he observes, "and I was deeply fortunate to be able to spend the last seventeen years of my career as a professor at West Point. That portion of my career spent with the 1st Division I consider the highest point of my commissioned service."

Appendix:
1st Infantry Division
Chronology,
May 1942 to May 1945

MAY 1942
15   1st Division officially redesignated an infantry division.

JUNE
21   Division moves to Indiantown Gap Military Reservation, Pennsylvania.

30   Division command post (CP) at Indiantown Gap; advance detail departs for overseas movement.

JULY
1   Advance detachment headquarters and 2/16th Infantry depart by ship from Brooklyn, New York, for Liverpool, England.

14   Advance detail arrives in Liverpool.

30   1st Division troops begin departing Indiantown Gap.

AUGUST

2   Division troops depart New York City on HMS *Queen Mary*.

8   *Queen Mary* arrives in Gourock, Scotland. Division troops proceed by train to Tidworth Barracks, Wiltshire (division CP).

10   Division maneuvers, Inverrary, Scotland.

OCTOBER

22   1st Division departs Glasgow, boards transports in Firth of Clyde, Scotland, for invasion of North Africa (Operation Torch); advance CP aboard SS *Reina del Pacifico*, alternate CP aboard HMS *Warwick Castle*.

26–27   Operation Torch invasion convoy departs Clyde; arrives off Algerian coast November 7.

NOVEMBER

8   Allied invasion of North Africa begins; 1st Division lands at Les Andalouses and Arzew, near Oran, Algeria; CP at Tourville.

10   French forces in Oran capitulate.

11   French sign armistice with Allies, all resistance by Vichy troops ceases at 7 A.M.

23   Throughout month, 1st Division committed piecemeal to Tunisian front, with elements involved in fighting in Medjez el Bab vicinity; 5th Field Artillery Battalion joins British V Corps in Tunisia, to remain with British until February 7, 1943.

25   After flying to Youk les Bains in southern Tunisia, 3/26th Infantry sets up outposts guarding south and east approaches to Atlas Mountains.

DECEMBER

22–25 Battle of Longstop Hill (Medjez el Bab vicinity), 18th Infantry Regimental Combat Team participating.

JANUARY 1943

18–25 Remainder of 1st Division moves into southern Tunisia, concentrating in Guelma area; division elements committed to action over area extending two hundred miles from Medjez el Bab in north to Gafsa in south; notably, toward end of month division elements involved in fighting in Ousseltia River Valley, central Tunisia.

FEBRUARY

14 Germans attack in Faid vicinity, advancing through Sidi Bou Zid toward Kasserine Pass; elements of 26th Infantry withdraw from Gafsa to cover southern approaches to Tébessa; others positioned to defend Kasserine Pass. 1st Division involved in subsequent Battle of Kasserine Pass (February 18–22).

16–18 Rest of 1st Division moves into Kasserine Pass area.

19 18th Infantry repulses German attack at Sbiba; 26th Infantry receives probing attack by Germans in Kasserine area.

20–21 Division CP (advance) established at Bou Chebka; Germans launch strong attack in Kasserine area; British forces with 1/26th Infantry withdraw northwest up Oued Hatab River Valley.

21 16th Infantry elements attack in Kasserine Pass vicinity.

22 German forces withdraw east through Kasserine Pass.

23 1st Division elements advance into Kasserine Pass.

MARCH

1 Division turns over positions in Djebel Chambi area to 9th Division, regroups at Marsott northwest of Tébessa;

for first time in Tunisian campaign, 1st Division is assembled as unit.

10   1st Division begins movement into Bou Chebka area.

18–19   1st Division occupies Gafsa, advances toward El Guettar.

20   1st Division attacks along Gabés road east of El Guettar.

23–25   Heavy fighting in El Guettar vicinity; Battle of El Guettar continues through first week of April.

APRIL

16   Lead elements of 1st Division take up positions northeast of Beja in northern Tunisia.

22–23   1st Division launches offensive to clear Tine River Valley and flanking hills.

MAY

3   1st Division captures Mateur.

7   Allies take Tunis and Bizerta.

13   Surrender of Axis forces in North Africa. (Since April 23, 1st Division has advanced ten miles in Tine Valley.)

13–19   1st Division returns to Oran vicinity.

25   16th Infantry near Saint Leu, Algeria.

26   16th Infantry undergoes amphibious training at Amphibious Training School at Port aux Pules, near Arzew, Algeria.

28   26th Infantry begins amphibious training near Mers el Kebir, Algeria; 18th Infantry begins amphibious training shortly thereafter.

JUNE

8   1st Division begins concentrating at Staoueli, Algeria; movement completed July 5; planning headquarters at Sidi Ferruch, Algeria.

24   1st Division conducts large-scale practice landing at Zeralda, Algeria, in preparation for invasion of Sicily (Operation Husky).

26   1st Division elements embark on transports; depart for Tunis next day.

JULY

5   Remainder of division embarks on transports; advance CP on USS *Samuel Chase*, alternate CP on USS *Barnett* (both in Algiers).

8   1st Division transports rendezvous with invasion convoy outside Tunis.

10   Allies invade Sicily; 1st Division lands at Gela.

11   Enemy counterattack at Gela beachhead repulsed.

11–12   Gela beachhead secured; 1st Division, supported by elements of 2nd Armored and 82nd Airborne Divisions, begins offensive action; takes Ponte-Olivo Airport.

13   18th Infantry takes Mount Ursitto, north of Ponte-Olivo airport; 26th Infantry fighting at Gibilscemi; 16th Infantry enters Niscemi.

14   26th Infantry captures Mazzarino, Mounts Figare, Canolotti, Gibilscemi; 18th Infantry takes La Serra.

15–16   26th Infantry captures Barrafranca.

17   16th Infantry takes Pietraperzia, south of Enna.

20   16th Infantry captures Enna, capital of Sicily.

28   16th Infantry captures Nicosia.

AUGUST

1   1st Division launches attack in Troina area with 39th Regiment of 9th Division; Battle of Troina begins.

3   Axis forces start evacuating from Sicily across Strait of Messina.

6   After repulsing numerous counterattacks, 1st Division and attached units capture Troina.

7   1st Division relieved by 9th Infantry Division, held in II Corps reserve in Troina vicinity until August 12. Division commander Major General Terry Allen and assistant commander Brigadier General Theodore Roosevelt are replaced by Major General Clarence R. Huebner and Colonel Willard G. Wyman.

13   Division elements (notably 18th Infantry and 32nd Field Artillery Battalion) advance east toward Randazzo.

14   18th Infantry advances from Randazzo to Moiot Rocca Bodia and Novara di Sicilia, reaching the junction of Franca–Villa Novara roads.

15   18th Infantry occupies Novara. This is the final action by the 1st Division in the Sicilian campaign; tactical employment of the division officially ends at midnight.

17   Allies enter Messina, ending Sicily campaign.

28   Division CP (advance) at Palma di Montechiaro, Sicily, through October 13.

OCTOBER

14–22   Division CP (advance) at Augusta, Sicily.

23   1st Division departs Augusta.

25   1st Division arrives Algiers, Algeria (does not debark).

NOVEMBER

8   1st Division arrives in Liverpool, England; proceeds to Dorset County to train and refit for invasion of France (Operation Overlord).

9   1st Division headquarters at Blandford, England, through June 2, 1944.

MARCH 1944

23 1st Division alerted to be ready to move on short notice to invasion marshaling areas.

MAY

7–11 1st Division moves to invasion marshaling areas; toward end of month division units move to Portland, Weymouth, and Poole for embarkation.

JUNE

3 1st Division troops complete loading of invasion transports; advance CP on USS *Ancon*, alternate CP on USS *Samuel Chase* (both in Portland).

5 Operation Overlord invasion convoys leave port.

6 D-Day: Allies invade France; 1st Division lands at Omaha Beach beginning 6:30 A.M.; pushes several hundred yards inland by nightfall.

7 1st Division captures Colleville-sur-Mer, Huppain, Surrain; reaches all D-Day objectives by nightfall, except in Formigny-Trevieres area.

8 1st Division elements capture Formigny and Tour-en-Bessin, advance across Aure River; all D-Day objectives now reached; division advances into *bocage* country.

11 1st Division advances twelve miles inland.

13 1st Division captures Caumont, twenty miles inland.

JULY

14 1st Division relieved by 5th Division, sent to Colombieres to rest and refit.

25–26 Operation Cobra, U.S. forces break out in Normandy.

26–27 1st Division captures Marigny.

28   1st Division and 4th Armored Division capture Coutances.

31   1st Division crosses Sienne River near Gavray.

August

1   1st Division captures Brecey; advances toward Mortain.

5   1st Division ordered to disengage from drive to Mortain and proceed to Mayenne.

7   1st Division crosses Mayenne River, advances to Saint Fraimbault de Prieres.

9   1st Division ordered to advance north via Couterne, Bagnoles, La Ferté-Macé.

24–25   1st Division advances ninety-six miles through Alençon and Mamers to Courville-sur-Eure.

26   1st Division advances east fifty-five miles to Étampes vicinity.

26   1st Division drives south and east of Paris and then wheels northeast into Mons area; movement completed September 2.

30   1st Division CP (advance) at Soissons, France.

September

3   16th Infantry mops up Mons pocket.

8–9   1st Division advances toward Liège.

11   1st Division crosses Meuse River, drives toward German frontier and Siegfried Line defenses.

12   Allied attacks on Siegfried Line commence; U.S. forces advance into Aachen vicinity, with 16th Infantry penetrating the state forest of Aachen, south of city.

15   1st Division cuts roads leading southeast out of Aachen; breaches Siegfried Line west of Munsterbusch.

16–21   1st Division attacks toward Stolberg and Munsterbusch.

21   Munsterbusch captured.

OCTOBER

10   1st Division captures Haaren, completing encirclement of
      Aachen; German garrison rejects surrender ultimatum.

12   16th and 18th Regiments repulse German attempt to
      relieve Aachen as 26th Regiment attacks directly into the
      city.

13–20 26th Infantry with attached elements advance through
      Aachen against strong resistance.

21   German garrison surrenders; 1st Division subsequently
      moves into Hürtgen Forest southeast of city.

NOVEMBER

16   1st Division launches attacks in Hürtgen Forest; drives
      toward Roer River in the Hamich-Gressenich vicinity;
      combat continues through first week of December.

DECEMBER

7   1st Division relieved by 9th Infantry Division.

9–16   Most of 1st Division in Henri Chapelle, Belgium, for rest
      and refitting; 16th Infantry quartered in Monschau area.

11   Major General Clift Andrus succeeds Major General
      Haebner as commander of 1ST Division.

16   Germans launch Ardennes offensive (Battle of the Bulge);
      1st Division alerted for movement from rest areas north
      of Eupen.

17   26th Infantry passes through Camp Elsenborn, takes up
      positions in Butgenbach on northern edge of German
      breakthrough; 16th Infantry occupies high ground south-
      west of Butgenbach and north of Weismes; 18th Infantry
      positioned south of Eupen to counter German para-
      chutists.

17–22 Germans launch several attacks down the Bullingen-But-
      genbach-Weismes road; repulsed by 1st Division.

20   Germans complete encirclement of U.S. forces in Bas-
        togne, Belgium.
23   Germans cease offensive operations in 1st Division
        sector.
25   German Ardennes offensive effectively halted.
26   U.S. counteroffensive in Ardennes breaks through to
        Bastogne.

JANUARY 1945

15–28   1st Division attacks south in offensive to eliminate Bulge.
28   Bulge liquidated; 1st Division turns east toward German
        border.
30   1st Division captures Hunningen, Murrigen, and Hons-
        feld on German border.

FEBRUARY

3   1st Division penetrates Siegfried Line, captures Hollerath.
5   1st Division relieved by 99th Infantry Division.
8   1st Division moves to forward assembly area; takes over
        defense of Untermaubach-Bergstein-Grosshau sector.
25   1st Division crosses Roer River, advances to Rhine River.

MARCH

1–3   1st Division attacks, captures Erp.
6   1st Division captures Dersdorf.
7   1st Division captures Bruhl, Berzdorf, Bornheim, and
        Alfter; reaches outskirts of Bonn.
8   1st Division enters Bonn.
9   Bonn garrison surrenders to 1st Division.
11–13   1st Division consolidates positions in Bonn area.
14–15   1st Division relieved by 8th Division; moves south to
        Remagen.

16   1st Division completes Rhine crossing at Remagen.

17   1st Division attacks German positions on east bank of Rhine to defend and enlarge Rhine bridgehead.

18   1st Division seizes high ground west of Eudenbach; captures Quirrenbach, Rostingen, Orscheid, Gratzfeld, Wullescheid, and Stockhausen.

19   1st Division captures Eudenbach and Nonnenberg.

24–25   Heavy fighting in Rhine bridgehead around Geisbach and Uckerath.

25   Rhine bridgehead secured.

27   Allied forces break out of Rhine bridgehead; 1st Division drives north-northeast into Germany.

APRIL

1   1st Division makes longest tactical march in its history, from positions east of Siegen into Buren area; 1/26th Infantry moves 115 miles; advance division CP moves 70 miles; division captures Ruthen, Hammern, Geseke and Steinhausen; U.S. First and Ninth Armies link, seal Ruhr pocket.

8   1st Division crosses Weser River, advances east toward Osterode and Harz Mountains.

9–10   1st Division crosses Leine River, captures Dassel, Northeim, and Einbeck.

11   1st Division reaches western slope of Harz Mountains.

12   1st Division captures Osterode and Freheit.

18–19   1st Division takes high ground overlooking Blankberg and Thale; enemy forces in Harz Mountains routed; elsewhere U.S. Third Army, spearheaded by XII Corps, enters Czechoslovakia.

20   Organized resistance in 1st Division's operations area has ceased.

22–23   1st Division moves to assembly area in Blankenheim vicinity to maintain order, prevent sabotage of important installations.

27   Division CP (advance) moves 155 miles to Markleuthen, Bavaria, near Czechoslovakian border.

30   Adolf Hitler commits suicide in Berlin.

May

1   1st Division on Czechoslovakian border.

4–5   1st Division advances east into Czechoslovakia on broad front, clearing Drenice and launching last attack of war against scratch force of trainees from German officer candidate school in Milowitz.

6   1st Division continues advance, encountering resistance along Cheb-Falkenau road; captures Eubabrunn, Klinghart, Plesna, Sneky, Mnichov, Sangerberg, and Kynsperk.

7   1st Division liberates Falkenau concentration camp; advancing toward Karlsbad when order received to halt in place and maintain defensive positions.

8   VE Day—Germany surrenders. 1st Division gets cease-fire order at 8:15 A.M. Later that day accepts surrender of German XII Corps (Seventh Army).

Index